**Person-Centred Approach
and Client-Centred Therapy
Essential Readers**
series editor Tony Merry

**Person-Centred Approach and Client-Centred Therapy
Essential Readers** is a new series of books making important and
exciting contributions to international person-centred literature by
authors who have already made distinguished additions to the
development of the person-centred approach.

The series is edited by **Tony Merry**, Senior Lecturer,
Department of Psychology, University of East London, A person-
centred counsellor, trainer and supervisor, and author of several
person-centred books and articles.

D0807965

Other books in this series:

FAMILY, SELF AND PSYCHOTHERAPY: A PERSON-CENTRED PERSPECTIVE

NED L. GAYLIN

PCCS BOOKS
Ross-on-Wye

First published in 2001

PCCS BOOKS
Llangarron
Ross-on-Wye
Herefordshire
HR9 6PT
United Kingdom
Tel +44 (0)1989 77 07 07
Fax +44 (0)1989 77 07 00
email: contact@pccs-books.co.uk
website: www.pccs-books.co.uk

Family, Self and Psychotherapy: A person-centred perspective

ISBN 1 898059 36 5

Cover design by Denis Postle.
Printed by Bookcraft, Midsomer Norton, Somerset, United Kingdom

CONTENTS

Dedication

This work is lovingly dedicated to my family: my wife, children, grandchildren, parents, brothers, sisters, nieces, nephews, grandparents, aunts, uncles, and cousins who are still alive in the usual sense, as well as those who live on in my memory and from whose existence is derived the weft of my fabric.

Acknowledgements

To Rita, my wife and editor of 43 years, to whom words are like notes to Bach, and for whom the word thanks is meaningless — for her help with this work, but oh, so much more, my eternal gratitude. And to Pete Sanders, whose gentle encouragement made this work happen.

PREFACE

A bit about me and my journey

My life has been delightfully unremarkable. Born the youngest of three boys (my brothers were six and ten years my senior), I was also one of the youngest of many cousins in two very large, closely-knit extended families — a veritable community of relatives who lived in close proximity to one another in Cleveland, Ohio. As a child, I always wanted a younger brother or sister; as a young teenager I satisfied these fraternal needs by babysitting and working as a camp counselor during the summers. I liked young children, and the feeling seemed mutual.

I had a penchant for drawing and attended art classes at the Cleveland Institute of Art which, when I was 16, offered me a scholarship. Coincidentally an application for early college entrance appeared on my desk. Both of my brothers had gone to medical school. Although not discussed, my family believed that a career as an artist could wait, perhaps indefinitely (as it did). Off I went to Shimer College — a small experimental college of the University of Chicago.

In my first semester, I read *Love Is Not Enough* by Bruno Bettleheim (1955), a lay child psychoanalyst. Bettleheim directed the University of Chicago's Sonja Shankman Orthogenic School, an internationally famous residential treatment school for severely emotionally disturbed children. The children he wrote about captured my interest and my heart.

A friend at Shimer, knowing of my growing interest in working with disturbed children, introduced me to her uncle, a social worker at Bellefaire Children's Home, a Cleveland facility similar to the Orthogenic School. At 17, I interviewed for a position at Bellefaire as a summer counselor. That interim job changed my life.

I returned to college, transferred to Chicago's main campus and took a job at the Orthogenic School as a part-time counselor and swimming instructor. I became so involved with the children, the work, and Bettleheim that I almost lost my undergraduate scholarship.

I continued at Chicago through graduate school in the Committee on Human Development, majoring in the study of the family and developmental and clinical psychology. As part of my graduate training, I enrolled in the practicum at the University of Chicago Counseling Center where I encountered Carl Rogers and client-centered therapy. The clients at the Counseling Center were primarily young adults. Despite some early work by Virginia Axline (1947), only one of the senior staff, Charlotte Ellinwood, provided therapy to children. No one worked with families.

Consequently, I took an internship at the Institute for Juvenile Research (IJR) in downtown Chicago and was introduced to the (then quite new) practice of family therapy. Carl Whitaker supervised me in that endeavor. But a heavy psychodynamic emphasis at IJR impelled my return to the Counseling Center where I felt more at home theoretically, professionally, and personally. At the Counseling Center my philosophical and professional identities solidified.

After graduate school I accepted a position with the National Institute of Mental Health (NIMH) to direct the section on Youth and Student Affairs within the division of Child and Family Mental Health. Two years later, I interviewed for the chair of a new department — Family and Community Development, now Family Studies — at the University of Maryland, where I have been for the last 30 years and presently direct the Marriage and Family Therapy Training program.

Not incidentally, along the way my wife and I married and raised our four children. We have since been blessed with two wonderful daughters-in-law and two delightful grandchildren. These intimates, along with my extended family (some living, many dead): my mother and father, my brothers, their wives and families, a multitude of aunts, uncles, cousins, and a quartet of grandparents, are the people who define my life.

A quick map of this book

This book is divided unevenly into three sections. The first section (Chapters 1–4) presents my ideas, beliefs, and feelings about the importance of the family to us as individuals, and its centrality to the very nature of our species. Chapter 1 is an intensely personal statement drafted early in my career upon the death of my mother. Its social-ecological focus frames the rest of the book. This opening chapter anticipates the second chapter that describes the role of the family as mediator and buffer between the individual and society. The second chapter identifies some of the stressors on the family in our times. Chapter 3 presents a brief history of the institution of marriage and explores the nonrational foundations of marriage — love and trust; it ends with some thoughts regarding the breakdown of these two cornerstones. Chapter 4 concludes this section and provides a developmental overview in cultural context.

The next section is brief but pivotal, comprising Chapters 5 and 6 which deal with the psychological foundations of the person-centered approach: the notion of the self and a positive conceptualization of emotionally well-functioning individuals. These chapters segue to the last half (Chapters 7–12) of the book and its focus: (a) principles and methods of therapy and (b) therapy with families. Chapter 13 concludes the book by re-emphasizing the personal and positive (rather than pathology-based) soul of the person-centered approach and suggests a methodology for exploring human behavior from that affirmative vantagepoint.

Introduction

The Rogersian mode

The core of Rogers' special genius was his ability to integrate complex ideas, distill their essence, and communicate this pith with simple elegance and charisma. He also was a great integrator who had the ability to draw upon and fully credit the ideas of others and still, somehow, reconfigure the concepts, thus forging an elegant theoretical platform uniquely his own. In conceptualizing *nondirective therapy*, as he first called his theory of therapy, Rogers drew upon the work of Otto Rank and Rank's student, Jesse Taft (1933). Later Rogers incorporated the ideas of Jules Seeman, Rosalind Dymond, and Desmond Cartwright (among others) and shaped *client-centered* and finally *person-centered* therapy. But the forging of these ideas into the practice of an optimistic, humanistic, and quite democratic form of interpersonal psychotherapeusis undoubtedly resulted from his deep respect for the individual and profound convictions regarding the basic positive nature of human beings.

Philosophical and historical perspective

At the twilight of the nineteenth century, the world was eagerly anticipating its entry into the *century of science*. At the dawn of the twentieth century, humankind naively believed that science would enable a utopian millennium wherein the frontiers of the unknown would come under the control of growingly omniscient technology.

In the neonatal field of clinical psychiatry, Sigmund Freud unabashedly convinced his publishers to falsify the publication date of his first major opus. The *Interpretation of Dreams* (*Die Traumdietung*, 1900), actually published in 1899, carried the date 1900. Thus Freud established himself as the harbinger of the science of psychology for the twentieth century — and indeed he was. For the first half of the twentieth century, in both Europe and America, psychodynamic theory dominated thinking in medical psychiatry, the social sciences, and even the arts.

Meanwhile, in animal laboratories at many American universities, the condition-response theory of Ivan Pavlov was being empirically tested and elaborated. Ensuing refinements by B. F. Skinner and others enabled behaviorism (as it came to be called) to establish itself as a legitimate branch of the growing science of psychology. Indeed, with as much confidence as Freud, Skinner believed that behaviorism offered the pathway to an idyllic society (Walden II, 1948). Thus, by the middle of the twentieth century, behaviorism and psychoanalysis were the two major forces in psychology.

However, at the mid-point of the last century, it was neither Freud nor Skinner who shaped our thinking and spoke to our anxieties. By that time, psychoanalysis had not only failed in its promise to enhance the human condition, it seemed to have sullied it. Even our most creative endeavors became suspect as neurotic *sublimations* of our more primitive instincts. Furthermore, giving names to and etiological explanations for our neuroses did not seem to improve our mental health but, rather, augmented the need for a larger mental illness industry. Neither were we optimistic that Skinnerian conditioning would enhance the quality of our lives. At about the same time, novelists such as Huxley (*Brave New World*, 1932) and Orwell (*1984*, 1949) were quick to point out the dangers inherent in technological control of human behavior.

Also shaken was our naïve faith in science's abilities to create paradise. We came to realize that letting science's technological genie out of the bottle had its dark side. With the unveiling of the technologically efficient atrocities of the holocaust and the unleashing of the atom via the bombing of Hiroshima, our optimism was transformed into foreboding.

In this climate the *Third Force*[1] in psychology had its birth. Seeking a more holistic, less pathological/mechanistic view of human behavior, some theorists of the time advocated a more positive conception of mental health (Jahoda, 1958) and a nobler image of the human condition (Maslow, 1962). This was the milieu in which Carl Rogers (1951) conceptualized and nurtured into practice client-centered therapy.

Rogers' ability to think and write about relatively complicated ideas in a simple straightforward manner drew heavy criticism from the mainstream to whom Rogers' ideas seemed iconoclastic, and indeed, even simplistic — *unscientific*. Nonetheless, in mid-twentieth century, when behavioral and psychodynamic psychotherapy were considered standard and mainstream, Rogers continued to advocate a model of psychotherapy in which the therapist would learn the client's language, rather than vice versa (see Fancher, 1995).

Rogers' earliest written endeavor (1939) reflected his interest in not only children and families but also the philosophical psychology of William James (1890), the organismic theories of Kurt Goldstein (1940), and the therapeutic style of Jesse Taft (1933). His theoretical base — *the necessary and sufficient conditions for therapeutic change* (Rogers, 1957) emphasized the interpersonal nature of the therapeutic relationship and the importance of caring and empathy by the therapist for the client.

First called *nondirective therapy*, Rogers soon considered this name inaccurate, observing that clients could read virtually everything the therapist did, from a simple 'uh huh' to a nod of the head, as somewhat directive. Thus, the term *client-centered therapy* was introduced in 1951 (Rogers, 1951) and is still used today. Later still, Rogers coined the phrase *person-centered* to indicate the use of his approach beyond the circumscribed limits of the professional psychotherapy hour and the *client/therapist* relationship.

---

1. *Third force* is a termed coined by Abraham Maslow to distinguish the humanistic phenomenological psychology advanced by Maslow, Rogers, and others, from the reigning hegemonies of psychoanalysis and behaviorism.

By electronically recording the therapy hour as a means of better observing and quantifying client and therapist behaviors, the client-centered approach introduced empiricism to the practice of psychotherapy (Rogers and Dymond, 1954). The subsequent development and use of ipsative as opposed to normative research methodology enabled a more comprehensive investigation of both psychotherapy process and outcome. Perhaps the greatest validation of Rogers' philosophy, theory, and method to the world of psychotherapy is that his ideas, once considered iconoclastic, are now considered self-evident.

Nevertheless, in today's systems-oriented family therapy community the client-centered approach is virtually without portfolio. This is ironic considering that Rogers' first published volume concerned the treatment of troubled children and their families (1939), and the most widely read and still-published volumes on therapy with children are those of his former student, Virginia Axline (1947, 1964).

Rogers' journey

Carl Ransom Rogers began his career in psychotherapy by working with children and their families. Although not widely known for this work, his first major published effort, *TheClinical Treatment of the Problem Child* (Rogers, 1939) was written while he was at the Rochester Guidance Center from 1928-1940. Client-centered therapy had not yet been born. Rogers dates that event as December 11, 1940 when he used the term in a talk he gave at the University of Minnesota. Although the term *non-directive* therapy was introduced then, its antecedents were clearly in evidence in the earlier 1939 book. In that initial work, Rogers made clear his discontent with the then highly-touted, psychoanalytically oriented, interpretive approach to working with troubled children, an approach proposed by Anna Freud (1935) and Alexander and Healy (1935) among others. Further, Rogers underscored the desirability of helping difficult children by practicing that which he referred to as *relationship* therapy, a concept drawn from the work of Jessie Taft (1933).

Rogers moved to Ohio State University in 1940 where he continued to explicate *non-directive therapy* (Rogers, 1942). In 1945 he moved from Ohio to the University of Chicago to direct its Counseling Center. There *client-centered therapy* (Rogers, 1951) was officially born, and an emphasis on empirical research (Rogers and Dymond, 1954) brought Client-Centered Therapy to full flower. During the Chicago period, Rogers' client-centered principles stimulated other theoreticians, researchers and practitioners, attracting them to the Counseling Center to observe and study. Among them was Virginia Axline, who later published her influential works on client-centered therapy with children (1947, reprinted in 1969).

Rogers moved from Chicago to the University of Wisconsin in 1957. There he focused his attention on the application of client-centered principles to his work with severely disturbed, institutionalized clients. Heretofore, virtually all client-centered practice and research had been conducted in non-medical settings. In 1963, Rogers left Wisconsin for La Jolla, California where he applied the term *person-centered* to his efforts in education, group facilitation, and world peace.

Rogers' final endeavors concerned applying person-centered principles towards the promotion of international peace. He was near the end of his life and relatively taciturn about these efforts, but I recall an anecdote he related at one of his final professional appearances. He told about a group of high-ranking officials from a variety of antagonistic nations who had convened to work together towards establishing some degree of mutual understanding. He recounted how, during the formal portion of the meetings, the air was electric and the participants wary and stiff. He noted that this atmosphere continued during the initial phases of the mandatory social period that followed. He then observed a couple of generals (from opposing nations) in conversation. One of them pulled out a picture of his grandchildren from his breast pocket. Grinning with pride and doting, he proffered the photo to the other who smiled appreciatively, reached into his own pocket and did the same. The atmosphere between them palpably relaxed and their conversation became more animated, earnest and warm. This behavior, Rogers noted, carried over to the subsequent formal meetings where the two officers became noticeably more empathic and cooperative with each other. The impact of their shared personal experience also seemed contagious within the assemblage at large. Concern for those whom we deeply cherish — our families — can, indeed, provide a positive common denominator.

From client-centered to family-centered to person-centered

I began my career as a child therapist and have spent the vast majority of my professional life working with children and families. Early on I learned that a family approach was a far more efficacious means of working with troubled children: working directly within this intimate interpersonal context maximized potential for positive and lasting change. I later found this to be true in psychotherapy with adults as well. As a result I was discomfited at the change of nomenclature from *client-centered* to *person-centered*. The idea of a family as client is workable, whereas *person* is clearly singular. Thus, working primarily with couples and families, the concept of a *person-centered family therapy* seemed disjunctive and contradictory. But a series of events led me to rethink that position.

I am at home and congruent with the philosophy and tenets at the heart of the *person-centered approach*: respect for the individual and appreciation for each person's uniqueness and idiosyncratic process of growth. However, like George Herbert Mead (1934), it is my belief that there can be no person, no *self*, outside of the interpersonal context. The very nature of the human condition is totally and completely interpersonal; basic and paradigmatic to the interpersonal nature is the context in which that nature is shaped — the human family.

Thus, I recall screwing up my courage and confronting Rogers about his emphasis on the individual. It was 1986 in Chicago at the first meeting of the Association for the Development of the Person-Centered Approach (ADPCA). Someone had asked him to define the *healthy* or *fully functioning person*. I remember being taken aback at the enormity of the question. But in his typically thoughtful manner, Rogers did not flinch but went on to think aloud. At the top of his list was the quality of *independence*. I began feeling uncomfortable and remember interrupting him with the suggestion that the concept of an independent human being was antithetical to the human condition — indeed, interdependence defined our species. I expected an argument from Rogers. Instead, he paused, cocked his head, thought for a moment, and agreed. That was it, just a simple agreement.

But I think I wanted, perhaps *needed*, an argument or at least some dialogue on the matter. Despite Rogers' acquiescence, the person-centered philosophy really does stress the independent nature of the person.[2] Furthermore, I think that this emphasis on the individual is a hindrance to the actualizing of person-centered ideation into a more comprehensive theory of the human condition. Thus, for a relatively long time, I continued to use the older and (for me) more comfortable *client-centered therapy* designation in which the client may be an individual, a couple, or a family. Briefly I used *family-centered* therapy (Gaylin, 1989, 1990). However, the more I thought and wrote about family therapy, the more comfortable I became with the idea of a *person-centered family therapy*. The self emerges and develops within the context of the intimate environment of the family. Appreciation of our lifelong interdependence gives dimension, understanding, and consequent effectiveness to practicing therapy with individuals in the family environment. Thus, I came to realize that *person-centered family therapy* (Gaylin, 1993) was, rather than a contradiction in terms, a more consonant form of family therapy than any of those commonly practiced today.

Much as Rogers simplified our understanding of individual psychotherapy, the person-centered framework clarifies our understanding of family therapy. Nonetheless, the *systems* perspective — drawing upon cybernetics theory that evolved in the middle of the twentieth century — has dominated the theory and practice of family therapy to date. The basic assumption underlying family systems orientations is that the family unit — rather than its individual members — is the primary focus of the therapeutic endeavor. By contrast, the person-centered family therapist sees each individual as part of a complexly interconnected milieu and proceeds to respond empathically to family members as both individuals and interdependent agents in the context of their relationships within the family. Because the family is the progenitor of all interpersonal relationships, working within the intimacy of the family enhances potential for effective intra- and interpersonal growth. Furthermore, the person-centered family therapist effects change by working one-on-one in the traditional empathic client-centered manner while simultaneously modeling behaviors that may be sustained within the family unit beyond the therapy session. Thus, person-centered family therapy empowers the family *and* its individual members.

---

2. This underlying emphasis on individual independence as a quality of the fully functioning person may be seen in continued discussions on 'autonomy' and 'personal power' (e.g., Rogers, 1977, Natiello, 1987).

The Quality of Life and Death[1]

1

*Death ends a life, but it doesn't end a relationship, which struggles
on in the survivor's mind towards some final resolution, some clear
meaning . . .*
R. W. Anderson, *I Never Sang for My Father.*

Introduction

On a Friday afternoon more than a quarter century ago, I finished gathering some
notes and prepared to leave my university office. I planned to spend the weekend
drafting a talk I would deliver the following month. Just at my departure moment,
I answered the phone. I listened as my brother informed me that our mother had
died while visiting with his family in New York.

My experience of the week that followed was one of the most intense of my
life. During that week I began reflecting upon not only my mother's (and father's)
life and passing but upon my own life and its meaning and quality. And because
the day I was to give my talk coincided with the final day of the second period of
mourning per Judaic custom, it seemed both appropriate and meaningful to share
some of that experience.

The talk's original theme dealt with issues of competence and the ability to
cope with the depersonalization and anomie that result from an increasingly
industrialized and institutionalized society. My intent was to address some concerns
regarding the increasing disenfranchisement of the family and the community from
their educative and socializing responsibilities and the subsequent dangers of
isolation, loneliness and hopelessness inherent therein. Further, I intended to rebut
some of the popular attacks on the family, especially those that impugn it as
functionless and lacking survival value in our contemporary world. Although the
agenda for the talk remained the same, the approach took a different tack.

The assembly-line American[2] family

As a family professional, my interest has largely focused on quality-of-life issues,
particularly those related to the near environment — home, family, and community.

1. First published in *Family Relations*, July, 1975. Reprinted by permission of the publisher.
2. Footnote overleaf.

Such concerns start with basic human pragmatics: our needs for adequate food, clothing, and shelter which are as germane now as they have been to all human beings throughout history. Yet with the possible exception of the now-waning field of home economics, few academic disciplines deal with these issues.

The need for nutritional awareness is as critical now as ever, despite the modern innovations of vitamin-fortified foods (e.g., Product 19, Space Bars, and Wonderbread). The easy availability of vitamins and nutritional supplements does not seem to mitigate the continuing trend in western nations towards overfed, yet undernourished, children and adults. What is more, far too many people remain poorly housed, ill clothed, and badly in need of health care, despite large sectors of overall affluence in developed nations. The yellow brick road which modern technology has led us down to the Oz of overproduction and consumption for the sake of profits becomes badly in need of paving when we confront the ruts and potholes of energy crises, world famine, and pollution of air and water. Although contemporary America may have a plethora of supposed work-saving gadgets in more and more homes, studies indicate that today's families are no happier than their predecessors with regard to time spent on household chores. Statistics on divorce and the increasing numbers of families applying for therapy do not suggest that science and technology have significantly enhanced the quality of our home-lives in the last millenium.

What has happened that deflects us from the good life? The nub of the problem seems to be that which has been referred to as the crisis of modernity where, in but one short century, technological advances have outstripped our abilities to cope with the enormous powers gleaned therefrom. In earlier days we were concerned with efficiency. The Gilbreth's (1911) showed us ways to conserve time and energy in both industry and the home. But it seems that we have never really come to grips with the true meaning of efficiency. We have somehow managed to translate means into ends. One of the means-ends phenomena that I have often referred to as the *assembly line mentality* permeates not just our manufacturing of goods and materials but the way we deal and relate to each other, as well.

On an assembly line, each worker performs a single, specific task ideally with machine-like precision. The more precise the performance, the higher the efficiency rating. More often than not, those on the assembly line have little knowledge of the totality of the product upon which they are working. As a consequence, there is little opportunity to develop that which we now nostalgically refer to as pride in one's craft. There is little sense of accomplishment and a corresponding lack of self-esteem. Each worker becomes a super-specialist: a gear inserter or label inspector. Lost is the sense of the whole, a sense of integrity. And we have

---

2. My apologies to those of other cultures who may read this and the following chapter and conclude that I am being an American chauvinist. Having lived virtually all of my life in the United States, I can speak knowingly only of my experience within this culture. However, as the world shrinks through technology, I suspect that all of us will come to appreciate the degree to which the same forces, tensions, and contradictions discussed in this and the next chapter exist in other post-technological western cultures.

generalized this mode of mass production. Not only do we build our cars and houses and process our food this way, (even worse) we train our children this way.

The efficiency of mass production and modern technology has certainly given us much. True, we still have our poor, but, in fairness, never have so many lived so well. However, there have been tradeoffs. Like the sorcerer's apprentice, we do not know how to stop the beast. The line must keep moving and producing, developing all kinds of commodities and goods we neither need nor want but have been trained to want and need in order to keep the machine well oiled and going. We now have a plethora of work-saving tools and gadgets, even artificial fibers and foods, but somehow we also have a corresponding loss in our sense of self.

The worker on the assembly line has little association with his colleagues at the beginning or end of the line — only with those nearest. There is no sense of starting, no satisfaction in completing, and little sense of belonging. We have come to emulate the machines that we created and now serve. It is this crisis of automation that strikes at the core of our humanness. Of all the creatures in the biosphere only humans have an awareness of the whole of it. Of all the beings on this earth it is only we who understand birth and anticipate death. We have knowledge of our past, and although we may not know the future, we generally presume its existence and try to envision and plan for it. Indeed, apart from our opposable thumb and the technology that it has enabled, it is our self-awareness that sets humankind apart from the others with whom we share this planet. But in embracing technology, we seem to have lost something — our sense of purpose.

Despite the fact that telephones, electronic mail and the media enable us to communicate with one another more easily, we do not seem to have enhanced our understanding of each other. Despite the fact the we can get more places faster, we do not seem to know why we are in such a hurry, or indeed where we want to go, or why we need to get there. But we must be on the move. The whole idea of *standing still* is imbued with slovenliness and lack of progress which are bad for the country's economy. We equate progress with technological advances and with *things*. To be productive and acquire those things we have been trained to want, modern parents work each day from dawn to well past sundown.

We have tended to merge our concept of the quality of life with a commodity orientation. The name of the game is acquisition. We acquire not for permanence but for change. To make life easier or have more fun we must have a new home, car, TV, computer, or cell phone. But life does not seem to be getting easier. Nor do we seem to be having more fun. We find it somehow more difficult to cope as these commodities inundate us with ownership and maintenance. We appear to have somehow lost control of ourselves and the world around us. We no longer can tinker with our cars; they have become the purview of expert mechanics. Any but the simplest plumbing or electrical task (that is, changing a washer or light bulb) is beyond the expertise of most homeowners. And we no longer make jokes about such ineptitude. It is an accepted given.

We have come to the point where mass production has made it easier and less expensive to get rid of the old and buy a new one than repair the old. The disposable world is upon us. From dishes to diapers, from clothing to cars and computers — it is easier and somehow more desirable to throw it away than to keep it working. It is also patriotic, for it helps the economy. Then suddenly, one day, we awaken and find ourselves up to our progressive necks in waste and garbage. Perhaps it is walls of waste that have separated us from one another, led to a sensed loss of control over our lives and our world, and left us with corresponding feelings of loneliness and incompetence.

Pre-technological people were, by and large, generalists not specialists. They made use of the world at large in a holistic way. No scrap of material was considered waste. When they burned wood to cook the mutton and keep themselves warm, they used trees they had cleared from the land they had plowed. They saved ashes to make lye that they combined with the residue of fat from the sheep that they ate to make soap with which they washed the wool from those same sheep. There was an ecological elegance to the way they understood the workings of their environment, an understanding and articulation between them and their world that we have lost through specialized technology. When the preschool urban child is asked where does milk come from, we smile when he or she responds 'from cartons'. Yet how many adults are aware of the simple process of making soap? A better question might be how many of us are aware that wanton consumption of gasoline by the gas-guzzling engines lavished upon us by auto-makers creates an increase in the price of our children's new wash-and-wear clothing? The two questions are basically the same: they ask that we again see our resources and ourselves as parts of a reciprocating ecosystem. The answers, like the handwriting on the wall, are harsh reminders that we can no longer be complacent about how our system operates or take any part of our world for granted.

To suggest that we return to making our own soap and spinning our own wool is patently absurd. But through super-specialism, by continuing to exacerbate our lack of awareness of the interconnectedness of modern humankind to its world, we rebuild the tower of Babel in modern technological terms. This is not so much absurd as tragic. From Moses and Plato to the framers of the *Magna Carta* and the *United States Constitution*, people were concerned with the quest for *the good life*, but somehow differently than we are today. What do we mean by *the good life*? Do we take it to mean doing, making, and using more things more quickly or, rather, producing a better society for the benefit of all, a society in which our relationships to each other and the environment have some sense of integrity and meaning?

If we train, rather than educate, not concerned citizens but technicians, each with his or her own single area of expertise (replete with specialized jargon), then we have been ensnared by the assembly-line mentality. Then our talk of the quality of life, like the tower of Babel, becomes an edifice of hypocrisy — a structure with no function, reaching for pie in the sky while ignoring bread on the table. The world of the generalist may be long past, but the world of the isolated specialist has been with us long enough to assess the results, both positive and negative, that have brought us in either case to the present crisis of modernity.

To this end, the family as interface among individuals, society, and the environment is the focal point. In the face of claims that the family is a dying institution, we need note that research consistently indicates that everything from eating habits to social skills and morals are learned around the family table. Families teach these lessons with far more effectiveness and staying power than do classrooms that use elaborate, commercial visual aids to extol the virtues of the *food pyramid* or media campaigns that urge the curbing of drug use by 'just saying no'. System analyses of decision-making paradigms may appear sophisticated, but they only continue to tell us what we already know but refuse to believe: we impart values from generation to generation by the ways in which we deal with our children in our homes. And these are the values that directly affect the decisions we make regarding everything from how to dress and whether or whom to marry. Thus, despite its being knocked about by prophets of gloom, the family unit is still the most potent force for (and last bastion of) an integrated and purposive modern humankind.

However, the family, like all other elements of society, is not immune to the splintering effects of specialization. To survive and to ensure that its individual members survive, the family must adapt to the larger ecosystem. It has, thus, streamlined itself from the deep-rooted, extended structure it once was (steeped in history and tradition) to the shallow-rooted nuclear or single-parent module of today. The post-technological family has become increasingly isolated from its kin network so that a specialized kind of peer-oriented constellation of age-mates predominates in today's urban and suburban communities. This horizontal nature of the modern family contrasts sharply with the more vertical age-articulating structures common to the extended family of the less megapolitan town of the past.

The modern family is geared toward training its children to be independent of any vertical family structure. To a great extent this facilitates the kind of physical mobility needed to jockey for position in our extensive national marketplaces. A nuclear family, like a module in an assembly line, must be prepared to *plug in* where it will function most effectively within the larger system. Thus, its vertical extended family ties must be loose while, simultaneously, it must be easily able to establish horizontal peer ties that will result in flexible mobility and speedy adaptability. We have, indeed, translated a technological concept of efficiency into our human relationships and called it *human engineering*.

The cost to society has been discussed by social analysts: *Future Shock* (Toffler, 1970), *Pursuit of Loneliness* (Slater, 1970), and *We The Lonely People* (Keyes, 1973). When reflecting upon the cultural climate of the time, these social critics came to roughly the same conclusions (implied by the titles of their books): American society suffers from a growing sense of shock, isolation and loneliness, and a desperate search for connectedness. Each author uses somewhat different metaphors. For Toffler the family becomes, appropriately enough, the *giant shock absorber* of the mobile society. Keyes' central theme is the quest for community through the local McDonald's or 7-Eleven store. Slater uses the toilet, rather than the assembly line, as the touchstone and symbol of humankind's isolation from itself and its world. He contends with far less humor than one might suppose that indoor plumbing, by providing us the ability to flush our waste away, has led to a kind of sterilizing concept that we apply to the whole of society. He compares our mental institutions, nursing homes, and old-age communities to gigantic societal toilets where we flush away our distasteful human wastes. We have transposed increasingly sophisticated technological control over our physical environment to a similar state of affairs in our personal environment, where all but the most basic familial ties have been severed through institutionalization. The ramifications of a sense of personal fragmentation and social isolation are enormous and frightening.

The crisis of morality which some social critics blame for the ills of modern society — everything from divorce, drugs, and violence — is actually not a cause but, rather, another symptom of a total lack of the concept of connectedness from which a true sense of integrity must emanate. When we lose our personal sense of cause and effect, we may find it overly easy to justify actions that result in our immediate gratification and, consequently, may erode (even obscure) our sense or appreciation of personal right and wrong. Thus, self-serving behavior in even one aspect can have exponential impact upon the whole of society. Twentieth-century technology has hardly softened the curse of Cain.

As a family advocate, I have struggled with potential solutions to our collective modern dilemma. We have turned over to our educational institutions those concerns once clearly under the purview of the family. Our schools now attempt to teach everything from decision-making to human sexuality to our young people, as a means of helping them cope with the complexities of modern life. With our children's alarmingly increased exposure to violence in the schools (e.g., Dunblane, and Columbine),[3] we are even allowing the schools to counsel our children about violence and death, topics once taboo there. But I wonder if the school is the appropriate venue in which to meaningfully deal with such intensely personal and important topics, issues once clearly under the purview of the family. I seriously doubt that the schools can embrace and educate our children about such intensely personal subjects. Thus, as I share my personal experience surrounding the death of my mother, I hope to convey the importance and centrality of the family to the quality of my life and that of those nearest me.

Death, grief, and mourning

Like many people today I had, as a youngster, little direct personal experience with death — the loss of one grandparent when I was six, and another at 18 while I was away at college. My first truly impactful encounter with death was when my father died of a heart attack at age 58 and I was 24. As a young man and product

---

3. Two contemporary massacres of children have proven our inability to shelter and protect even our young from the atrocities enabled by modern technology. One mass shooting of 16 small children and their teacher, occurred in Dunblane, Scotland (in 1996) by a deranged 43-year-old member of the community. The other took place in Columbine High School, Colorado, USA, where two emotionally disturbed students killed 15 people and wounded 28 others (in 1999).

of my culture, I had few handles to deal with my loss. I could relate his death to little. I was angry at the felt injustice of this situation and repulsed by the social and religious rituals surrounding it. The funeral, the mourning period, the enforced socialization of friends and relatives all seemed barbaric.

Fifteen years later, my thoughts were quite different that Friday afternoon following my brother's call about my mother's death. Driving home, my mind was racing. We had had some preparation for the event. My mother had a weakening heart. Yet, at 73, she seemed much younger, more active and vital, somehow not old. Just three weeks before, ironically, for the first time that any of us could recall, all of the family — my mother, her three sons, their wives and her nine grandchildren — came together to celebrate my niece's college graduation.

Speeding home on the expressway, I believed I appeared strange to the drivers in the other cars who could see that I was crying. (Now I doubt that anyone noticed.) A seemingly absurd idea occurred to me, the middle-aged father of four: I was an orphan. However, this notion was not absurd. Vital links to my past had been severed. A repository of knowledge and experience was lost: no longer was there a way of checking whether I had ever had the mumps or chicken pox or how old I was when Cousin Bert was married: never another taste of the magnificent pastry that my mother had learned to make only by watching her mother — the recipe for which, for some reason, never was translated into measured cups and teaspoonfuls. Little and large memories bombarded me. I became supersensitive to the past and who I was in relationship to her and the rest of my family. It was now I who was the older generation. It was this kind of thinking that was the harbinger of a week of such thoughts, islands of which even now — 25 years later — still occur.

We had prepared the children for this eventuality. Yet, as anticipated, each reacted in her or his own personal way. Although we had discussed the subject as openly as we could, no preparation could have been adequate for the Cleveland funeral, that they would have to experience. I was concerned about how they might react to seeing me, their father, in an emotionally overwhelmed, grieving state. My wife and I talked about it. We momentarily discussed the desirability of leaving the children at home. We then realized that we were being seduced into the dilemma of the modern parent: how to protect ones' children from the realities of life events and inevitabilities that would demand the ability to cope and test their sense of competence. In times past and in simpler societies even today, such questions never occur. Considering death and birth as functions of life, children experience them directly as part of maturation. Not so in the assembly-line toilet society where aging, infirmity, and death are dirty ugly words. They are links to the past that serve no apparent function in the present.

The next three days were intense, arduous and exhausting. First a seven-hour drive; the awkward greetings of my brothers and their wives who had flown in and had already begun disassembling the apartment; the funeral; the meeting of friends and relatives (many I hadn't seen for ten or fifteen years); and the final packing of a lifetime of memorabilia. Each moment was filled with myriad thoughts and feelings that only much later began to merge into some poignant totality. The day of the burial I was barely aware of my children. That evening, when we had time to talk before bed, my grief for them became tangible.

I had grown up surrounded by grandparents, aunts, uncles, and cousins — a veritable community of extended family ties. To my children, I thought, these people had little meaning; they were like shadows in a dream or characters in a play, only momentarily there. To me, that day, they signaled a journey into the past: talking of other relatives and friends now distant or dead, of old times, small incidents and large, holidays and vacations spent together. Relating to them was easy, exceedingly comfortable and comforting. Those people knew me in a way I had forgotten people could know one another: intimately, nonjudgmentally. It was as if the lapse of time between visits did not exist.

There was talk of the continuity of the generations, the physical resemblance of my children to me at their respective ages; there was connectedness that made me terribly aware of my children's deprivation. For me there had been aunts and uncles who would listen and understand hurt or anger at parents, siblings, or friends. I had had no need to run away, as do many children today. I had only to walk a block or two away from home for solace and still remain within the protection of my family. Just as in my own house, I was at home in any of a half-dozen homes within walking distance, and my parents were as assured as if I had been home. And if even in my own home I felt a bit deprived or wanting, I could always count on a grandmother or aunt to soften my parents' attitudes.

I realized that now there was one less giving person to spoil my children a little, and I became wistful for them. We talked more that evening. One by one they came to me to say goodnight and share some of their thoughts and concerns of the day, their inability to understand some of their own reactions and feelings. And I listened and heard them in a way that I never had before. In some ways their loss was indeed greater than mine. And I mourned more for them than for myself. In my relationship with my children, that night has become a watershed. I think of it often. How glad I was that the children had come with us. They had gained, I later learned from them, a bit of their past and who they were in relationship to it, even in this brief and seemingly disturbing experience. Their roots of self had sunk a bit deeper.

For me, the next day was the most difficult. There was the business of closing my mother's apartment. In many respects it was the interment through dissemination of the bits and pieces of her life. The three pairs of us were there deciding which of the tangible anchor points to our memories we wanted; there was little of great extrinsic value. There were no fights, as I understand are common in such instances. Nevertheless the situation was extremely difficult.

And as the chaos slowly disappeared into boxes, pair by pair we left: first one brother who drove my mother's car back to New York for my nephew, then the other whom we drove to the airport. In between we talked about the past and the future. As we dropped them off, my sister-in-law commented with great intensity, 'We must make the effort to keep in touch'. And I realized that, indeed, my mother had been a kind of mortar that cemented the bond between my brothers' families and mine over distance and time, a kind of clearinghouse of information and affection about relatives seldom seen. And I mourned again, this time for myself.

My wife and I returned to close up the apartment and finish the packing — the final stage. We both felt the need to have the place in the kind of order she would have had it if she had moved out. We straightened up and cleaned out the refrigerator, the final task. Whereas we had been practical in our decisions of what to save and dispose of previously, exhaustion and a need to be finished made us somewhat indiscriminate. All that remained were partially opened jars and bottles, sustenance to keep one alive — not objects. We were near the end. At the back of the middle shelf I came upon a large plastic canister. I opened it. It contained an enormous quantity of shelled pecans. I began to throw them away — but could not. I began weeping. Somehow this one item, foolish as it may sound, captured something of the past that nothing had before.

My mother had been a prolific and brilliant baker. Her tour-de-force was an inimitable pecan coffeecake. In my childhood she used to bake daily. How well I remember, even now, the smell of yeast dough and caramelized sugar upon arriving home from school. My father, the father of three during the depression years, was a firm believer of buying in quantity. Despite hard times our basement locker was always filled with vast stores of canned goods. We were not affluent but never wanted for food. Somehow the paradox of this large canister filled with pecans, nestled in the back of a tiny refrigerator sparsely populated with single-serving commodities, symbolized something of the memories and values which were as much a part of me as my genetic heritage, the color of my eyes, the shape of my nose. I could not bring myself to throw the container — now a symbol — away.

We closed the apartment, bare now except for a few large pieces of furniture and some clothing. The apartment had little meaning for me — it was not the house of my childhood. Now denuded of any remnants of the past it was a hollow, impersonal place. We picked up the children and prepared for the journey home. The trip was flooded with thoughts and conversations of the past few days. I began to realize that in some ways my senses had become activated, sensitized. Odors, a snatch of a song, a familiar road or landmark, all took on significance. The facial tissue that we brought from the apartment smelled of my mother's cologne, the road led to a trip once taken as a family. Somehow everything began relating to everything else. On the way home, we decided to stop at our cabin in the Pennsylvania mountains to catch our breath. At the cabin the next morning, the old carpenter and his helper arrived early to begin the deck we were attaching. A strange coincidence or fate: whatever one might call it, it was ironic that he came that Wednesday morning of all times. We had asked him to build the deck months before.

The groan of his chainsaw signaled his work. My youngest son, taken with machinery, was watching from the window. Suddenly he ran to his mother, tearing profusely. The carpenter was sawing down a large, old favorite, clump birch to make room for the deck. He, who until that moment had been the least articulate, was mourning and grieving for both that tree and my mother with profound intensity, and I understood and grieved with him. We talked of the loss of the tree and decided its wood would keep us warm in the winter, and that we might even make something of some of the logs. We would not waste that loved and familiar tree just as we would cherish the memories of his grandmother. He accepted that. He was learning to comprehend and cope in his own way.

Although not a religious person in the ritualistic sense of my faith, I took the remainder of the week, as prescribed by tradition, to mourn. I had never really understood the concept, so first I read on the meaning of the mourning periods. The traditions and rituals abound. They are specified and manifold. Too numerous to elaborate here, they are impressive. Essentially they state that during the mourning period the bereaved are to spend the time with family and friends and in prayer and study. The prescribed prayers are brief, and they do not deal with death but, rather, with life and the continuation of the generations.

I was somehow reassured and warmed to know that my ancestors had performed the same rites in the same manner for countless generations, and that someday my children would do the same in my memory. This awareness gave me a profound sense of continuity. The sensibility of the prescription was impressive and I followed it. I read Kubler-Ross (1969) again, and Aries (1962), and Buber (1937): religious and other scholars and philosophers of the past and others who had written on the topic of death, dying, and grieving.

I did not concern myself with the office, budgets, schedules, or students. The time was mine; I took it and savored it. It helped me put into perspective many of the thoughts I now share. It is difficult for me to phrase my feelings about those four days. When I returned to the routines of my life, I tried explaining to people what a positive experience it had been for me, but most of them were at a different place. They wanted to express their condolences and be done with it. I can understand that; I had often reacted similarly. Modern technological society does not look upon dying and mourning as positive experiences. It has few traditions or ceremonies for dealing with loss and death. One must pick up where one left off at the assembly line without missing a beat. I am not sure whether this is but another *symptom* of our lack of connectedness — our totally present orientation — or whether it is a *cause* for some of it. But I am convinced that disconnectedness is an integral part of our sensed emptiness (despite our affluence) and desperate search for meaning in our lives.

We have systematically stripped our lives of any traditions that link us to our past and, as a consequence, to our future. Although, for the vast majority in western society there is Christmas, it has been so commercialized as to become an orgy of promotion and consumption. We have, rather, a unique tradition of anti-tradition. And this I believe is a key element in our loss of connectedness and lack of integratedness. In the past, in classes on parenting, I have encouraged parents and students to establish secular traditions where the sacred do not already exist or where they seem inappropriate. It is often these little regularities which children most remember and which allow them a sense of familial attachment, integrity, connectedness, and rootedness. They are the embellishments of existence that take us beyond the level of survival and subsistence and into the realm of living, in the fullest sense of the word. They are the bases for the distinctions among coping, competence, and creativity, each step of which raises humankind above its animal cousins and therefore makes us responsible to both ourselves and them. Interconnection and intimacy with our world are what I think it behooves us to mean when we refer to the quality of life.

Cultures establish rituals and traditions that mark our coming and our going, our joining and our parting. These traditions enhance and facilitate the inevitabilities of life: birth, coming of age, marriage, and death. They give people a sense of what and who they are and where we are going. These are actually the rites of passage from one life's stage to the next designated by virtually all cultures. When a society systematically denies these embellishments, it deprives its members of their cultural essence and the very elements of their humanness. To recognize and anticipate our end as well as our beginning are one and the same and are vital to our continuance as a species.

Conclusion

The following sonnet by a contemporary poet is one which I had posted in my office for many years. Originally, I clipped it from a magazine because of my natural aversion to one of the miracles of modern society, plastic flowers. It sums, I think, my thoughts in 14 lines, simply, yet most eloquently:

> The man who invented the plastic rose
> Is dead. Behold his mark:
> His undying flawless blossoms never close
> But guard the grave unbending through the dark.
> He understood neither beauty nor flowers
> Which catch our hearts in nets as soft as sky
> And bind us with a thread of fragile hours.
> Flowers are beautiful because they die.
> Beauty without the perishable pulse
> Is dry and sterile, an abandoned stage
> With false forests. But the results
> Support this man's invention; he knew his age:
> A vision of our tearless time discloses
> Artificial men sniffing plastic roses.

> J. Peter Meinke
> *On the Death of the Man Who Invented Plastic Roses*

Apologia for the Family[1]

2

> *In the Götterdämmerung which overwise science and overfoolish
> statesmanship are preparing for us, the last man will spend his last
> hours searching for his wife and child.*
> Ralph Linton (1949, p.38).

Introduction

Written over a half-century ago, Linton's apocalyptic quote still has chilling power perhaps even more so now than then. During roughly the same period, I have been a student, teacher and advocate of the family. This chapter — a draft of which was written early in my career — was originally entitled *The Family is Dead — Long Live the Family*! A later extended version I called *Survival and the Discovery of the Family*. Each is an unabashed apologia for the institution of the family.

An American cultural paradox

The ethos of American culture demonstrates an essential tension between two basic cultural values, two poles which seem glaringly contradictory: a belief in the right to individual and different lifestyles (e.g., the *Bill of Rights*) versus the constraint to conformity (i.e., *the melting pot*). The first English settlers to the United States sought freedom to worship as they chose and codified this ideology a century and a half later in the *United States Constitution*. The *melting pot* notion began to crystallize during the nation's industrialization in the late 1800s and a subsequent wave of major immigration from Europe (circa 1900). The family, the mediator between the individual and society, continues to sit in the middle of this paradoxical tension.

Living amid the complexities of post-technological society, we rarely reflect upon these apparently conflicting ideologies. The velocity of social change initiated in eighteenth century England via the industrial revolution pales by comparison to the myriad cultural changes wrought by the twentieth century's technological revolution. Our long-standing cultural paradox is exacerbated by burgeoning technology that races faster than culture can accommodate. In an effort to lend

1. Revised version of paper first published as 'The family is dead — long live the family!' *Youth and Society, 3,* (1975) pp. 60–79. Sage. Reprinted with permission of publisher.

some semblance of control over our lives, as is the American penchant, we search for the root of the problem in order to fix it. But in our efforts to remedy the problem we use the familiar disease/cure model and focus upon a symptom rather than the problem's cause. One of our frequently (and mistakenly) preferred scapegoats is the already overworked and overburdened American family.

The family is a natural whipping boy for both professional and lay observers of the modern scene. In part this is because the family is familiar. Good or bad, we all have had familial experiences and have observed those of others. As mediator between the individual and society and by dint of its first social contact with the child, the family begins the civilizing process. Thus, when children do not seem to be adapting to the society of which they are a part, the first target for blame is the family.

Increasing and alarming violence among our young adds further credence to the hue and cry that the family is failing to fulfill its function adequately. Serious questions regarding modern parents' childrearing practices arise when data suggest that greater than previously-recorded numbers of highly motivated, middle-class children and youth now resort to violence and drugs or opt out of the educational marketplace before they complete their education. It therefore seems more than coincidental that professional interest in the analysis of family dynamics continued to increase dramatically during the past half-century.

Study of the family

The family, once primarily the purview of sociologists and cultural anthropologists such as George Murdock (1949), Margaret Mead (1950), and Talcott Parsons (1955) is under continuous scrutiny by behavioral scientists of all persuasions. Family therapy, a field previously dominated by pastors and a few vanguards like Nathan Ackerman (1958), Erika Chance (1959), and Murray Bowen (1961) is now an accepted means of intervention. In the last generation it has become a licensed profession in its own right; other mental health professionals in most community mental health clinics across the country also practice it.

The bulk of research regarding the tenor of the American family has been dominated by sociology. Early sociological views of the family were relatively simplistic and filled with generalizations and abstractions. Across cultures the family was considered the most basic of all institutions and the paradigm for all primary groups. Despite variations on this theme, the notion of the universality of the family went much unchallenged until fairly recently.

Early thinking was perhaps best embodied in and crystallized by Murdock (an anthropologist) who in 1949 summarized the four necessary and sufficient functions of the family in all its permutations in all cultures as: (a) socialization, (b) economic cooperation, (c) reproduction, and (d) sexual relations (Murdock, 1949). As shibboleth for the universality of the family, Aberle (1950) dubbed these four *functional prerequisites*. Similarly, Parsons and Bales examined contemporary society and suggested that family functions may be reduced to two: (a) socialization and acculturation of the young and (b) the stabilization and articulation of the adult members of society (Parsons and Bales, 1955). Later, Reiss (1965) in an ultimate simplification, proffered only one basic universal function of the family — *nurturant socialization*. He went even further by asserting that, in some cultures, the nuclear family appears unimportant, even absent.

The situation is at best confusing with regard to what contemporary social analysts think about the future of the family. A third of a century ago, there were those who saw the family as a progressively dysfunctional appendix to a post-industrial societal body. Even the more optimistic suggested a narrowing and specializing of the family's role in society (Rodman, 1965). Thus, in the view of some, it became primarily a *haven in a heartless world* (Lasch, 1977) or a *giant shock absorber* (Toffler, 1970) — and an overloaded one at that — for post-industrial Homo sapiens. At the beginning of the twenty-first century there are fewer predictions, but models abound in an effort to understand the family (see Cherlin, 1999). Most popular today are the family systems models (Burr, Day, and Bahr, 1993) and the feminist framework (Osmand and Thorne, 1993).

Although the work of such theorists may sometimes seem a bit removed from the everyday problems facing us, such theories demonstrate efforts to discern and explain the forces that, over time, shape our society, its institutions, and our world. The hope is that through understanding we may gain some measure of control. Simultaneously, behavioral scientists concerned with therapeutic intervention may agree with their sociological colleagues that the family is beleaguered and unable to cope effectively with the demands placed upon it in today's world. Thus, as more families seek help in dealing with problems of living, they turn to family therapy.

The clinical perspective
The clinician's approach to family study is far more pragmatic and somewhat less theoretical than that of the sociologist. Clinicians who traditionally have been concerned with the active, day-to-day functioning of individuals have set the stage for a change of emphasis from the individual's behavior to that of the family unit as a whole.

Until recently, family therapists had their moorings in the more classical branches of individual psychotherapy (e.g., psychiatry, psychiatric social work, and clinical psychology). Many, e.g., Fritz Redl (1951) and Nathan Ackerman (1938), began their work with children, believing that often the disturbed child was merely an outward manifestation of a disturbed family. Treatment of the referred child often disclosed even more severe pathology in other children within the family or was considered relatively ineffective without the inclusion of other family members. Others, such as Murray Bowen (1965), Donald Jackson (1961), and Carl Whitaker (1965), started with severely disturbed adult patients (i.e., schizophrenics) and noted little gains from traditional methods that did not include patients' families. Thus, the family eventually provided a framework from which psychotherapy might offer greater success.

Despite different theoretical origins and the 'bewildering array of diverse forms of family treatment' (Ackerman, 1970, p. 123), the current emphasis in family therapy concentrates (virtually) entirely upon the internal workings of the family. (For a detailed explication of the state of the art, see Goldenberg and Goldenberg, 2000.) Thus, conclusions drawn from both macro (the study of society) and micro (the study of the individual) perspectives lead increasingly to a refined examination of the family. But the situation is disorganized and confusing.

In the clinical arena, insidious dangers underlie and confusions result from such scrutiny. Diagnosis and prognosis without recommendations for habilitative strategies are primarily intellectual athletics. Focus on the family often encourages the inference that the institution itself causes difficulties within the larger society but, in reality, the family is a responsive institution grown overtaxed and overwhelmed by the many conflicting demands made upon it. Familial structures do not shape society. Rather, they reflect and respond to it. The family is (and is likely to remain) the primary socializing unit within any society.

The family as whipping boy
When during periods of social crisis we have concerns about the manner in which our society is functioning, we often look to the family as a primary cause of the problem. When, for example, violence, divorce, and youth alienation or underachievement increase, we presume our family structures are ineffective — even defective. But the family is a responsive institution — a mediator between the individual and the culture. Thus, rather than see the family as a causal agent and reproach it, perhaps we might better question whether it is adjusting perhaps *too* well, and is performing its functions too efficiently in grooming its children for society, the values of which may be somewhat askew. Perhaps no culture demonstrates this phenomenon better than that of Nazi Germany before and during World War II. Families either groomed their children for the state or were systematically destroyed.

Social science must question the appropriateness of its willingness to maintain a stance of *scientific neutrality* or social relativism with regard to the society that it is both examining and of which it is a part. When examining the institutions of society, are we also prepared to examine and evaluate the values of the society in which they operate? In past times such questions were under the purview of philosopher-statesmen. Today they are often left to gadflies. Thus, when Aldous Huxley (1932) and George Orwell (1949) proposed their societies of the future based upon technocracy and the assembly-line efficiency of Henry Ford, we were troubled but skeptical that their *Brave New World* or *1984* would ever be so close at hand.

American families and the communities that house them have primarily become suppliers of raw material for educational assembly lines that attempt to process greater and greater numbers of individuals. Education has become more and more bureaucratized and, in its attempts to serve larger and larger numbers, has resorted to techniques that seem more efficient but are often less than effective. Far too often we rely upon poorly standardized tests, inadequately evaluated curricula, and ill-defined goals and objectives in establishing mass educational policies. We then become discouraged with the extremely disappointing results. Simultaneously, we encourage our families to proffer their young to our educational institutions (earlier and earlier), and then castigate the family for its ineffectiveness in socializing our young appropriately.

The developmental vantage point

Unlike many Asian nations where, until recently, the system of age grading was a relatively straight ascending line, i.e., the older one became the more status and respect one attained, our system reflects a normative or bell-shaped curve. From this perspective, the relatively narrow age range (roughly 35 through 55 years of age) becomes the pinnacle power years. These are the years when one reaches one's acme in the production-consumer society in which we live. Those on either end of this age range are often seen as dependent in some way or another. Edwards (1967, p. 509) has phrased the situation succinctly if perhaps somewhat brutally:

> In many instances it is not too much of an overstatement to consider as objects those that have not yet developed exchangeable resources (the young) and those who have exhausted theirs (the elderly). Even those occupying the middle ground, however, are not necessarily in an enviable position, for their relationships often lack all but a vestige of emotional interchange.

Thus, for a third of our lives, maturing means gaining independence, power, and respect. This is the phase that we refer to as *growing up*, and it is imbued with the dreams and expectations of becoming a person. The middle phase of our lives is marked by intense activity — often fraught with anxiety and the desperate need to achieve. Achievement, usually measured by monetary success and conspicuous consumption, is paired with raising children and ensuring their successful launching.

Our children's transition into their teens and twenties and subsequent autonomy (that which has been referred to as the *empty nest* phase) has become, in our society, the prelude to their parents' retirement. At this stage we refer to parents as *growing old*. Growing old in contemporary society is imbued with negative connotations: lack of vitality, vigor, and productivity. Thus, the worship of youth becomes the order of the times. We continually emphasize our unique tradition of anti-tradition in this way: that which is new (i.e., young) is better.

Other ramifications of condensing the productivity years are manifold. There is desperation to achieve and a need to do it quickly. Whereas stability of employment was once looked upon as the ideal, now if young workers do not change positions frequently, they are not considered *go-getters*. Thus, it is not uncommon for families to make a number of geographic moves to maintain and jockey for position and power in the economic marketplace. Increasingly, American culture is marked by a proliferation of dual-career parents attempting to achieve professional fulfillment and maintain an appropriate consumer-oriented standard of living.

Geographic moves and dual careers are additionally characterized by parents who are often more than willing to entrust much, if not all, of their children's socialization to professionals — the educators. This in turn encourages consistency and conformity in our educational systems so that children may move among different schools frequently. Such children are expected to adapt quickly to changes in venue, and their schools are expected to accommodate them quickly and easily in that adaptive process. Our overworked and (ironically) underpaid teachers are, in turn, forced to look for more efficient teaching methods that will allow them to process more children through our school systems faster.

Our primary and secondary schools have begun taking on the role of *in loco parentis* but without the moral authority to do so. Parents expect the public schools to educate and prepare their offspring for the competitive world but disallow any imposition of discipline or inculcation of values.

Nonetheless, teachers are the primary adult role models for our young during their developing years. Yet, because we have disenfranchised them from any but the most basic tasks of conveying information, and we disrespect them by poorly remunerating their efforts, they become ineffective as both models and mentors.

Geographic mobility is usually at the expense of extended family ties and commitment to community, thereby isolating the family further from a sense of belonging, rootedness, and tradition. Emotional interchange between generations is primarily expressed among the few people in the nuclear family. Grandparents, aunts and uncles become people to be e-mailed, called on the phone, and visited perhaps once or twice a year. Mostly, they are nonpresent.

This lack of articulation among generations leads to a paucity of caring adults available to mentor, model, and counsel our developing young, reinforcing a locked-in peer group or horizontal social structure. Troubled young people have few adults with whom they can share and discuss their problems and concerns. Friends or siblings are their primary avenues for expression. Grandparents are no longer sought for counsel, advice or decision-making. Rather they have been encouraged to let their children lead their own lives. Instead of the middle-class, working mother using her own mother to help raise her children, she turns (once again) to the professionals (e.g., nursery schools, day-care centers, nannies, etc.).

Horizontality and bureaucratization

Our children are thus well prepared for our peer-oriented culture. Home has become the place where one sleeps, grabs a meal on the run, watches TV, and chats with one's friends on the phone or the net — usually in one's own room. It is the place from which one leaves for day care and after care, nursery, elementary, middle and high school and then later, college and graduate school. It is also the place where one returns at day's end after myriad part-time extracurricular activities that may even include a part-time job. Consequently, after the first two or three years of a child's life, most parents probably spend less time with their offspring than do their teachers.

The modern western family stresses what has been referred to as the *instrumental* as opposed to *expressive* (Parsons, 1955) cog-wheeling of the institution: the distribution of funds and commodities, the planning of extrafamilial schedules, etc. Ubiquitously, the peer group becomes the primary emotional support system for the developing young. From nursery through graduate school, close association with anyone but nearest age-mates is exceptional.

The effects of increased horizontal association and lack of cross-generational ties are far reaching and troubling. They severely delimit the choice of experiential models to emulate and interactive individuals to lean on for emotionally supportive relationships. Thus the field is left open to the ever-present media for emulative objects. The TV industry has continued that which the movie industry began in the early part of the twentieth century. Unrealistic fantasies about love, marriage, and family life are assimilated by experience-hungry young. Sexual interaction — increasingly more specific and graphic — is often substituted for real emotional interchange. What's more, increasingly detailed and graphic depictions of violence are available in films, TV, and video games. Research regarding the effect of TV violence on children leaves little doubt regarding the negative impact on these young people (Huesman and Miller, 1994). Adding insult to injury, this kind of programming is constantly injected with machinegun-like selling by advertisers who stress and capitalize on the need to acquire, the desirability of newness, and the be-like-everybody-else-on-the-block mentality. Thus we allow our chidren to be conditioned by hedonism and immediate gratification.

From early on, children are catapulted into our highly competitive, achievement-oriented society. They are bereft of supportive adult relationships in their daily lives. They are bombarded by stimuli laden with sex, violence, and unrealistic expectations regarding interpersonal relationships. Increasingly, they are diagnosed with depression, attention deficit disorder, anorexia and other psychopathology. Our answer to this alarmingly growing number of maladapted young people is typically technological. Far too often we medicate these children to address symptoms which may be more a reflection of social malaise than individual psychopathology (see Garber, Garber and Spizman, 1996; Valenstein, 1998; and Wilens, 1999).

Childrearing practices
During the last half of the twentieth century, advice-givers offered numerous books on childrearing and stressed the magnitude of the importance of psychological development of the young, particularly during the first five years. Thus, parents know well that in this short five-year period they must inculcate the values they deem important before society (i.e., the school and the peer group) takes over. The effect is to instill anxiety in parents who, because of the horizontal nature of their own rearing, have had little first-hand experience with children. Now, when needed, they have little contact with their own parents, older siblings, and/or other extended family who may have had greater experience and could possibly furnish emotional support.

Modern parents thus turn to nonpresent authorities — books, manuals on child-rearing. These manuals are filled with developmental checklists, formulae and warnings, do's and don'ts. Because all situations cannot be covered, parents are left to interpret and extrapolate. As parental awareness increases that their offspring represent a formidable responsibility, they often adopt formulaic measures prescribed by various published authorities, hoping thereby to reduce their anxiety. For years parents have been warned that rigidly scheduled feeding and toilet training can stunt creativity and create *neurotic* behavior patterns in adults. As a result, flexible and child-demand schedules may too easily become exercises in lax or laissez-faire parenting. At the same time, the child may interpret freedom to mean license. Infants become unsuspecting tyrants ruling by the cudgels of guilt and uncertainty that have been instilled in confused and isolated parents.

When these undisciplined young become preadolescents and adolescents who have been repeatedly assured that we wish them to be creative, nonrestricted and unhampered individuals, we reverse ourselves and begin enforcing more authoritative behavior patterns. As parents we are then dismayed when our children do not heed our rules or seek our advice and counsel. In turn, our children resent the newly imposed standards that to them seem to have been suddenly and arbitrarily established. To make matters worse, we are hurt that (also seemingly suddenly) we play only a small part in their lives. Just as we put the finishing touches on the horizontal independence of our young, we recognize, too late, that we have created a gap between us.

We have, as parents, turned the childrearing process topsy-turvy. We have denied our young the benefit of structure and controls — of psychological protection — in infancy and toddlerhood, when it is most needed. Rather, we have delayed the process until the later years, the time when we should be granting more freedom and expecting more decision-making on the part of our youth.

The distinction between love and license must be made and the need for consistency in parenting emphasized. However, in light of cultural values and anxieties in our consumer-commodity society, parental love may erroneously be expressed by the doling out of goods. Through the most subtle form of behavior modification, the young have been trained to prize what parents have been substituting for discipline, guidance, time and understanding. Time is heavily structured in planned activities, generally away from the home. The result is a frantic shuttling between activities (Elkind, 1981) rather than the development of interaction between the generations and the creation of mutual interpersonal respect.

During times of social crisis, the family often becomes the object of concern for social critics, academics, and policy makers. We lament the loss of traditional *family values*. This is hardly a new phenomenon. William Goode (1963) referred to 'the classical family of western nostalgia'. Despite the observation that the family is a constantly changing mediating institution, we create cherished stereotypes embellished by our happiest memories and fantasies. A hunger and wish for affiliation, connection, and belonging, shape such icons.

Our children are being raised in communities where anonymity and the constraint towards conformity are the order of the day. There is no longer a spirit of neighborhood. As our communities grow larger and larger, and along with them our schools and universities, they become more like horizontal high-rises. Anonymity increases. The quest for individuality is mistakenly perverted into the pursuit of privacy that becomes almost obsessional. The result is increasing isolation and a growing sense of normlessness and confusion — anomie.

The young, having been trained in the model, associate with their peers. The old withdraw. We shake our heads when we see others' children playing with matches or chasing balls in the street, rather than take the time to correct their risky behavior. These are not our children and we have not the right to castigate them, just as we would not expect our neighbors to reprimand our own children for their inappropriate behavior. Recent attention has been brought to such behavior in our borrowing of the African slogan 'It takes a village to raise a child', but post-technological societies are no longer nations of villages. Only in times of great stress or emergency (when snowbound or during power failures) do glimmers of that spirit of neighborhood return.

What happens to our affiliative needs the rest of the time? To a large degree, we place the burden on the nuclear family and, like an obliging scapegoat, it desperately attempts to meet the need without questioning the role it is being asked to fulfill or recognizing the impossibility of the task and the unreasonableness of the request. Then the critics step in and condemn the family for its failures. Poor academic achievement, drug abuse, and violence have all been used as arguments that the modern American family has failed to meet the needs of post-industrial humankind. One compendium on the family contends: 'Not only is the nuclear family a faultily constructed piece of social engineering, but it also, in the long run, contains the seeds of its own destruction', (Skolnick and Skolnick, 1971, p. 29).

The protean family
The family's place in our personal and collective odysseys is of particular interest during times of social flux. Certainly the third millenium qualifies as such a time. Alvin Toffler (1970) predicted our *future shock* and Margaret Mead (1970) dubbed us *immigrants in time* inadequately prepared for a future totally different from our experience. It is in this context that we are told the family is incompetent to deal with the world of tomorrow.

Robert Lifton has gone so far as to propose that we are psychologically evolving to accommodate to our time. He sees a breed of Homo sapiens developing that is constantly in flux, shifting identity, uncommitted, continually experimenting with itself as well as the world around it. Lifton calls this person of the future, *Protean Man*, after Proteus,[1] the man of the sea in Greek mythology, who had the ability to change his shape to all forms of being and matter and know the past, present, and future.

---

1. We know of Proteus from the fourth book of the Odyssey, wherein Menalaus is told to seek him in order to find his way back home. Homer's tale is basically one of return to home and family.

However, Lifton suggests that our new protean persons pay a price for their chameleonesque abilities. They experience a

> break in the sense of connection which men have long felt with the vital and nourishing symbols of their cultural tradition — symbols revolving around family, idea systems, religions, and the life cycle in general. In our contemporary world one perceives these traditional symbols . . . as irrelevant, burdensome, or inactivating, and yet one cannot avoid carrying them within or having one's self-processes profoundly affected by them (Lifton, 1968, p.16).

Lifton never resolves the dilemma because, despite the cogency of his observations, he has misread the metaphor of the myth of the demigod, Proteus. Neptune was his father and the sea his mother — source of all life on this planet. Proteus' very name has been used by modern science to signify that which is the basis of all life, *protein*. Humankind is neither God nor demigod but the seeker of God. Humankind (like Menalaus and Odysseus) is the questioner, the wanderer.

The family, not humankind, fits the protean metaphor. The family knows past, present, and future. Through parents and grandparents and uncountable generations before them, the family relates us to our heritage — back to the first man and woman and beyond that to our protozoan past — in a continuous and unbroken chain. So too, does the family (and the many familial analogues by which we order our societies) engage us with our present, through siblings and extended family. Our language is replete with continual reference to familial bonds. Finally, the family speaks to our future through our children and their children's children. The family is the only representative of immortality presently available to us.

At different times and other cultures, the Protean family may indeed take various forms: from that of a large extended multigenerational clan to the smallest two-person, single-parent-and-child unit. Nonetheless, each functions as a family. The family is the whole that defines us as an interdependent species. The family is the place wherein rites of passage define us as human beings. These rituals mark our beginnings, our coming of age, our joining, our generating, and our parting.

Societies may attempt to constrain and mold their institutions to some idealized pattern of utopian ends, but when such constraints strike at the heart of familial priorities, they invariably fail. Thus, for example, the communal structures of Russia, Israel and Czechoslovakia showed signs of devitalization and eventually reorganized or collapsed as more and more parents in those societies wanted a greater share in the rearing of their children. So too, do companies in the United States meet resistance in their moving of executives, as families protest the sense of anchorlessness that such moves create.

This is not to suggest that there is some ultimate family form towards which we must direct ourselves. Indeed, that which makes the family so pivotal to us as a human species is its very adaptive protean quality. It is this very same quality which makes it so difficult to legislate policy that will facilitate the family's task of mediating between the individual and the culture. Thus, talk of the decline or demise of the family is as diagnostically naive as talk of strengthening it prescriptively is misleading.

What is therefore needed is not so much a plan for strengthening families but rather a societal and governmental attitude for enabling them. Strengthening implies knowledge of endpoint or ideal. We have no such knowledge. With all good intention and far too little knowledge we have intervened in cultures of other societies and in our own subcultures by imposing social standards that, at a given moment, may seem appropriate to a select number of policy makers. Enabling, on the other hand, suggests a multiplicity of facilitative means for preventing problems. It implies mitigating impediments rather than structuring solutions. It is freeing rather than constraining.

Conclusion

Mutual interdependence defines the human condition. The family is a social institution that nurtures, protects and cherishes its individual members while simultaneously meeting their needs for interpersonal intimacy. At least two reasons may explain why an institution is not meeting the needs of a society: (a) the institution is inadequate or (b) the ideologies, values, and priorities of the society in which the institution is operating may be awry. It is the second of these alternatives, I am firmly convinced, that we have not explored adequately.

The debate with regard to the universality and viability of the family may well continue among social scientists and critics. Suffice it to say that for all intents and practical purposes the idea of family is indigenous to the human species. Indeed, the family is perhaps the most satisfactory institution to which we have fallen heir. It is surely far more functional than any other we have as yet devised.

MARRIAGE: SAFEHOUSE OF LOVE AND TRUST[1]

3

That is why man leaves his father and his mother and attaches himself
to his wife and the two become one.
Genesis: 2:24

Introduction

The preceding apologia for the family discussed the centrality of the family in our lives, irrespective of the forms it may take. The present chapter adduces historical evidence of that centrality. We begin with the institution of marriage, defined as the public and conscious taking of a life partner. It is a safehouse of love and trust.

The institution of marriage

Although cross-cultural comparisons reveal all manner of variations on the typical monogamous unit we have come to know, marriage remains the most basic of all human institutions. No other social institution is either so indigenous to us or so defining of us as a unique species. For all cultures, marriage serves the universal function of maintaining responsible intimacy.

Recent trends, primarily the precipitous rise in divorce rates in the last half-century, have caused many observers to question the viability of marriage as an institution. To question its viability is tantamount to questioning the viability of civilization as we know it. It is not that we are not marrying; we are marrying, divorcing more frequently, and remarrying. We are continuously seeking the right relationship, the eternal match. A force that impelling — the romantic quest for the ideal state between man and woman — surely speaks to who we are and where we are going.

All mammalian species mate for sexual reproduction, and it belabors the obvious to note that this biological imperative is requisite for species continuance. Although some infrahuman species have analogues to monogamous marriage (e.g., certain species of birds tend to mate for life) there is little evidence that any have the special consciousness of the future which the bonds of matrimony imply. Thus, marriage is palpably different from parallel mating behaviors in other animals.

---

1. First published as 'Marriage: The civilizing of sexuality'. In M. Farber (Ed.), (1985) *Human Sexuality: Psychosocial Aspects of Disease,* NY: MacMillan and Co.

Marriage is a conscious contract that has an explicit past as well as an implicit future. Marriage transtemporally bridges the past by recognizing ancestry, the present by joining individuals and families, and the future by anticipating and producing heirs. Marriage, because of its link with the past and its projection into the future, is humankind's attempt to overcome the limitations of the lifespan. By marrying, one establishes a relationship with ramifications greater than either partner's individual longevity. Thus, conscious transtemporality and generativity enable marriage to bridge and connect individuals, generations, families, communities, and even empires. Marriage and its usual sequel, the family, are the social paradigms which, together, serve as the keystone in the arch of civilization.

Historic perspective

The western family as we know it today had its roots in ancient Hebrew, Greek, and Roman civilizations. What little is said about marriage of prewritten history is largely inferred from scanty anthropological clues combined with ethological and biological speculations. Some investigators (Washburn and DeVore, 1961) go so far as to date the origins of marriage within the Middle Pleistocene period (roughly 300,000 years ago). They believe that for even the most primitive of marriage and family forms to have been generated, humankind must have developed distinctly different roles for the sexes. That is, women would have to have been gatherers, planters, and tenders of the young; men would have to have been hunters of game. Hunting, particularly large game, would have required bands of men working cooperatively. Accordingly, such cooperative efforts would have been predicated upon exogamous (outside the family group) mating in order to establish affiliative bonds and enlarge the community. Most investigators (e.g., Washburn and DeVore, 1961; Morris, 1967; Ardry, 1970) assume that this same prehistoric period also saw the inception of the incest taboo which continues to preclude inbreeding as a means of enhancing communal expansion.

The incest taboo, its function, origins and centrality to understanding human interaction, have been widely discussed and debated by biologists, anthropologists, psychologists, and sociologists. There are some animal behaviorists who observe the tendency for exclusively exogamous behavior in a few infrahuman species, particularly those prone to relatively small close groupings (e.g., lions, certain monkeys, and apes: Wilson, 1980). Despite rare exceptions (e.g., the ancient royalties of Egypt, Peru, Sumaria, and a brief imperial period of Roman history), virtually all scholars of marriage and family accept the universality of the incest taboo. There remains wide debate about reasons for the inception of the taboo, but few disagree with its importance in (a) preventing of disruptive sexual rivalry and role confusion and (b) enlarging the marrying group, thus facilitating its and species survival (Stephens, 1963).

Comprehension of propagation and lifelong concern for the physical and psychological well-being of mate and offspring differentiate humankind from all other mammalian species, even our closest infrahuman cousins. The crucial distinction is the idea of *lifelong* concern, which requires the fulmination of a special kind of consciousness: transtemporal awareness. This includes the cognizance of history (a form of memory unique to humans) as well as a cognitive ability to anticipate and plan for the future. With this kind of consciousness, the development of complex communication — nonverbal, spoken, and written language — is associated.

Written history yields firm support for conjecture that marriage is an institution central to humankind. The period of the ancient Hebrews is the first for which we have appreciable extant written information (Old Testament; Pritchard, 1955). These writings introduce the perspective by which we view marriage today, especially with respect to structure and male-female role delineation. Even though it is assumed that the Old Testament patriarchs practiced polygyny, most biblical tracts imply a preference for monogamy. Emphasis on primacy of the patriarch-matriarch pair, and the likelihood that the majority of men were not affluent enough to maintain more than one wife, support the likelihood for a propensity toward monogamy. Though probably idealized and romanticized by biblical poets, ancient reports also recount a gradual evolution from a nomadic lifestyle to an agrarian and then urban society. From the times of the ancient Hebrews through those of the Hellenistic City states and the Roman Empire, the dual practice of polygyny and monogamy continued. Concubines were not uncommon among the wealthy, but the marital dyad was generally the norm, perhaps because of economic necessity, moral rightness, and/or natural proclivity.

The early writings of Hebraic, Greek, and Roman cultures make plain the highly defined differences between male and female roles and the superior status of the males, although there is evidence that these premises were, at least some of the time, questioned (Old and New Testaments; Plato, *The Republic*). By the time of the Roman Empire (27 BCE–395 ACE), however, continued urbanization and expansion saw a very gradual shift in gender role designations. Men went off to war and left women to manage households and gain greater visibility in governance than they had had earlier. Also a concurrent shift from barter to monetized wealth took place and probably gave impetus to the codification of the laws of family lineage and inheritance. Separated from the land, wealth and power became symbolized through money and, thereby, also became portable and more easily inheritable.

What the latter part of the Roman period began, Christianity continued. Women were at least nominally accorded a more focal role and greater status than previously. Christianity also intensified the notion that marriage had divine sanctity. Sexuality was considered subservient to parenthood; the main purpose of marriage was procreation. Subsequently, in the next millenium (400–1400 ACE) the medieval Church, emphasizing the morally correct role of the marital dyad, made divorce (previously a relatively easy option, at least for the male) far more difficult to obtain. These trends continued through the Renaissance (1400–1600 ACE). The Church solidified marriage as an institution (Bardis, 1964). Further, the economic rules of the feudal manor combined with the laws of inheritance to ensure the consolidation and continuity of family wealth along patrilineality. Thus, in addition to fulfilling religious and moral obligations, marriage (at least for the more prosperous) was as much an economic as an affectional institution.

These are the historical foundations of marriage and family that we have inherited. The growth of urbanization, the nation state and industrialization saw the continuation of those trends begun at the beginning of the Common Era. Men continued to leave the home — not to hunt game but to work in trades. Despite small changes in women's status and visibility, their vocation remained primarily that of family nurturer, caring for the young, the old, and spouses. Role delineation was still highly circumscribed. With the emergence of Protestantism, followed by the industrial revolution, the way was paved for dramatic changes in gender role differentiation and economic opportunity.

First, Protestantism extended the concept of vocational *calling* outside of the priesthood and thus dignified the earthly ambition of earning money (Weber, 1930). Then machinery began to minimize some of the biological differences (primarily brute strength) which had kept women working inside and men working outside the home. Travel for economic as well as for religious and political opportunity established the marital pair and its issue as a functional and portable unit of civilization, the nuclear family. These trends continued into the New World and intensified in post-technological society (Aries, 1962, 1979).

Love and trust

The truncated outline of humankind's odyssey through the millennia, as sketched above, does little justice to the elements that make marriage so central to our lives. What has been presented so far is primarily an intellective or rational view of the voyage. The nonrational or affective perspective — the poetry of our development — is as fundamental, if not more so, to an understanding of modern marriage and family.

There are two basic elements to a workable, satisfying, and lasting marriage: love and trust. How these elements articulate within a given cultural context determines the effectiveness of marriage and the family as institutions for people of a culture. The family has become one of the few remaining bastions of interpersonal security — the safehouse of love and trust, the hearth against the chilling winds of loneliness.

Love

Love is a word, an abstraction and, like all words, its meaning is derived from complex memories of myriad sensations: smells, touches, sounds, and images — stored in our individual and collective histories. Thus, while there is a timeless and universal quality to our common understanding of love, there is also a mutable quality, which can subtly modify our view of it, both as members of groups with common histories and as individuals with unique histories. Our collective histories are perhaps best embodied and crystallized by artists, musicians, and poets who project on recognizable screens before us our universal experiences and remembered feelings. Thus, for most westerners, David's love for Bathsheba,

Tristan's for Isolde, Romeo's for Juliet, etc., resonate with a form of common experience imbued with personal overtones.

Extrapolating from ethological evidence, Morris (1967) and Wilson (1980) note salient affective features of human sexuality that are distinctively different from those of animal sexuality. These features include: visual over olfactory arousal cues resulting in a more personal (face to face) mating, prolonged courtship employing highly complex vocal/verbal cues, and absence of a relatively circumscribed estrus or heat period making sexuality more or less continuous and less focused on reproduction. These characteristics all lead to a lesser dependence on instinctive bonding and a greater emphasis on conscious awareness of the loving process.

By contrast, Sigmund Freud considered the animal sexual drive at the root of all varieties of human love from coital to altruistic (1962). He took sex out of the box and infused it into all areas of life. Although his intent was to put human sexuality into perspective, the impact of Freud's work, in many ways, was just the opposite. Sex became ubiquitous. We not only became conscious of sexuality in a different way, we became self-conscious. Thus, psychoanalytic ideation, which dominated much of psychological thought for the first half of the twentieth century, promoted (and we accepted) the notion that we, like our animal ancestors, were motivated by lust. Furthermore, our nobler accomplishments were little more than sublimations of our animal drives.

Freud recognized the dependency period of the immature organism as vastly important for later social bonding. However, it was the neo-Freudian theorists (e.g., Erikson, 1964; Sullivan, 1953) and researchers working directly with both animal (e.g., Harlow, 1962a, 1962b; Lorenz, 1952) and human (Bowlby, 1952; Spitz, 1945) mother-child pairs who demonstrated the full power, intricacies, and ramifications of the early parent-child relationship on later socialization skills. The closest we can come to imputing love to lower animals is to observe the attentive, nurturant, or passionately protective behaviors exhibited by animal parents (generally mothers) for their young. Animal courtship and the copulation which follows do not even come close to comparison. Thus, although sex may be the basis for species survival, the parental bond is the foundation on which civilization rests.

The biological imperative, which is part of the initial attraction of male and female, is by its very nature fleeting and limited. Although none would deny the impelling quality of the sensual pleasure of the arousal state or the ecstasy experienced in the orgasmic moment, this momentary exultation cannot wholly account for the continuous concern, tender tactile attentiveness, nostalgic bittersweet reverie of separation, and the anticipated joyous reunion of human lovers. Neither does the biological imperative explain the conscious desire of those in love to actualize their love for each other through the creation of children. Our awareness of the differences between biological and nurturant love tends to affect all human sexuality and particularly love in the context of marriage.

The nature of the parent-child bond is the crucial ingredient in the transcendence of love over sex. The two uniquely human qualities of transtemporal consciousness and the protracted dependency of the young, lead Homo sapiens to an awareness of kinship ties well beyond the bonding period. Memories of comfort, sustenance, and caring by parents are carried with the human organism throughout life. It is the awareness of past nurturance and anticipation of future giving and receiving of pleasure, which make love a far more complex phenomenon than sex. How this complex love evolves in the child must be discussed more fully in a developmental context.

Knowledge of the rudiments of human love would, perhaps, not be so important if love did not play so central a role in our lives. To say that its origins are *either* sexual or nurturant, rather than *both* sexual and nurturant, changes our understanding and, consequently, the way we relate to one another in all interpersonal dealings. Our written history is replete with efforts to comprehend love.

Most social scientists consider Greece of the fifth century BCE the source of modern ideas about love. Plato, in the *Symposium*, defines love as the inspiration of virtue and delineates its hierarchy: (a) common, earthly, or sensual love (both homosexual and heterosexual), each of which contributes to but does not constitute, divine or heavenly love, and (b) spiritual love, the noblest of pursuits. Reiss (1980) and others contrast composite love with the hedonistic, sensual pleasures depicted by Ovid in pagan Rome of the first century CE. With the establishment of Christianity, the concept of love was revolutionized. The varieties of love that Plato portrayed as a continuum, early Christianity reinterpreted as polar opposites. On one extreme was celibacy, the only pure manifestation of spiritual love; on the other was physical desire, the sole appropriate expression of which was limited to the conjugal bed. This dichotomization of love, with sex as a necessary evil (1 Cor. 7), led the way to the establishment of love as a sacrament with procreation in marriage its primary purpose (a view which remained unchallenged until the Reformation and continues to be the position of the Catholic church today).

The next watershed contributing to our present ideology of love is considered by many (Biegel, 1951; Clayton, 1975; Lederer and Jackson, 1968; Linton, 1936; and Reiss, 1980) to be the period of the twelfth century, the age of chivalry. Although the erotic element is present in the literature of this period, it remained secondary to the hero-knight's pursuit of virtue, embodied in the image of the beatific female. This period is considered a turning point because it introduced the idea of gentleness and restraint into the consciousness of the male.

It is only with the Renaissance (fourteenth to sixteenth centuries) that the epic quest became the search for a marriage partner, thereby integrating the spiritual qualities of love with the sensual. While the periods of the Reformation and Enlightenment (sixteenth to eighteenth centuries) showed changes in the institution of marriage, this integrated view of love endured. The glorification of this 'ideal love' in the art, literature, and music of the nineteenth century, with its emphasis on the ecstasies of emotion, is considered the culmination of that which we have inherited as romantic love between woman and man (Clayton, 1975). The compelling and enduring presence of the romantic ideal, as well as the evolution of the dyadic relationship based on affection, suggest that love has been a major part of selecting a mate for a large part of the population for several hundred years.

Although our intellectual conceptualization of love has undoubtedly changed somewhat over time, perhaps the change has not been as great as that which we may have been lead to believe. As Gay (1983) has observed, often what we know of the past comes from the writings of a relatively few sources, generally social critics of the time. For example, in his analysis of 'private diaries, family correspondence, medical texts, household manuals, religious tracts, and works of art', Gay provides different pictures of Victorian private lives from those portrayed by public images. He found that in the privacy of their homes, Victorian individuals lived sensually fulfilling lives and were less dominated by conformity and repression than by guilt and anxiety (as had previously been thought).

Furthermore, the fact that the Old Testament,[2] a major source of information regarding the customs and mores of earlier times, is hardly ever mentioned by most social scientists (Clayton, 1975) suggests the need for further scrutiny. This is not to suggest that the development of romantic love as presented by historians is inaccurate or unimportant to the understanding of our present ideas of love, nor even that the Old Testament gives an accurate accounting of love. What is important is that the stories of the Old Testament (which include perhaps as many of the facets of love as those proffered by Plato, Ovid, Paul, and Shakespeare) undoubtedly have had a profound impact on what we think and feel about ourselves. From the florid erotic ecstasies of the *Song of Songs* to the *courtly* love of Jacob for Rachel, the *friendly* love of Jonathan and David, the *fraternal* love of Joseph and Benjamin, the *filial* love of Abraham for Isaac, and the *heavenly* love of man for God, all are elegantly explicated. Because these depictions are familiar and common to the vast majority of westerners, they are perhaps as much a part of that which comprises our ideation of love as are the histories and tales of the Greeks, Romans, early Christians, and Elizabethans.

Our individual and collective expectations of marriage and family are shaped by our histories. These same expectations affect our satisfaction and happiness. If we are led to believe that marriage can meet all human affiliational needs perfectly, we are placing an enormous burden on that institution. Over-idealization or unrealistic expectations can too easily lead to disappointment and a sense of failure. That marriage and family have become the *giant shock absorber* (Toffler, 1970) of modern American society is a much discussed phenomenon. The question is can it take the load? Perhaps it is best, then, to leave this discussion of love on a simpler note. The theorist and psychotherapist Harry Stack Sullivan (1947) defines the state of love as existing, 'when the satisfaction or security of another person becomes as significant as is one's own security'. Perhaps, as Kaufmann (1958) and Levi-Strauss (1969) suggest, it would be better still to leave it to the poets.

---

2. The Old Testament is assumed to have pre-dated Plato by anywhere from three to five centuries, i.e., 950–750 BCE.

Trust

In contrast to vast material from widely varying sources regarding love and our understanding of it, trust as an interpersonal construct has virtually escaped or eluded attempts at scrutiny or study. Yet, ironically, throughout history we are aware of loveless marriages arranged for the purpose of establishing trusting unions between families, clans, or nations. Although few have had much to say with respect to the issue of trust in marriage, without the former, the latter is at best a fragile contract of questionable viability. Perhaps because trust is so basic to human interaction and society in general, its necessity and existence simply have been assumed and taken for granted.

Erik Erikson was one of the few behavioral scientists to recognize how essential trust is in intimate human interactions. He traced the roots of trust to the first feelings of a child towards its mother. For Erikson the first year of life is characterized by adult-child interactions that engender the establishment of basic trust. Trust, according to Erikson (1964, p. 220), is fostered by 'consistency, continuity, and sameness of experience', and 'the quality of the maternal relationship'. Thus, whenever a sense of basic trust is not established in early infancy, healthy human interaction throughout life is in jeopardy. In working with monkeys, Harry Harlow (1959, 1962) confirmed Erikson's observations. Later, Ables and Brandsma (1977) drew a parallel between the early establishment of a sense of trust between infant and mother and the ability to establish a similar relationship in marriage.

The most extensive treatment of the subject of trust in marriage appears in Lederer and Jackson's book, *The Mirages of Marriage* (1968). Although Lederer and Jackson identify trust as an essential ingredient of a workable marriage, they take issue with the Eriksonian concept of infantile trust, describing it as unilateral — the child has no choice but to trust the parent for its basic needs. They further contend that trust occurs interactively between marital partners only when there is equivalence or mutual confidence regarding the expectations and behaviors of the other person. As such, trust is dependent upon continuous communication and honesty between partners.

Reliance on confidence as a synonym or even as a test for trust is dangerous, however. Confidence tends to be a specific and transitory feeling, whereas trust is more encompassing and comprehensive, implying greater permanence. For example, one may have little confidence in a spouse's driving skills yet still maintain a basically trusting intimate relationship. Trust rests on the accretion of confidence-building past experiences and projects itself into the future as faith. Thus, it falls somewhere between the specificity of confidence and the less tangible, simple feeling state of faith. Trust has both a retrospective base and a projective thrust.

The most dramatic breach of confidence or trust in a marriage is adultery that strikes at the very heart of the union. For this transgression we even have special terminology: *unfaithfulness* or *infidelity*. One may tolerate extravagance, alcoholism, neglect (sometimes for the sake of career) and differences about childrearing, and extended family relationships. Such difficulties may be replete with insensitivities, broken promises, even lying, thereby stretching the confidence aspects of trust. When strained to the extreme, the marriage base may eventually erode to the point of dissolution. But often spouses are far more forgiving of these kinds of infractions than of those associated with infidelity. What distinguishes faith from both trust and confidence is that faith does not require proof or logic — it is there and, like love, it tends to be blind.

Faith is what makes marriage the ultimate contract. Virtually no one enters marriage today without the belief that the union will be permanent. It is unlikely that either partner would marry, otherwise.[3] Modern marriage vows have evolved over time but, broadly speaking, the nature of the marriage contract, assumptions of its permanence, and the necessity of having it a public affair (i.e., witnessed) seem to be roughly similar throughout history and across widely varying cultures. It is the sanctification of pledging troth publicly that gives the union life.

Correspondingly, when faith is broken, there is significant loss akin to that which one experiences when someone close dies. The ingenuous old union no longer exists, and for a new union to be formed there are necessary conditions. Blind faith must be replaced by built trust. But, even then, the totally rational process of developing confidence to the end of establishing trust must often be accompanied by some form of ritual burial of the old union and ceremonious birth of the new. Although some believe that the therapeutic process alone helps perform these tasks, other professionals (e.g., Haley, 1976) take the need for a ceremony more literally.

We live in trying times; the stress placed upon intimate relationships is often chronic and insidious. We have a strong belief in science and in the rational — we need to understand ourselves, others, the world. Twenty-first century society tends to reject the nonrational aspects of life. Under such circumstances, faith — unabashed and naive, given without proof or logic — is the relatively rare commodity that Erikson referred to when he discussed the basic trust of the infant. It is there, a priori.

As we grow and experience more of the world around us, our faith in others and ourselves may, at times, feel shaken. Our parents' love can seem to grow conditional, dependent upon our behavior and their moods.[4] As we age we become aware that misplaced, unequivocal faith can lead to disappointment, hurt, and anguish. Yet we continually look to others as objects of that unconditional faith: first, a best friend or *chum* (see next chapter); later a prospective spouse. Through experiences fired by hope and anticipation, but dampened at times by disappointment and hurt, we gradually learn to temper blind faith with trust, a

---

3. The recent trend, particularly among the very wealthy, of marriage, divorce, and remarriage — now termed serial monogamy — accompanied by prenuptial contracts, seriously undermines the foundation of the prospective union, and sullies the institution of marriage as we have come to know it.

4. It is this conditionality which Rogers refers to as *conditions of worth*. These conditions of worth, according to Rogers, are the blueprint for later psychological incongruence and distress (see Chapters 8 and 9).

more rational and conditional feeling based upon the accretion of confidence-building experiences. It is trust, referred to by Lederer and Jackson (1968) that needs constant nurturance and validation through essential anchors of a successful, workable marriage: honesty, communication and caring.

Marital strain and divorce

Marriage is the ultimate form of intimacy between adult members of society. As such it is a primary counteragent to loneliness and isolation — states anathema to the human condition. Marriage is a bulwark that serves as buffer to crises and stresses (both normative and aberrant) which occur during the adult years. Marriage is, however, also a responsive institution that may be positively or negatively affected by life's vicissitudes.

One of the first stressors on marriage is the adaptation the newlyweds must make to each other. Within each person's responses to the mundanities of life there will be behaviors to which the other of the newly married pair must learn to accommodate. Often individuals are attracted to each other because their differences and styles are complementary. A relaxed person often finds an intense person interesting; a loquacious person may find a taciturn individual fascinating and vice versa. However, common life stressors can turn healthy complementarity into conflictual polarization. Attributes that were considered charming, attractive, or humorous during courtship (and even through early marriage) may prove to be sources of irritation and conflict later when the pressures of daily living mount. Even though conflict is inevitable in intimate personal relationships, we are neither educated in its understanding nor trained in its resolution (Bach, 1968). However, with a mutually engendered intimate and loving relationship and a willingness to confront and resolve conflict, most marriages are capable not only of withstanding but also of mitigating the expectable and unexpectable stresses and crises which are inevitable in life.

For the newly-married one of the more dramatic accommodations is sexual reciprocation. A mutually satisfying sexual life is a major source of joy when successful and, correspondingly, a source of anguish when not. Sexual satisfaction is also pivotal because it may be adversely affected when the couple experiences stress in other areas. As a result, other problems may be exacerbated rather than resolved (Belliveau and Richter, 1970). Although our society affords maturing members few opportunities to prepare for this aspect of their mature years, both nature and society do offer some time for the newlyweds to accommodate to each other sexually. Furthermore, while greater numbers of young people are entering marriage with some sexual experience, still a large percentage is virtually inexperienced in this most crucial aspect of the marital relationship (Cherlin, 1999).

Unlike our animal cousins, our awareness of the importance of sexuality often creates self-consciousness, awkwardness, and a sense of failure during initial interactions. For males, who in our culture are expected to be skilled, sophisticated, and satisfying lovers and who also must be psychologically and biologically primed, the anguish can be devastating. Likewise, disappointment, hurt, and feelings of failure are not uncommon for the female who also now is expected to be an adept orgasmic full participant in the lovemaking process.

Catastrophic events are rarely anticipated, hardly ever prepared for, and usually devastating to those directly involved. Such events include those indigenous to society (some tragically so, like war or murder) or to life on this planet (like natural disasters, severely debilitating illness, or untimely death). Regardless of origin, when a catastrophe affects one individual in a marriage, the catastrophe also impinges on the marriage itself. Paradoxically, marriage, family, and society as a whole, are the individual's best source of protection, support and comfort against such contingencies. One might even go so far as to say that it is in response to these adversities that marriage and society, in general, came into being.

Some crises and the potential strains they create are both inevitable and therefore expectable. Those anticipatable, commonly stressful nodes in the branches of growth that mark our development through the lifespan are often termed *normative crises*. The impact of crisis and stress upon the institution of marriage and the manner in which the institution and its members respond and cope with these events have received increasing attention by theorists and researchers (Figley and McCubbin, 1983). McCubbin and his associates summarized the major life events considered sources of stress: '(1) transition to parenthood, (2) child-launching, (3) post-parental transition (i.e., "empty nest"), (4) retirement, (5) widowhood', and '(6) relocation and institutionalization', the last category being associated with aging (McCubbin et al. 1980, p. 858). These issues are discussed in the Chapter 4.

Despite few reports in the research literature, the popular press and mental health professionals have observed that annual events such as holidays and changing of seasons can be sources of intense personal stress. At these times, an individual's nostalgic fantasies or expectations often contrast sharply with the less than ideal realities experienced. Thus, for example, Christmas and spring are times that are apt to bring on feelings of loneliness and despair, particularly if one's interpersonal relationships are found lacking.

Another stressor with more insidious erosive qualities is that of economic insecurity. In our highly monetized society, economic insecurity as a form of stress does not refer just to those experiencing poverty. Any abrupt change in living standard or any event likely to cause the anticipation of such a change (e.g., change of job, temporary or long-term unemployment, illness) can impose strain severe enough to deleteriously affect the marital relationship. This scenario tends to be particularly true of men, for whom self-esteem is highly dependent upon the ability to provide for their wives and children. Ironically, in its most severe form, such strain can lead to aggression and physical abuse of loved ones within the family (Prescott and Letko, 1977).

Although marriage is the most basic and perhaps the most resilient of all social institutions, it is not immune to failure. Historically, divorce, the dissolution of the *eternal* bonds of matrimony, has always been recognized as an option, even if an unhappy one. Because of the importance we place upon marriage (even to the point of divine approbation), heavy sanctions have generally been levied (heretofore) against divorce. Even today, as divorce becomes a relatively common occurrence, it is nevertheless looked upon with considerable disfavor and heavily imbued with the notion of both personal and interpersonal failure.

However, it may be wise to reconsider recent figures on divorce that are often used to attest to the failure of marriage as an institution. Although demographers themselves warn against cursory examination of census figures and note difficulty in their interpretation, misunderstanding and misuse of these figures abound (Norton, 1983). For example, the high divorce rate found in the first two years of marriage often leads to an interpretation that these years are the hardest. This conclusion directly contradicts the results of studies on marital satisfaction which indicate that these are the most satisfying years. Since the process of divorce takes months, a final decree in the first year or two after marriage suggests that the relationship would have to have been problematic at its inception. We are also aware that while the figures are difficult to obtain, many young couples marry post-pregnancy. Actually, the only reason for the marriage may have been the pregnancy. Therefore, it is likely that a good many of those marriages that fail in the early months had the seeds of failure sown before the union was legalized. Thus, rather than attest to the failure of marriage as an institution, these results may indeed indicate the contrary — that marriage may have been successful as a means to legitimize a child and give it a name.

Divorce, by nearly any standard, must be viewed as a highly negatively charged life event. It certainly qualifies as a *discontinuity of cultural conditioning* (Benedict, 1938). Although we have cultural tools for facilitating an appropriate entry into marriage (i.e., ceremony, social witnessing, etc.), we have none for easing our exit. If we are to address divorce as a necessary cultural phenomenon, we must comprehend both its rational and nonrational aspects. From an emotional perspective, divorce typically represents an extreme form of personal loss. Like any other such loss, divorce may also require a grieving and mourning period before rehabilitation can be anticipated.

Finally, in a discussion of divorce there is also the possibility of remarriage. As noted in the introduction, the increase in the divorce rate seems to have done little to disenchant us with the idea that marriage is the best way for man and woman to live together. Nearly 90 percent of all divorced men and women remarry (Carter and Glick, 1970), and recent figures indicate that nearly one third of our annual marriage rates are comprised of remarriages for either one or both partners (Price-Bonham and Balswick, 1980). These figures seem to suggest that it is not the institution of marriage we consider a failure but, rather, our abilities at it or our preparation for it.

We do not know much about the quality of life for remarrieds. There are certainly aspects of it that would make it different from first-time marriages for the individuals involved. Often the marital pair starts out with a preformed or blended family: one or both spouses enter the new marriage with children from an earlier relationship. This instantly structured new family may pose strains regarding the children's acceptance of the new spouse as parent (decision-maker, disciplinarian) and as intimate partner to the child's original parent. The newlyweds often have little time and even less privacy in which to try to accommodate to each other. Moreover, the failure of the first marriage may cause worry and anxiety about the second. On the other hand, the spouses are often older, wiser, and probably more realistic about their expectations (see Sager, et al. 1983).

Conclusion

Few would dispute the universality of marriage and its centrality to our lives — even those who question its viability at the present time. Historically, our collective, cultural memories continuously allude to marriage as the ideal state of intimacy between men and women. The partnership of men and women is the foundation upon which civilization rests and we, as caring adults, depend.

FAMILY: ITS DEVELOPMENT AND CULTURAL CONTEXT[1]

4

Grow old along with me!
The Best is yet to be,
The last of life, for which the first was made.
Robert Browning, *Dramatis Personae.*

Introduction

The previous chapter discussed love as the watershed of social encounter and marriage as the fulcrum of societal development. The identification of social structures and delineation of their functions and interactions can give us a comprehensible picture of society. Its developmental framework within the cultural context adds dimension and breaths life into our understanding. Morphology without development is a Galatea without a Pygmalion.

The present discussion of development is divided into those stages that precede and follow marriage. However, it should be mentioned that development is a gradual and continuous process with few easily identifiable points along the way. Nonetheless, all stage theories demarcate the inclined plane of development in discrete comprehensible steps; the orientation presented here is no exception.

A developmental overview of the family

Premarital (Family of Orientation) stages

Despite a relatively limited range of socio-emotional responses at birth (i.e., contentment versus distress), human neonates display a predisposition to empathy. As early as one day of age, infants have been observed to cry empathically at the sound (real or simulated) of other infants' cries (Sagi and Hoffman, 1976) and to respond bodily to adult voices (Condon and Sander, 1974). By as early as ten days of age, infants will also mimic adult lip and tongue motions and facial expressions (Meltzoff and Moore, 1977). Despite this kind of early responsiveness, the human infant is totally dependent on its caretakers. Such complete helplessness and the

1. First published as 'An intergenerational perspective of marriage: love and trust in cultural context' in *Marriage and Family Therapy Review, 16,* 1/2, (1991) pp. 143–59. Reprinted in Pfiefer, S., and Sussman, M. (Eds), *Families: Intergenerational and generational connections.* New York: Haworth Press. Reprinted with permission of the publishers.

child's innocent physiognomy are highly evocative of parental nurturing and caring (Gaylin, 1976). These factors create an intense symbiosis between mother (or other caretaker) and child during the first year of life that is crucial to the child's appropriate future psychosocial development. Children's total dependency continues for nearly two years; their relative dependence may last, in western cultures, for at least another 15.

Although the infant's discovery of itself as a separate entity undoubtedly begins somewhere in the first year (through self-exploration of body parts), self-awareness and a sense of a separate identity are probably not fully crystallized until about the end of toddlerhood. Since the child under three remains dependent upon the parent(s) for nurture and security, the child receives love and looks for approbation but is really not much of a reciprocal actor in the process. It is within this period of total dependency that basic trust is established (Erikson, 1964).

At about two to three years of age, the distinctly human biosocial phenomenon of toilet training begins, and expectations of self-help skills are made of the child. This is the period that Sullivan (1953) regards as the true beginning of the child's self: the 'good me', ' bad me', and 'not me'. It is the 'good me' and its enhancement which are, for Sullivan, the beginnings of self-esteem which, in turn, form the basis for the child's ability to love. The child as reciprocator begins to take social form first in the bosom of the nuclear family, then in the extended family, and finally with peers. The process is impelled through play: first solitary, then parallel, then cooperative, and finally competitive. First the child imitates, then emulates and identifies with others, and (ideally) eventually develops a *true* sense of empathy.

Although virtually all investigators commonly observe sex cleavage (the exclusive association of boys with other boys, and girls with other girls), little is subsequently made of it. For Sullivan (1953), however, the establishment of this intense homo-affiliative behavior during preadolescence is crucial to the appropriate development of mature love in the well functioning adult. Sullivan sees this preadolescent homo-affiliative behavior highlighted by a unique relationship: the same-sex best friend, or *chum*. Few other theorists have attended so carefully to this period or its uniquely focal, chum relationship. The importance of the chum, whose well-being becomes as important as the preadolescent's own, is for Sullivan both the paradigm and precursor of true heterosexual love. Initially, it is the finding comfort with, and caring for another who is like oneself which enables the later caring for another who is different from oneself, as in mature heterosexual love. Thus, the transition from preadolescence to adolescence is effected.

Gradually, through socially sanctioned means such as school dances and sports events, etc., the two gender groups begin to co-mingle, often with the more physically and socially mature females taking leadership in heterosexual pairing. One or two of the more mature couples begins to seek privacy although, for a long period, group dating is the norm. The onset of pubescence tends to finalize the move from homo-affiliative to heterosexual patterning.

Perhaps no developmental phase receives as much attention in modern culture as adolescence. The term itself is rather new, circa the fifteenth century.

Adolescence means growing up: it is the bridge between immaturity and maturity. It is also the one stage of development experienced by both males and females that is marked by a series of clearly observable biological events. The events constitute puberty. The onset of puberty (emerging roughly between 11–14 years of age) and its occurrence earlier in girls than boys pose a good many problems for our post-technological society. In other cultures and other times, social readiness for parenting more closely corresponded to biological readiness. Courtships in those societies were either short or ceremoniously instantaneous, and parents often prearranged marriages. On the other hand, the hiatus between biological and social readiness (as defined by our society) is often half a generation (ten years) or more in length! Until recently, western culture placed heavy sanctions against premarital sexual experimentation and practice while simultaneously encouraging ever-increasing intimacy through dating, where privacy was both expected and given. Thus we exacerbated strain between individual biological readiness and social sanctions against sexual practice at specific developmental stages. In so doing, we highlighted a *discontinuity* of our *cultural conditioning* (Benedict, 1938). Some mitigation of this discontinuity seems to be occurring of late, undoubtedly as a result of the increased availability, ease, and knowledge of contraceptive techniques and the feminist movement of the past 40 years.

Prior to 1960, the reported rates of female premarital intercourse remained at about the 20 percent level. After 1960, this rate more than doubled. Although some increase has occurred in the frequency of premarital coitus by men, it is not nearly so dramatic as that by women, and the percentage of men entering marriage with no sexual experience still remains lower than that of women (King, Balswick, and Robinson, 1977). With the relaxation of the concept of *in loco parentis,* the years of college (which now the majority of young experience) appear to provide as much a sexual as an educational or vocational apprenticeship (Clayton and Bokmeier, 1980; Macklin, 1980). It is well after college that couples in the United States are marrying. Furthermore, in the last half of the twentieth century the median age of marriage has been steadily increasing from about 21 years of age for women and 23 years for men to about 25 years for women and 27 years for men. Recent findings indicate that more than half of American couples cohabit before marrying — figures eight times greater than those calculated for 1960 — and that cohabiting is becoming more acceptable (Olson and Defrain, 2000).

At whatever ages, respectively, couples do decide to marry, the practice of prenuptial ritual in many postindustrial societies varies widely from elaborate to nonexistent, unless one wishes to count the procurement of blood tests and a civil license. However, ceremonious weddings for first-time marriages are the rule rather than the exception. That this is so speaks to the emphasis (and the burden) we as a culture and as individuals place upon the institution most central to our humanity: marriage.

Postmarital (Family of Procreation) stages

After the wedding, our society looks differently upon married individuals. They now constitute a socially recognized and sanctioned unit. Despite the fact that the couple may have been cohabiting, the public announcement of their commitment to each other makes a difference — not just socially but to themselves as well. They are now Mr. and Mrs., Mr. and Ms., or sometimes just M/M, although even this is changing somewhat as more and more women are choosing to retain their family of orientation names (viz., *maiden names*). Thus, our etiquette or operating procedures and social conventions built over the years speak to the fit of the husband and wife union as an indigenous part of our lives. But, as yet, we have no rules or conventions for dealing with couples living together absent the rites of marriage. Our cultural confusion is evidenced by our social awkwardness, e.g., making an introduction with reference to the kind of relationship the two individuals share, extending a formal invitation to a cohabiting partner for an event to which only family relatives are invited, etc. It is interesting to note that a similar awkwardness occurs in dealing with a formerly married pair.

In direct contrast to our social ambivalence regarding premarital sexuality, that period immediately following the wedding, the honeymoon, receives our open (although sometimes more subtle) recognition of its sexual nature. Our own romantic fantasies, memories, and humor surrounding the honeymoon are cultural indicators of our (albeit discreet) social approbation and recognition of the marriage bed as the right place for sexual activity. Our children are finally adults and expected (after a sanctioned brief period of experimentation) to produce children of their own. Although some may question the validity of pressure towards pregnancy following marriage today, procreational expectations from parents, other family members and society at large are nonetheless present and, to varying degrees, explicit. As the sole tangible means for continuity or immortality, grandchildren represent a sense of completion and can serve as a source of profound gratification to the new couple's parents. Society still tends to look with question and concern upon a childless union.

The period of the childless dyad used to be relatively brief for most marriages, although towards the end of the twentieth century, dual-career couples extended that interval. Although couples may naturally experience the strains of getting to know how to live with and accommodate to their partners, young marrieds tend to report these years as happy. As might be anticipated, sexual activity is reported to be the highest during this period. Although the blending of the two extended families often requires some fine-tuning, newlyweds are generally given social latitude by relatives and friends. Everyone, including the new husband and wife, considers the couple's happiness and success at settling into marriage priorities (Mace and Mace, 1974).

Furthermore, for most marriages, the childless period used to be relatively brief because both the biological and social imperatives make the dyad unstable. Although biology sets the lower baseline to nine months, most American marriages extend this childless period to about two to three years (Duvall, 1971; Norton,

1983). With more and more women seeking careers and with the increase of dual-career marriages, in western cultures many couples are delaying marriage — choosing to cohabit — and delaying the birth of the first child after marriage (Cherlin, 1990; Lindsay, 2000; Turner, 1991).

With the birth of the first child, the honeymoon seems to be over. The dyad of lovers is now irrevocably transformed into the triad of family. The lovers are now parents with responsibilities not just to themselves but to the next generation as well. The new child places severe constraints upon the couple's time and economic resources. Childrearing is demanding and absorbing, particularly for the relatively isolated nuclear family of our complex world.

Most family developmentalists see the childrearing phase of marriage as having anywhere from two to as many as six discrete periods (depending upon the children's stage of development) in the progression of the married progenitors' lives (e.g., Cavan, 1969; Duvall, 1971; Price, McHenry and Murphy, 2000; Rodgers, 1962). In all, the childrearing stage may comprise as many as 25 years of a couple's married history. Increasingly, however, childrearing no longer consumes proportionately the longest period in the marital career. The trend towards fewer children has decreased the childrearing years on the one hand, while greater life expectancy has increased non-childrearing years later. Thus, the marital career is now longest at its end for a growing number of couples.

Research on marital satisfaction and adjustment indicates that the middle marital stage (childrearing years) is often the most problematic for many married couples. Indeed, until recently, investigators contended that marital satisfaction and consensus between partners decreased to their nadir during these childrearing years, never to return to their former early-marriage high (Rollins and Feldman, 1970; Spanier, Lewis, and Cole, 1975; Udry, 1971). If, as stated earlier, the quintessential function of the family is 'nurturant socialization' (i.e., childrearing), the finding that the childrearing years are also the least satisfying period for many couples certainly seems ironic and deserving of scrutiny.

Undoubtedly, one of the sources of dissatisfaction during childrearing is that the marital pair has less time to focus on itself and its needs. Sexual activity decreases in this period relative to the childless years as a result of both familiarity and fatigue (i.e., greater demands on time and energy, Greenblatt, 1983). Part of the problem seems to arise out of another major discontinuity of cultural conditioning: there is inadequate preparation for the role of parent and a lack of anticipation of the intensity of its demands (Russell, 1974). The small, relatively isolated nuclear families of orientation of today offer little first-hand exposure to, let alone experience with, child care. Short of books on the subject and paid childcare, there are few sources of help for the first-time parents. This contrasts sharply with cultures (both past and present) where extended family members and communities that are smaller and more intimate are available to help.

In short, once past the honeymoon and the first few years of marriage, the family of procreation is alone and has little support in performing its tasks. This strain is exacerbated by romantic fantasies about love, marriage, and childrearing perpetuated by popular mythology. Unrealistic expectations create frustration and anguish, particularly when one is tired, money is short, the baby is crying, and one's spouse is angry about one thing or another. Yet, although the childrearing period may frequently suffer extramarital affairs and divorce, it is perhaps an attestation to the institution of marriage that most marriages survive this period. Furthermore, it is also worthy of comment that many couples report that the rearing of their children, while perhaps arduous, was the most rewarding of their lifetime activities.

The final stage of marriage, when the children leave home, is often conceptualized in two or three phases, named for the events common to them (i.e., *empty nest*, retirement, aging, widowhood, etc.). This period, when the marital dyad finds itself alone once again, at one time was considered basically the time of preparation for death. Both members of the dyad were believed to be experiencing growing demoralization over loss of personal generativity. For women menopause was the issue, for men retirement. Loneliness and isolation were often considered typical of the aging marital pair. Contemporary studies have indicated that these assumptions are baseless, at least for the present generation of middle-aged couples. Indeed, the reverse tends to be true: marital satisfaction appears to increase after the last child is launched (Schram, 1979; Spanier and Lewis, 1980). Although adjustments must be made to the aging process (e.g., decreasing vigor, increasing infirmity, and the eventual death of the spouse, other intimates and/or family members) most couples in the early phases of this stage of marriage seem to find pleasure in renewed mutual intimacy. Having fewer demands on their time and economic resources they seem to have a more relaxed attitude about sexuality and freedom to enjoy each other more.

The cultural context
No exposition of modern marriage would be comprehensible without elaboration of what has come to be perhaps its greatest source of strain, that is, gender role delineation. Although the conflict between male and female is hardly a new one (Aristophanes, 411 BCE; reprint, 1964), the intensity with which the battle of the sexes is being played out in contemporary marriage demands a clearer understanding of the nature of the conflict.

Most discussions of sex or gender role delineation begin with basic biological distinctions between the sexes and then deal with the socialization process. The scientific study of these issues is probably best traced to Darwin (1859; reprint, 1952) who represented the nature side of the controversy. Sexuality and the essential tension between the sexes was introduced into psychology by Freud (1905; reprint, 1962) who juxtaposed nurture against nature. The crystallization of the concept of gender role is attributed to George Herbert Mead (1934). It was he who enabled our understanding of the different socialization processes that continue to exist for men and women respectively. Historically, these processes have defined consistent sets of male and female behavior, adhered to still in various contemporary societies. Today, the argument of nature versus nurture, although not dead, is rarely a heated one — at least for most scholars who take a combined or biosocial approach (perhaps best embodied by Wilson, 1980).

Recent advances in the biological sciences, particularly in the field of neuroendocrinology, are telling us more and more about the basic biological differences between men and women. Those which have the most significant impact on gender role are those which have remained constant, namely menstruation, ovulation, gestation, and lactation which irrefutably are human female, not male characteristics. Although far less important now than in earlier times, a larger skeletal frame and greater body mass of striated musculature are characteristics of the human male. Thus, premodern humankind left women those tasks relating to child care and the home, while men were naturally relegated the more physically strenuous and demanding tasks of maintaining the mother and child unit via gathering, farming, and hunting. Later, with the introduction of money and industry where previously there had been only barter and agriculture, many men turned to industry and politics, while women continued their roles in the home. As has been succinctly stated by Reiss, despite the widely varying distribution of labor in various cultures throughout time to the present, 'Two features of gender roles in all cultures then, are: (a) female ties to childrearing and (b) male ties to economic power' (1980, p. 62).

It is only as recently as the middle of the nineteenth century that most historians mark the public questioning of classic gender role distinctions. The industrial revolution had an enormous repercussive impact on work in general. With the advent and aid of machinery, greater physical strength and speed lost their gender specificity and thereby their importance. By and large, women could perform virtually any of the skills formerly reserved for men. As in the end of the Roman period when women took over many of the managerial functions of their husbands who had gone off to war, so women also took their spouses' places on the assembly lines in America during World War II. For better or worse, the twentieth century saw the final reduction of gender specific behavior in human beings to those surrounding reproduction (and modern science seems to be pushing these, too).

Any change, by its nature, creates strain. The dramatic and rapid changes that occurred in gender roles in the last two centuries have put an equivalent load on that most basic of human institutions, marriage. Heinz Hartmann (1958) explicated how, out of necessity and for expedience, the individual places certain behaviors out of awareness. This submergence frees the individual from being overloaded with continuous decision making. A chain of decisions is organically learned and, as Hartmann termed it, *automatized* at a preconscious level, thus enabling the organism to perform complicated acts. So, for example, although the beginning driver finds the process overwhelming at first, the complexities once mastered become second nature, rarely to be forgotten. The result allows the driver to attend to the road, dodge obstacles, and navigate without having to attend consciously to the clutch, brake, accelerator, etc. However, during a crisis such as a skid on a slippery road, the discrete actions may be brought to conscious awareness for re-evaluation. To draw from Darwin, as ontogeny recapitulates phylogeny, so too may phylogeny parallel ontogeny. Thus, role delineations have served as automatizers for our species. In previous times men have, by and large, known what was expected of them and what they might, in turn, expect of women (and vice versa).

Social automatization, in its specific reference here to male/female role structuring, was crucial for the development of civilization. Cerebral decision-making can maximize options but also paralyze through overchoice. Somewhere, then, it is necessary to strike a balance between flexibility and rigidity in everyday decisions. Just as automatization is necessary for the individual's functioning, so too is some form thereof necessary for society's functioning. Social automatizers assure a degree of expectability and predictability. They reduce anxiety, increase comfort, and at the same time mitigate or even eliminate the need for continuous decision-making. These automatizers (or norms) develop over time and are gradually modified to facilitate adaptation. This is a natural evolutionary process. On the other hand, norms can become entrenched and inflexible, rigidly adhered to, anachronistic and dysfunctional. When this happens we often have revolutions. When automatizations for good or bad reasons are de-automatized, that is, brought into awareness, our identity is called into question. This can happen at both an individual and a cultural level. When identity is called into question, it affects our ability to care and to love. When we are so concerned about ourselves and who we are, egoism eclipses altruism (see Lasch, 1978 and Maslow, 1971).

In many respects, we are in a state of de-automatization today. We are in the process of discarding operating procedures that are centuries old and gender specific. If we are to move on, we will have to find new roles and rules to replace the old. Emile Durkheim (1951) discussed these ideas in the framework of norms, noting that when a society, for whatever reason upsets its established norms, it creates anomie. Anomie can occur at any level within a society from the interpersonal to the economic and political. In the former situation we may observe an increase in divorce; in extremes of the latter, we may see an increase in suicide. Both observations may be made of contemporary American society.

Social automatizers may also be seen as a means by which humankind has compensated for the loss of instinctual behavior — the tradeoff for the growth of the cerebral cortex. The development of rituals, ceremonies, and traditions may be viewed in such a manner. Here, too, contemporary western civilization, particularly in America, is relatively lacking in the use of ceremonies to smooth out the normative crises of living such as birth, coming of age, marriage, death. The age of science has put religion, once our primary source of ritual or ceremonial practice, in a secondary position. What little ritual we retain (especially to facilitate public interactions) more aptly falls under the heading of social convention (see Goffman, 1971). Conventions are more like social habits than social automatizers. Although they serve many of the same purposes as automatizers, they do so at a much more superficial level and are more easily subject to change from one generation to the next. Societal conventions are less intrinsic than automatizers and lack their timeless ability to stabilize. Further, conventions bear little of the richness and aesthetic appeal of ceremonies.

All societies have ceremonies to mark passages through life, although some have more than others. It is often noted that those subcultures in our own society which have retained more ritual practice tend to demonstrate greater family cohesion, better individual adaptation, and a lower propensity to social deviance. Traditionally, the Chinese, Japanese, and Jewish ethnic groups are noted for having greater family integration and correspondingly lower rates of alcoholism, delinquency, and divorce. These same subcultures tend to surround birth, marriage, and death with rich ceremony. It might be countered that these groups have generations of religious tradition on which to draw. However, one of the few studies of secular traditions of non-ethnic American families demonstrated similar findings: i.e., that secular (as well as sacred) 'ritual is a relatively reliable index of family integration' (Bossard and Ball, 1950, p. 203).

One of the few ceremonies that most Americans still retain is marriage, although even this practice appeared to be diminishing for a while. Indeed, marriage seems to be the last rite of passage that we continue to ceremonialize to any real degree. It remains the one step in our biological and social development that American culture at large recognizes as focal and best marked by ritual embellishment from the prenuptial arrangements to the exchanging of vows and rings to the honeymoon, etc. Few young first-marrieds and their families seem inclined to dispense with the choreography involved in such rituals and with good reason. Marriage, in our society as in most others, demarcates the leaving of childhood and the entering into the adult world. Furthermore, the public witnessing of marriage has the impact of affirming and renewing the marriages of those who witness; their vicarious participation in the vows engenders a sense of community.

By and large-society has dispensed with the ceremonializing of the premarital developmental passages common to the majority of cultures in previous times, including the biological coming of age. Ironically, the closest thing we have to such a rite of passage is the obtaining of a driver's license. (Indeed, we might have more responsible drivers if we were to celebrate more richly the adolescent's initiation into independence via physical mobility. It might contrarily be argued, however, that marriage licenses do not guarantee success despite all of their ritual accompaniment.) Thus, marriage has become a highly loaded fulcrum with few structural supports to aid it in its work of gracefully moving both individuals and the culture through the lifespan journey. Over half a century ago, Ruth Benedict (1938) explicated an American dilemma that she called our *discontinuities in cultural conditioning*. Calling them normative crises, she noted discontinuities in all cultures surrounding various turning points in the lifespan. She explained the importance of these normative crises and the need for all cultures to facilitate their members' recognition, anticipation, and preparation for the impact of these crises. She observed that those cultures which did this best demonstrated smoother functioning, and their members experienced greater well-being. Cultures with disjunctive turning points often accomplished the transitions effectively by attending them with elaborate ceremony.

In discussing American culture of the time, Benedict (1938, p. 163) noted three major discontinuities between childhood and adulthood: (a) 'responsible-nonresponsible status role, (b) dominance-submission, and (c) contrasted sexual role'. Thus we expect childhood to be a time of play and relative irresponsibility (*the best years of our lives*), a time of submission to adult authority (the power struggles we lament with our adolescent children), and a time of asexuality (despite high heterosexual social contact). Benedict depicted American culture as one with great discontinuities and few sources of mitigation. That is, our transitions were abrupt and painful, we had little preparation for them, and little celebration of them.

It is not suggested here that we develop a more ritualized society as the only appropriate method for dealing with our discontinuities. Indeed, ceremony and ritual might appear somewhat disjunctive to our scientifically oriented culture. Benedict's point was that if a society does not adopt the means with which to mollify normative crises inherent in life transitions (especially if the society demands radical change during those transitions), enormous strains will be placed on both the individual and society. This is particularly true of the transition from child to adult status. For several decades, many have advocated family life education as a way to moderate through preparation the rather difficult child-to-adult passage. However, by and large, such programs have not received the support of our educational institutions or of the public at large (Gaylin, 1981). This notwithstanding, the social indicators of our time all validate Benedict's premise. Our protraction of adolescence well beyond its biological years and our inability to ease the transition may well account for the recent increase in rates of adolescent drug abuse, crime, suicide, and other social ills. With little or no role preparation and few ceremonies with which to soften cultural discontinuities, the burden of expectation we place on our children to become overnight successes as spouses, breadwinners, and parents may be too great for some of our fledglings to bear.

Conclusion

Marriage and the family are institutions worthy of being worked at. They are not to be taken for granted. From our earliest moments of awareness, the bonds of our earliest years and our attitudes about them shape our futures as persons. Few would deny that loneliness is perhaps one of the most tragic of human conditions. Mutual interdependence is central to our concept of who we are: indeed it is how we define our selves.

DEVELOPMENT OF THE SELF AND ITS CONTEXT[1]

5

You shall no longer take things at second or third hand,
nor look through the eyes of the dead,
nor feed on the specters in books;
You shall not look through my eyes either,
nor take things from me;
You shall listen to all sides, and filter them from yourself.
Walt Whitman, *Leaves of Grass.*

Introduction

Person-centered theory and method of psychotherapy are anchored in respect for the uniqueness of individuals and their life experiences. They fall within the category of self-psychology. In this book, the foregoing chapters on the family describe the crucible in which that self is forged — a vessel often overlooked in our understanding of self. From birth on, the family engenders the self and shapes the individual.

Carl Rogers was one of the first psychotherapy theorists to recognize the basic caring nature of the therapeutic relationship and articulate its power to liberate the actualizing tendency of psychologically distressed individuals (Rogers, 1942, 1957, 1961). Yet Rogers' writings barely touched upon the significance of the intimate family-based relationships from which the self evolves. The natural emergence and development of the self in the intimate context of the family underlie and parallel an evolutionary process that culminates in self-actualizing. The family-shaped self and the self-actualizing process (Gaylin, 1990) require explication if we are to better understand the fully functioning person and the human condition.

Basic concepts

Basic to person-centered theory are the concepts of the self and its actualization. Traditionally, Rogersian self-psychology easily casts itself as a psychology of the individual, although it can really be viewed as a psychology of humanness and, therefore, of people in relationship to one another. Furthermore, self-psychology

1. First published as 'The self, the family, and psychotherapy' in *The Person-Centered Review,* *3*(1), (1996), 31–43. Reprinted with permission of the editor.

should define and examine the developing self in the context of others because of the interdependent nature of human existence. Therefore, the person-centered approach warrants review that underscores the central position of the interpersonal elements of the development of the person.

The actualizing tendency and self-actualization[2]

Often our understanding is blurred regarding two key concepts of the person-centered approach: the actualizing tendency of the organism and the self-actualization of the individual. Goldstein, when he introduced the terms (1939, 1940), tended to use them interchangeably. Later (1959) Rogers appropriately distinguished between them, noting that the actualizing tendency is the innate press in all organisms — from plankton and amoebae to sequoia and Homo sapiens — to fulfill their biological destiny. For the human organism the actualizing tendency gives birth to a very special feature, the *self-system*, from which the uniquely human process of self-actualization derives. According to Rogers, early in life

> . . . a portion of the individual's experience becomes differentiated and symbolized in an awareness of being, awareness of functioning. Such awareness may be described as self-experience . . . This representation in awareness of being and functioning, becomes elaborated through *interactions with the environment, particularly the environment composed of significant others* into a concept of self, a perceptual object in his experiential field [emphasis added],(1959, p. 223).

Self, role, subself, and self-complex

Self-recognition, the ability to perceive one's own entity as distinct from other entities, is primarily a human characteristic, although it has been observed in a few infrahuman animals (see Gallup, 1977). Self-awareness, the ability to distinguish ourselves as both actors and objects of actions, is a more complex and sophisticated concept and to our knowledge a solely human attribute. In 1890, William James introduced the behavioral sciences to a new conceptualization of the self. Central to James' psychology of human behavior were two concepts: (a) the *hierarchy of selves* which gives complexity and (b) the *stream of consciousness* which maintains integrity to individual functioning.

James' brilliant conceptualizations of consciousness and self-awareness were, however, eclipsed by Freud's (1900) delineation of the subconscious and the tripartite functions (id, ego, and superego) of the human psyche as a schematic for understanding all human behavior. Nearly half a century later, George Herbert Mead (1934) borrowed heavily from James' 1890 treatise and reintroduced the concept of the self to the social sciences. Mead, like James, distinguished two

---

2. Later, in Chapter 8, I will introduce and discuss another facet of the human actualizing tendency — that of family actualization, an indigenous aspect of self-actualization.

primary aspects of the self: the *I*, subject of actions, and the *me*, object of actions. Mead also crystallized the idea of the centrality and multifaceted, interpersonal nature of the self and its components.

In the first half of the twentieth century, however, the battle between the concepts of *ego* and *self* was no contest in the therapeutic community. Freud's ego won, and psychodynamic psychiatry dominated psychotherapy. As late as 1953, Harry Stack Sullivan attempted to introduce self-psychology to the psychiatric community via his theory of interpersonal psychiatry and human development. However, despite his efforts, the tripartite function of the psyche with the ego as controller retained its hold in medical psychiatry and had a virtual monopoly on the practice of psychotherapy.

Nonetheless, in academic psychology, the battle continued (see Allport, 1943 and 1955; Bertocci, 1945; Chien, 1944; Koffka, 1935; Sherif and Cantril, 1947; and Symonds, 1951). It was Rogers, first in 1942 and later in 1951, but most persuasively in 1959 and 1961, who integrated the concept of the self into psychotherapeutic practice, made it fundamental to a theory of personality and, in the process, changed the face of psychotherapy.

At roughly the same time that Mead (1934) proposed his theory of the self, Bateson (1936) introduced the concept of social role to the behavioral sciences which embraced it. Today, unfortunately, social role is often used interchangeably with, or as a substitute for, the concept of self, resulting in a merging of the two ideas and a disservice to both. The concept of role and role playing, elaborated by Bateson in 1936, and again with Ruesch in 1951 (Bateson and Ruesch, 1951), is far different from the theory of a multiplicity of selves posited by James and Mead.

According to Bateson, *role* is a sociological concept that refers to a set of expected behaviors attendant to a particular status. A role is a kind of mantle offered by the culture and donned by the individual. The mantle may alternately be taken on and removed, in the same way that an actor assumes a role in a play.

Yet the array of roles which society recognizes, defines, and ascribes is dramatically different from the many selves which each of us, as individuals, identifies experientially from within and continuously integrates into our being. Each of our selves and our judgments concerning them constitute an amalgam of self that gives rise to our attitudes, judgments, and feelings about who we are. Reciprocally, such identifications shape the ever-evolving amalgamated self.

Attempting to understand the process of change in both individual and family psychotherapy requires closer scrutiny of the distinction between the concepts of role and self. Mead's (1934) discussion of the concept of role (p. xxi) focused on 'role-taking' and clearly delineated a process not unlike empathy, whereby one person perceives and, to some degree, is able to take 'the part of another'. Today, the word 'role' is often used loosely in two ways. The first, adopted by sociology, is used to designate an outward aspect of the person, a position which one fulfills. These are generally functions assumed by the individual or ascribed by the culture as a means of identifying a person as parent, worker, teacher, etc. The other, more psychological use of role is as a part of the self, i.e., the entire experience and associated behaviors of being children, siblings, parents, etc. Rather than roles we assume, these are identities that emerge within us as we interact with our environments; they then become an integral part of the way we think of ourselves. Therefore, these identities may be more accurately termed *subselves*, the amalgam of which may be termed the *self-complex*.[3]

Working from within the amalgamated self-complex, we develop a sense of worth or self-esteem grounded in our overall sense of adequacy, sufficiency, or competence — our recognition and assessment of self and who we believe we are. Disappointing or pain-laden self-evaluation, not simple role confusion, can result in an attenuation of self-worth or self-esteem that may cause people (individuals, couples, or families) to seek relief from their anguish through psychotherapy.

Self-esteem

Perhaps no other construct in psychological theory has received more attention in the past generation than that of self-esteem. Poor self-esteem is a term more bandied about by the general public than discussed in the literature of the behavioral sciences. Poor self-esteem is considered to be the cause of virtually every intrapersonal and interpersonal problem from scholastic underachievement to adult sociopathy (Coopersmith, 1967). Although not identical to Rogers' concept of incongruence it is related to it (see Chapter 7).

William James (1890) first empirically defined self-esteem according to the following mathematical formula:

$$\text{Self-esteem} = \frac{\text{Success}}{\text{Pretensions}}$$

The formula weighs perceptions of our accomplishments (*Success* in the numerator) against that of our aspirations (*Pretensions* in the denominator) to determine our feelings of self-worth. More simply put, the more we believe that our successes measure up to our expectations for ourselves, the better we feel about ourselves. About this equation, James (1890, p. 310) notes that:

> Such a fraction may be increased as well by diminishing the denominator as by increasing the numerator. To give up pretensions is as blessed a relief as to get them gratified; and where disappointment is incessant and the struggle unending, this is what men will always do.

In other words, identifying unrealistically high standards that we have at times set for ourselves and subsequently lowering them can effectively have the same impact on our feelings of self-worth as meeting high standards.[4]

---

3. Sampson (1988) has argued for a similar concept called the *ensembled self* (see Chapter 8).
4. Footnote 4 on next page.

Each of our many subselves contributes to our overall sense of self-esteem or self-doubt. An intricate, delicate, and unique interaction is created by our own evaluation and derived sense of competence regarding each of these subselves and the self-complex as a whole. Furthermore, maintaining integrity and balance within the self-complex defines our sense of psychological well being at any moment in time. Aspirations may compete for a person's time and energy. If, for example, a person's short- or long-term goal is to be a good parent, that person may simultaneously have to care less about being a successful worker or vice versa. At such a juncture, the individual's less emphasized subself would carry less weight in the computation of the self-esteem of the total self-complex.

Although our culture and social milieu may shape our aspirations, it is the individual who continuously delineates the components that make up the intricate, idiosyncratic equation of self-esteem. Therefore, depending upon subtleties of biological state, context, mood, etc., the accomplishments of the numerator and/or the aspirations of the denominator in the formula may change abruptly or subtly over time. At different times, depending on our sense of purpose and ambition, we may invest differently in each of our subselves and give more weight to one than the others.

Since each of our many subselves may be the focus of our attention and energy at any point in time, the self-complex is always in a fluid state, continuously amending and reintegrating itself. Thus, one cannot simply average the sum of the various evaluations of the many subselves and the perceptions of their adequacy or inadequacy to obtain a single measure of self-esteem for a given individual. Rather, an ongoing and, perhaps, constantly changing and subjective evaluation must be performed and the results ascertained only by the amalgamated self in question. And when the result of that ever-active evaluation causes anguish which the individual or the family cannot relieve despite valiant efforts, they then may be impelled to seek psychotherapy.

Thus, the self and self-evaluation are central to our understanding of psychological well-being, the fully functioning person, and the therapeutic enterprise. This recognition of the centrality of the self has led to what Seeman (1988) refers to as 'the rediscovery of the self in American psychology' during the last quarter of a century (see especially Neisser, 1993).

Developmental issues
The beginnings of the self
In the study of individuals, it is difficult to avoid using the word *self*. Consequently, there is a tendency to get caught up in tautologies when discussing how the self develops. Etymologically, the word *self* is so basic to our communication that it is impossible to determine when the word was introduced into our language.

---

4. James' formula for self-esteem is essentially that employed by Butler and Haigh (1954) in their Self-Ideal Q-Sort. Their adaptation of Stephenson's (1953) technique proved to be one of the most productive empirical measures of psychotherapy outcome (see Chapter 13).

Appropriately, the Oxford English Dictionary (1971) starts by defining the word *self* as *the primary sense.*[5]

Those who study development naturally assume that one's experience of bodily self is mandatory, precedes and leads to an awareness of oneself as a being separate from all others. Infants in the first few months of life may be seen engaged and absorbed in explorations of their bodies. These explorations are further assumed to be precursors to the development of our young ones' notions of first the *I* and then the *me* aspects of self. The *I* sense, observed in the first few months of life, is that of active agent who acts upon others and objects. The *me* sense develops somewhere in the second year and treats the self as an object of information and assessment (Berk, 1999).

The developmental progression continues. According to traditional thinking, the transition from simple self-awareness to a sense of separateness of being is followed by the offspring's awareness (about the middle of the second year) of its position and place in the family. Until recently, this clear distinction about self was believed to occur at the age of three or four years with the conclusion of toddlerhood and the onset of the preschool years. During this period many developmental theorists (e.g., Erikson, 1950; Mahler, Pine, and Bergman, 1975; Piaget, 1951; Werner, 1948) maintained that children begin to distinguish in meaningful ways between self and significant others in the environment. Development theorists also suggested that the late toddler/early preschooler actively takes the part of others, first through mimicry and then through language and games, implying the concomitant development of empathy and social interaction.

However, evidence suggests (Sagi and Hoffman, 1976) that the processes of differentiation and imitation begin much earlier in life: despite a relatively limited range of socio-emotional responses (i.e., contentment versus distress), human neonates display a predisposition to empathy and interaction from birth. Furthermore, rather than the previously assumed long period of self-centeredness thought to be characteristic of the very young, recent investigators' observations note the beginnings of an interpersonal empathic process by as early as the first birthday (Brunner, 1986; Zahn-Waxler and Robinson, 1995). Thus, although there is presently no way of discerning whether or not the self is innate in the human organism (Mead, 1934; Zimring, 1988), there is little question that we are biologically primed to be socially interactive from birth, if not before (Condon and Sander, 1974; Meltzoff and Moore, 1977). The natural conclusion is that the propensity for self-definition through interaction with others is, indeed, somehow inherent in the human organism.

Maturation and the development of the self-complex
We first become aware of our bodies — our physical selves — through primary

---

5. There are those, however, who contend that individual consciousness, including self-awareness, is a relatively late occurring event in our phylogenetic development. Lewis (1967), and later Stephenson (1980), suggest that *group-consciousness* or shared meaning precedes our sense of self. See Chapters 8 and 13, later in this volume.

somatic experiences: feelings of distress, (e.g., hunger, cold), and corresponding relief and comfort (e.g., satiety, warmth). Soon thereafter, we begin to experience ourselves as beings with physical parts (e.g., vocal cords, mouth, fingers, toes, etc.). Thus, our earliest self-awareness develops. But only in relation to others do young children define themselves as persons rather than simply other beings (Gibson, 1993). The difference between our awareness or sense of being and our recognition of ourselves as interactive people is what distinguishes the actualizing tendency (the biologic) from the self-actualizing tendency (the psychosocial). This distinction is what makes us sentient and uniquely human and creates characteristically human joy and anguish in evaluating the quality of our lives.

From the earliest body awareness of ourselves, we begin to experience and subsequently recognize our subselves by interacting as dependent children in relation to primary care-giver(s), generally our parent(s) (Trevarthen, 1993). Gradually, then, we also become aware of other significant persons in our life space. Through our relationships with them, we continue to identify a variety of subselves. Thus, if we are not first born or if we are and a sibling enters the household, our subself as brother or sister usually forms early within the family environment. We interact with our siblings, indeed, out of an awareness of our own sibling subself in relation to them. With other kin (e.g., grandparents, aunts, or uncles, cousins) we establish relationships that they and we reinforce with each new encounter, thereby defining new subselves. Thus, we approach each interaction from the relational positions that we have assimilated into our set of subselves, i.e., the self-complex.

Although many of these inter-familial subselves are formed very early in life, usually within the first two years, many other subselves continue to evolve throughout the lifespan. As social, physical, and intellectual maturation continue, the subselves of playmate, friend, neighbor, student, etc., also become parts of the self-complex, typically in the preschool years. Beginning with puberty and the onset of physical maturation, the subselves of girlfriend/boyfriend, lover, spouse, worker, parent, and grandparent are gradually added, via new experiences, to the repertoire of perceived and identified subselves. As we mature, incorporating new subselves augments and enriches the self-complex; we relate to larger interpersonal networks in more complex ways, with each increment fleshing out the continuum of self-growth and redefinition of previous experiences and definitions of the self-complex (see Neisser, 1993). Thus, we self-actualize.

We can never divest ourselves of the interactionally derived subselves of our self-complex even though the principals may die. Death may end active interpersonal exchange with a person, but it does not terminate the relationship because each relationally created subself lives on within us. In our minds we remain the child of our parents even after their death. We are forever child to our parent, brother or sister to our sibling, etc., even though sharply conflicting grievous conditions could create a wish to divest oneself of these subselves. A perceived egregious and, therefore, unwanted subself may in fact result in dissonance or incongruence sufficient enough to drive an individual or family to seek relief through psychotherapy.

These formulations of self may employ some of the same appellations as those under the banner of societally ascribed roles, but the former are, nonetheless, substantively different from them. These experiential, relationally defined entities are not, like roles, exogenous to our being: rather, they are indigenous subselves that become integral, though not always integrated, parts of our self-complex forever. Even when we assume various exogenous roles (i.e., student, friend, worker, spouse) on a trial basis, the minutes, hours, or years operating from that perspective serve as a subself which automatically is incorporated into the self-complex. Thus, we naturally transform many (if not most) of these roles into additional and meaningful subselves. However, depending on (a) whether or not our evaluation of our self-worth flourishes when we match our aspirations to successes in these roles and (b) we wish these to be meaningful aspects of our lives, we may also cast off the exogenous nature of these roles. Nonetheless, even those that are rejected by us contribute to our conceptualized complete self by helping us to distinguish among who *we have been*, who *we are not*, and *who we are*.

Out of a need to understand such an evolution of psychological growth, theorists like Freud (1900), Sullivan (1953), Erikson (1959), and Havighurst (1971) developed theories of how individuals relate and adapt to their interpersonal environments throughout the lifespan. This development of the self-complex is the crucial and virtually overlooked aspect of the self-actualizing process in person-centered theory and practice.

A psychology of well-being

The understanding of the self-complex, including the subtle interactions of our various subselves within that self-complex, is pivotal to an understanding of psychological well-being. Our self-esteem at any given moment in time is affected by an ever-changing constellation of selves, idiosyncratic to each of us and dependent upon unique history, internal constitutional environment, and the external environmental context in which we are operating. Thus, our internal states (e.g., hunger and fatigue) as well as external forces (such as weather, interpersonal threat, etc.) may affect our self-evaluations. Furthermore, self-evaluation is complicated by which of our many subselves we deem pre-eminent at any given moment. For example, when I am at home, my spousal or parental subself may be pre-eminent. At the university, however, my teacher or collegial subself may take precedence as the locus for my evaluation of self. These evaluations are continuously fluid, changing with time and environment, as well as with biological state and mood.[6]

The question that arises concerns how the self-complex managed. How do we maintain some sense of self-integrity, wholeness, or self-identity? This question

---

6. These ideas are neither new nor unique to the person-centered approach. Indeed, they form the antecedents to the person-centered thinking of Rogers. They draw upon William James' *hierarchy of selves* (1890), G. H. Mead's *interactive self* (1934) and H. S. Sullivan's development of self through communication (1953).

has intrigued the earliest philosophers and is the engine that continues to drive psychological theorists. The answer involves our sentience. Part of human uniqueness results from our individual and collective ability to remember the past and anticipate the future. This human sentience is intimately related to our basic biological distinctiveness that results from not only our highly developed cortical functioning but our long neonatal dependence, as well (Gaylin, 1985, 1991).

James (1890) referred to our awareness of being as a *stream of consciousness* that keeps our selves intact, flowing from one experience to another and incorporating past experiences in the process. My metaphor for the self is that of a woven fabric or tapestry, the warp threads of which are shaped by our biologic constitutions and genetic heritages and laid out by our earliest interpersonal experiences within our families. The warp thus forms the foundation of our fabric, and successive experiences serve as the weft. Our consciousness, then, is like a continuously embellished cloth maintaining integrity over time despite changes in texture, color, and design.

Implications for understanding the psychotherapeutic process

Rogers considered the importance not only of the family and interpersonal relationships in the self-actualizing process but the applicability, as well, of his theory to family life (see Rogers, 1953; and Rogers, 1959, p. 241). He noted the importance of parent-child interactions particularly the parents' *unconditional positive regard* for their child that supports the child's continuing *orgasmic valuing process* — thus enabling self-actualization. On the other hand he considered the negative impact of parents' expressed *conditions of worth* that he believed sowed the seeds of personal incongruence. However, these elements of family context appear to be afterthoughts or footnotes rather than integral to his theoretical formulations of human functioning and the psychotherapy process. The paucity of information in person-centered theory regarding the development of the self also yields little explanation of how understanding the development of the self helps enable more effective psychotherapy.

Ideas regarding the self and the context in which it develops are intimately connected with those elements of the therapeutic process that Rogers (1957) deemed psychologically restorative (i.e., *the necessary and sufficient conditions for personality change* — see Chapters 9 and 10). Understanding not only the development of the self but the manner in which people's self-complexes interact during the therapeutic process can have extensive ramifications for the manner in which we think about, perform, and evaluate psychotherapy.

Theoretically, I am not proposing different methods with which to conduct traditional person-centered therapy, but I am conceptually recasting a therapy of self into the intimate interpersonal context of the family wherein that self was conceived and developed. A more elaborate explication of the manner in which these concepts are expressed in the family therapy hour is presented in Chapter 11.

Also, it well may be asked why is it important to determine or understand these internal dynamics? Put more pragmatically, how or why does knowing the workings of the self affect the manner in which we do things — specifically, how does it affect the manner in which we conduct ourselves as psychotherapists?

The person-centered approach is an interesting alloy of self and experiential postulates. Basically, since the self-complex is composed of many subselves that are formed and constantly reshaped by continuing and varied interpersonal experiences, the process of psychotherapy becomes one more of those experiences despite, ironically, its focus on the process of experiencing itself. The client is the active examiner of self in an interpersonal environment that enables the re-experiencing of the multiplicity of subselves in the client's self-complex. Indeed, psychotherapy is perhaps only a pale analogue of other interpersonal experiences that, long before the invention of psychotherapy, had healing qualities. Examples of such relationships are loving familial relationships, intimate friendships, and communion with God (or those designated as God's representative).

In psychotherapy, clients examine their life experiences (both immediate and past) with a relative stranger called a psychotherapist. How much more powerful or efficacious might the therapeutic activity be if one were to examine some of these experiences with those people who share (or shared) one's most intimate life space? For these reasons I choose to provide person-centered therapy in the context of a marriage or family.

Indeed, when individuals call me for therapy, I often invite the caller to bring a spouse or significant family member along, if the prospective client can feel comfortable in doing so. If the presenting problem concerns an interpersonal relationship, I may suggest that the caller bring the individual with whom the difficulties exist. Sometimes, of course, this is neither desirable nor realistic. If one is experiencing difficulties with one's boss, it may be neither easy nor desirable to bring the boss to the therapy hour. Similarly, if one is unsuccessfully trying to divorce, leave, or in general disengage from a relationship, the last thing one might want is to have that person in the room. On the other hand, had we a different way of looking at the power of the therapeutic process, it might be exactly the thing to do. Since much therapy deals with issues of interpersonal relationships, the inclusion of others should be looked upon not as unusual and negatively complicated, but usual, natural and appropriate.

Generally, I am matter-of-fact about the suggestion that another person attend the hour and look upon such an accompaniment as a means of making myself familiar to other family members and significant others. Once the session is underway the individual client, who until then may have considered such a session somewhat unusual, soon discovers the usefulness of having a familiar person with them. In these sessions the guest is often turned to for validation of perceptions and may have experiential details that facilitate the client's examination of self from both perceived contexts with no additional thought given to the presence of the other person. From here the process naturally continues.[7]

---

7. Interestingly, teenagers without any prompting from me will often spontaneously bring a friend of the same or opposite gender to their session.

The person-centered approach has used the interpersonal milieu in more traditional settings, specifically with groups of individuals (Bebout, 1974, and Beck, 1974).[8] Thus I am puzzled by how few of my person-centered colleagues venture into working with couples and families. In part, I believe that work with families is not only consonant with the person-centered approach, it also augments our understanding of the individual client.

Conclusion

The person-centered approach derives from self-psychology and includes a positive growth-oriented perspective. Implicit in that perspective is the interpersonal context in which the self is shaped as the individual develops. Conceptually the interpersonal nature of the individual needs to be better articulated in order to understand the true nature of the self and develop a more efficacious psychotherapy. Finally, such an approach leads the way to an understanding of a positive psychology of well-being rather than a deficit psychology of disease/illness.

---

8. Even though we tend to use person-centered methods in our own groups (i.e., when we are together as professionals), I continuously wonder why group work in the person-centered approach to therapy is not more widely employed. Once again, I suspect that we are subtly trained to view the individual as independent of the interpersonal environment.

CREATIVENESS AND A PSYCHOLOGY OF WELL-BEING[1]

6

An ulcer, gentlemen, is an unkissed imagination taking its revenge for having been jilted. It is an unwritten poem, a neglected music, an unpainted watercolor, an undanced dance. It is a declaration from the mankind of the man that a clear spring of joy has not been tapped, and that it must break through, muddily, on its own.
John Ciardi, *An Ulcer Gentlemen Is An Unwritten Poem.*

Introduction

Perhaps no other major psychotherapy orientation views the human condition more positively than does the person-centered approach. Basic to the foundations of person-centered therapy and theory is the conviction that an inherent thrust towards maximizing potential exists within all individuals. The implications, though rarely enunciated, are that psychological health and basic creativity border on being synonymous and that both are embodied in the fully functioning person.

Few would argue against the merits of psychological health. Yet ironically, although creativity in the abstract is considered one of the most highly prized human attributes, many of the most creative people are regarded with a specialness that is far from positive. That is, despite research and theoretical arguments to the contrary, the clichéd association between genius and madness persists.

This paradoxical association has both historic and phenomenological bases that derive from increased societal constraints upon the individual and implications of the present-day practice of psychotherapy. An understanding of the impact of these forces upon the development of psychological theory and individual behavior is necessary if we are to develop a psychology of human potential rather than one that emphasizes maladaptive behavior. This chapter presents a more positive approach to human behavior and psychotherapy than is commonly accepted. Such an approach is based on three premises: (a) when successful, psychotherapy in essence facilitates the client's creativeness; (b) this creativeness, by nature, is

---

1. First published as 'On creativeness and psychological well-being', in D. Wexler and L. Rice (Eds), *Innovations in Client Centered Therapy*, New York: John Wiley and Sons, (1974). Reprinted with permission of the publishers.

therapeutic and enhancing; and (c) this creativeness is the same process which Rogers has referred to as the actualizing tendency.

Of genius, madness, and history

Traditionally, the practice of psychotherapy has been thought of as a means of making whole the psychologically infirm. It was conceived in the framework of physical medicine and, despite attempts to conceptualize it in more positive terms, the illness-treatment model maintains a firm hold on the minds of most people, including those who are actively engaged in its practice. This view is perhaps natural, as those who tend to seek psychotherapy are generally looking for relief from emotional anguish that impairs their functioning. But to equate health solely with the absence of infirmity is similar to asserting that love is merely the absence of hate. Although the absence of obvious disease may be a starting point for a definition of health, health also carries with it implications of robustness from which the organism may enhance its future growth and potential.

The concept of mental illness is relatively recent. The Greeks as far back as Plato showed a certain tolerance, even a reverence, for aberrant mental states. However, as western society grew more complex, it correspondingly became less able to tolerate the aberrant individual. During the Middle Ages, the insane were viewed as receptacles of evil; their behavior was considered a sign of consort with the devil. In the renaissance, psychopathology was viewed primarily as a moral failure. The most extreme cases were treated much as criminals; punishment was considered an appropriate form of *therapy*. According to psychological historians, it was Pinel in the latter half of the eighteenth century who first considered the insane *mentally sick*. With that appellation, their separate institutionalization and the creation of mental hospitals began.

The early pioneers of psychology and some recent counterparts have seen in the concept of mental illness a means of dealing more humanely with the problems of individuals who are socially maladaptive. They have attempted, therefore, to conceptualize aberrant psychological conditions in a manner similar to physical illnesses: that is, a condition not despised but evocative of sympathy and concern. Such a parallel also implies anticipation of treatment and cure. From all I can gather, by and large, these efforts have been a failure. In 1961 The Final Report of the Joint Commission on Mental Illness and Health notes that: '...mental illness is different from physical illness in (at least) the one fundamental aspect that it tends to disturb and repel others rather than evoke their sympathy and desire to help', (1961, p.xviii). Little seems to have changed since that report.

The medical sciences have traditionally focused upon malfunction as a means of determining normally functioning behavior. It was, thus, natural for the study of mental illness to operate from a similar perspective. However, that which originally helped to clarify has become a source of confusion, as was aptly pointed out by Zubin in a compendium on the definition and measurement of mental health.

> Disease is usually defined in terms of etiology, structure, and symptomatology. In most mental disorders etiology is unknown, the

structure of the organs of the patient as far as we know is unaffected, and symptomatology is the only available basis for the definition. Mental diseases whose etiology and structural defects become known are usually lost to psychopathology. Thus disorders like general paresis, pellagra with psychosis, epilepsy, even PKU are now largely in the hands of other disciplines. Only the diseases of unknown origin remain in the field of psychopathology. Furthermore, there is also the question of whether mental disorders are in fact diseases or merely reaction patterns (Zubin, 1968, p. 71).

Freud, in the early 1900s, conceptualized and articulated his mental illness paradigm. Freud's dissection of the psyche led to a structural and nomenclatural system analogous to that of the biological systems of medicine. Despite initial difficulties in its acceptance, its definitiveness made it attractive. Thus, as many practitioners even today acknowledge, the metaphors which Freud developed to account for the conflicting forces which shape the personality have come to be virtually existing organs (e.g., id, ego, superego).

Freud's is inherently a drive-reductionistic, conflict-based theory. All behavior is grounded in the satisfaction of the instinctual drives which, in turn, are observed to conflict with the constraints of the social system. Under such a theory, the best that can be hoped for is a dynamic (and precarious) balance or equilibrium. The emphasis on pathology is pre-eminent and its potential always an impending threat. Furthermore, despite Freud's emphasis on the importance of the first five years of life and his enhancement of the thoughtful study of children's psychological development he, himself, never worked with the young. It was natural that his views of child and human development should be slanted towards psychopathology, considering that he reconstructed them from the recounted experiences of patients whose early childhood, by definition, had been problematic.

While remaining associated with the Freudian conflict-based model, others — especially those working primarily and directly with children (e.g., A. Freud, 1946; Hartmann and Kris, 1945; Spitz, 1945) — began to perceive a more positive or, at least, more neutral formulation of psychic development. Thus they introduced less pathology-oriented concepts such as the *conflict-free ego sphere*, *regression in service of the ego*, etc. These *ego* theorists (as they came to be known) developed their ideas during the 1930s and 40s. Simultaneously, the locus of psychological activity (both theoretical and practical) was shifting from Europe to the United States where the ongoing emphasis was on experimental and behavioral psychology.

Psychological thinking was becoming more and more subject to empirical observation; it was being tested in light of recent animal studies and couched in terms of educational psychology. Sociology and anthropology began incorporating and applying many of the heretofore unchallenged *universal* concepts regarding personality development (e.g., the Oedipal conflict, dream symbols). It became increasingly apparent that even with continued reworking, there was much in analytic theory that could not account for certain behaviors exhibited by apparently healthy individuals in various societies. The impact of these divergent schools of thought coming together in a climate totally different from that of Victorian Europe generated a new ideational approach, that which Abraham Maslow referred to as the *Third Force* of psychology.

Although the Third Force has no one prophet, it is probably best embodied in the theorizing of Maslow (1954, 1962) and the empirical and clinical work of Rogers et al. (1951, 1954). It is heavily grounded in the philosophy of William James (1890) and the observations of Kurt Goldstein (1963) in that it presents a more positive and holistic view of the development of the personality. It postulates a drive considered but later rejected by Freud — that of a push towards growth or *actualization* by the organism. This drive is present in all human beings, both healthy and ill. The tendency is ever present. Basically, the Third Force maintains a humanistic and optimistic view of human behavior. Its stance is that psychological health is more than the mere absence of disease. It is, rather, a condition in which the individual approaches the acme of productivity — i.e., creativity. Whereas Freud's metaphor for the human condition is a blank slate upon which society writes its mark, Rogers' is more like the metamorphosis within the chrysalis.

Adherents to the Third Force are the self-theorists, like Rogers, who stress the process of becoming. This functional approach may, in part, account for the lack of an elaborate theory of personality as rich in embellishment as that posited by the analytics who stress the structural components of the psyche. Thus, for the analytics, there exists a highly technical delineation of psychic components for which appropriate development is considered crucial to adjustment and normative social behavior. For the self-theorists, no such dissection is attempted. The former tends to lead to theories of structural deficiency: the latter focuses instead on the process of becoming (Allport, 1955).

In part, differences between these two schools of thought may well explain why the mental disease modelists can best launch their ideas when discussing the kinds of populations observed in mental institutions. There, residents' behaviors tend to be extremely different from those individuals who appear able to function with at least minimal adequacy within society. As suggested by Zubin (above), the more we learn about neurochemistry and the brain, the more we may be able to identify constitutional anomalies in both institutionalized individuals and those whose behaviors (e.g., clinical anxiety and depression) we once considered psychogenic. Increased emphasis on human potential and its enhancement leads to a fresh look at the creative individual, not so much as an accident of genetic and societal forces but, rather, as the possible idealized combination of these forces which might be systematically facilitated and encouraged throughout growth and development. To understand the evolutionary thinking about creativity and unravel the reasons for the stubborn persistence of the specious correlation between creativity and emotional disturbance, it is necessary to trace the history of humankind's attitudes regarding the creative process and its manifestations.

On the surface, the connection between genius and madness is patently absurd.

This association suggests that all of humankind's augmented understanding of the world and the technology enabled by that understanding, as well as everything that people have treasured in art, music, poetry and literature, are products of deranged members. Yet, despite the obvious illogic, the cliches of the mad scientist and the temperamental artist linger on. Virtually no research has been done on the subject. Freud probably aided and abetted the notion via his continued use of the artist's work as clinical *case* material: e.g., Da Vinci (Freud, 1932), Dostoyevsky (Freud, 1956a), Michelangelo (Freud, 1956b), etc. He also introduced of the concept of *sublimation* as justification for the common relationship between the products of artists and their neuroses (Freud, 1958). However, he merely lent a semblance of scientific credence to a pre-existing societal prejudice.

More likely, the myth arose sometime during the late eighteenth or early nineteenth centuries. For the early Greeks the word *ars* (from which the word *art* developed) bore little resemblance to its modern counterpart. Rather, it meant a specialized skill or craft. Carpentry, cooking, and surgery (all kinds of handiwork) as well as poetry and sculpting were embodied in this notion, and little or no distinction was made among them. In medieval times, the Latin *ars* took on the idea of any special form of knowledge gained from books (e.g., astrology and magic as well as logic and mathematics). With the renaissance, *ars* again took on its older meaning. Most art historians mark the renaissance as the time when artists took on special identities as craftspeople. The refinement of this definition into the *fine arts*, as opposed to the useful arts, did not become fully established until about the nineteenth century in the west (see Collingwood, 1958).

Socially, the renaissance also demarcated the shift from a medieval, unspecialized, agrarian economy to an emerging industrial-commercial era and the rise of Calvinism with its belief in a divine *calling*. These events gave rise to the Protestant work ethic. The respectability of earning money and a corresponding emphasis upon thrift, responsibility, and sobriety radically changed humankind's view of its role on earth. For the first time, worldly success could be associated with a divine morality; the lack thereof became associated with moral frailty or failing (Weber, 1930).

The advent of the nineteenth century and the Industrial Revolution (really the final consolidation of the evolution noted above) completed the transition from a stable, agrarian, trade lifestyle to an urban factory-centered one. Accompanying economic and human labor specialization produced the technological society of the twentieth century with its highly refined division of labor. Also at this time, the role of artist as separate from the productive craftsman was finally synthesized. Artists were no longer the *interior decorators* of the church or the *photographers* of the nobility. Technology had freed them from any such defined job in the production-consumption spheres. Although elements of a former image lingered, the idea of *art for arts sake*, for better or worse, had arrived. With this transformation, the artist was separated from the mainstream of life, and a kind of dilettantism developed surrounding the artist's image and work.

The shift in our thinking about creativity, the arts, and psychopathology coincided with the dramatic worldwide social and economic changes. Since neither the artists or the deranged could play a productive part or a defined role in a production-oriented society that thrived and relied upon burgeoning specialization and role definition, both groups became alienated from mainstream society at large. Add to this the similarity of their behavior at times: the eccentricity of artists and their singular driveness when in the throes of endeavors that often had none but remote and abstract relevance to the world around them. All of this embued artists with an aura of the onanistic behaviors associated with those who were mad. Furthermore, artists' insistence at times (even in the face of poverty and rejection by their immediate society) on the merits of their efforts tended to corroborate the association. It was also easy to point to examples of the coexistence of severe emotional disturbance and genius (e.g., Van Gogh, Kafka, Beethoven) to lend credence to the argument. But, in the process, those who lived a less flamboyantly notorious and relatively stable existence (e.g., Dickens, Renoir, Haydn) were forgotten. Few thought to question the possibility that for those artists who experienced emotional anguish, the disturbance may have resulted from lack of familial and/or of social acceptance of their impelling life direction rather than the root of their ill-understood talents.

A short time after the Industrial Revolution in a Victorian Europe noted for its emotionally repressive atmosphere, Freud developed his theory of personality. As a product of his milieu, it was perhaps natural for him to perceive 'work and love' as the primary parameters of successful adaptation. It is ironic, however, that this pioneer of personality theory, who was quite taken with the works of creative individuals, had so much to do with the association of genius and mental illness. He went so far as to conceptualize artistic endeavors as outcomes of neurotic diversions of libidinal energy.

Thirty years after Freud, Ernst Kris (through his work with children) developed a more positive theory regarding creativity. This change required the introduction of a less conflict-based model of impulses than that of Freud's. Kris (1952) introduced the idea of a fluid preconscious, not unlike James' earlier (1890) *stream of consciousness*, and posed a constructive notion of regression *in service of the ego*. Additional exposition by Hartmann (1958) and Kubie (1958) led to such refinements as *the conflict-free ego sphere*. These cumbersome elaborations of classic psychodynamic theory were an effort to couch the process of creativity in positive rather than neurotic terms. These efforts were harbingers of a fresh approach to the study of creative behavior — one of human potential rather than conflict. It is this position which will be elaborated upon in the following sections.

On creative synthesis and psychological integrity

The phrase *psychological well-being* is introduced and employed here in lieu of *mental health* because: (a) unlike the concept of mental health it is not associated with a converse concept (i.e., disease or illness) and, (b) it has a certain easy-to-understand, straightforwardness. Furthermore, it tends to avoid (a) negative concepts such as *problems in living*, suggested by Szasz (1960) or (b) the implications of ability such as those of *effectiveness* (Smith, 1968) or *competence* (White, 1959), although I think they were all attempting to define similar states.

For similar reasons, I prefer the term *creativeness* rather than creativity. Creativity is a term that has been colored with the specialness of genius, a connotation that more often than not confuses discussions of a more universal capacity — creativeness — that I believe is inherent in all individuals.

The concept of psychological well-being draws heavily on the formulations of Allport (1955), Hartmann (1958), Jahoda (1958), Szasz (1960) and Sells (1968). No attempt will be made here to describe some of the elaborate and well-developed detail in the above-cited works. Instead, the reader is referred to Rogers (1959) for summation and a more complete explication of the basic premises and terminology of the person-centered theory.

As presented in the person-centered approach, major assumptions regarding the psychology of well-being are relatively few. The *actualizing tendency* is the only motive or drive that is postulated in this theoretical system.

> While it includes such concepts as . . . need-reduction, tension-reduction, drive-reduction (e.g., Maslow, 1954, *deficiency needs*) . . . It also includes however the growth motivations which appear to go beyond these terms: the seeking of pleasurable tensions, the tendency to be creative, the tendency to learn painfully to walk when crawling would meet the same needs more comfortably (Rogers, 1959, p. 196).

Person-centered theory is a holistic approach reflecting the entire state of the organism at any given moment. Rather than simply drive-reductionistic in its view, it introduces the idea of a positive drive referred to as *self-actualization* which incorporates the notion of stimulus hunger or *adience*. Investigators (e.g., White, 1959; Butler and Rice, 1960; Fiske and Maddi, 1961) have empirically and experimentally demonstrated adience and go so far as to suggest it supersedes basic homeostatic drives.

Rogers also defined a special form of the actualizing tendency — *self-actualization*. 'Following the development of the self-structure, the general tendency toward actualizing expresses itself also in the actualization of that portion of the experience of the organism which is symbolized in the self' (1959, p. 196). The hypothetical goal of the actualizing tendency is the *fully functioning person*. The *process of becoming* more fully functioning is emphasized and characterized by another focal concept, increased *openness to experience*. As the exact opposite of defensiveness, this openness means that every stimulus, internal or external to the organism, has entrée to the individual's awareness without filtering or distortion.[2]

Based upon the above premises, the operational definition of psychological well-being used here will mean a sense of personal worth or self-esteem. This is

---

2. Openness to experience presumes that individuals are free to attend selective to available stimuli and that the individual's sensory-perceptual processes are basically unimpaired.

not to imply a state of smug self-satisfaction but, rather, an ever-fluctuating awareness of who we are as individuals in relationship to our environment (both physical and interpersonal). It is a relative concept, one that contains (in varying degrees from individual to individual) upper and lower limits rather than a static endpoint. Self-worth also implies a constellation of values (some conceptualized, some amorphous), an *ideal* towards which the individual strives and against which the perceived self is evaluated. There is always some discrepancy between these perceptions; when the discrepancy is tolerable the individual experiences psychological well-being (also relative); when intolerable, psychological anguish or distress is experienced. Such a definition generally articulates with society's standards as they are often incorporated into the individual's value system. However, it allows for possible exceptions as in the case of individuals of vision or genius who may be psychologically more sound than their environments.

Psychological well-being stresses adaptation rather than adjustment. It includes, along with the adaptive and perceptual elements of self-actualization and openness to experience, a third focal concept, *internal locus of evaluation*. While allowing room for society to influence individuals' assessment, acceptance, or rejection of the values of their milieu, the valuing center remains solidly internal rather than external to the individual. Rogers describes the fully functioning person experiencing psychological well-being as follows.

> He would not necessarily be 'adjusted' to his culture and he would almost certainly not be a conformist. But at any time and in any culture he would live constructively, in as much harmony with his culture as a balanced satisfaction of needs demanded. In some cultural situations he might in some ways be very unhappy, but he would continue to move toward becoming himself, and to behave in such a way as to provide the maximum satisfactions of his deepest needs (1961, pp. 193–4).

It should come as no surprise that for Rogers (and others like him) the similarity between psychological well-being and creativeness borders on equivalence. 'The mainspring of creativity appears to be the same tendency which we discover so deeply as the curative force in psychotherapy — man's tendency to actualize himself, to become his potentialities' (1954, p. 253). Barron puts the relationship as follows, '. . . The moment of health is the moment of unconscious creative synthesis, when without thinking about it all we know is that we make sense to ourselves and to others' (1963, p. 5). For Schachtel it is the essence of growth, 'The problem of creative experience is essentially the same for all the human capacities . . . it is the problem of the open encounter of the total person with the world' (1959, p. 240).

There is simple straightforwardness to relating psychological well-being and creativeness. The relationship implies a growing integrity between the organism and its environment; it also suggests a maximizing potential with all the powers available to the individual. It goes beyond the simple correlation of the two, implying (though few have directly explored the possibility) that the very curative force of psychotherapy is self-integrating creativeness, the embodiment of the actualizing or growth motive within us all. Although it may become temporarily thwarted, this creativeness continually seeks expression in the person's drive towards wholeness. Such a formulation also implies a conscious and deliberate growth or enhancement rather than a passive one. It requires self-awareness that, to our knowledge, is a uniquely human characteristic. It is perhaps from such awareness that biblical poets inferred humankind was created in God's own image.

Because of the difficulties in defining or operationalizing the kind of creativeness discussed above, investigators have often turned to the study of successful artists, writers, scientists, etc., those individuals most readily identified as creative. As a consequence, the focus of much inquiry in the area has become field specific and dependent upon products defined by society as creative. Here lies the root of much of our confusion about the differences between the kind of creativeness discussed above and creativity as it is commonly thought to be. This is the distinction that the rest of this chapter will attempt to elucidate.

Individuals engaged professionally in the activity of creating generally combine with their innate creativeness special talent and skills — qualities that are often related to but not synonymous with creativeness. Maslow (1962) refers to these qualities as *special talent creativeness* that will be referred to here as *creativity*. It tends by nature to be rather easily identified and is often defined as the epitome of creativity or genius. Thus the process and state of creativeness has become confused with the attributes of skill and talent and the end products thereof.

However, Maslow suggests another kind of creativeness not unique to individuals in special fields and consequently not so easily identified. He calls this *self-actualizing creativeness*. Self-actualizing creativeness is a pervasive process found in all individuals. It is closely related to the process of becoming less defensive, more open to experience, and more fully functioning — the process of becoming more psychologically healthy. The suggestion offered here is that the creativity observed in those who seem talented is only a special form of creativeness and the latter underlies all creative activity regardless of field of endeavor, be it cooking or sculpting.

Creativeness, the driving force inherent in the human organism from birth, leads to creative acts and experiences. These creative acts and/or experiences need not be those which in the past two centuries have been defined as the work of the artist or scientist. Rather, they may be observed in developing children as they grapple with all of the motor tasks involved in actualizing their human condition.

Thus, the act of walking is a universal human behavior that is also inherently a paradigm of an individual creative act and experience. As such it requires the synthesizing of a multitude of more basic skills. It is also the precursor to the dance. If one doubts this, one has only to regard the toddler executing their first connected steps. The accompanying delighted facial expressions may range from distinct wide-eyed surprise to gales of laughter from the moment that the awareness of synthesis and mastery has registered. And careful observation shows that no two infants pursue this process in exactly the same way, despite the similarity of the end result. Correspondingly, one might call all true learning (as distinguished from training) a representation of creativeness but not creativity. Creativity requires the added dimensions of originality or uniqueness, as well as the implementation of creativeness through expression (as will be explained below).

A creative act or experience is an extension and representation of all individuals inherent creativeness as it directly relates to their actualizing tendency. Thus, a creative act may be an action or some form of experience but it does not imply a product and, correspondingly, has little or nothing to do with societal or cultural values that define it as aesthetic, worthwhile, or innovative. The recognition and identification of the creative act or experience is totally dependent upon the individual. The locus of evaluation is totally within.

This formulation of creativeness is similar to Goldstein's (1963) *biological knowledge*, Maslow's (1957) *peak experience* and the *eureka*, or *aha!* phenomenon. It is learning in the true sense of the word, meaning discovery and synthesis, not training or memorization which include little, if any, of the above-mentioned attributes. It is this kind of experiential learning that Dewey (1939) so ardently advocated. And, most importantly, it is the kind of learning that is prelude to the creativity that has advanced our culture (see Werner, 1948). It is the impetus for the actualizing process. Thus, as creativity is the actualizer of society, creativeness is that for the individual.

As each creative act or experience becomes synthesized and incorporated it becomes a part of the organism's repertoire to be further built upon by additional and often more complex acts or experiences. If the individual combines these acts and experiences with talents and skills, some kind of product creativity may result. An example is in order. When children spontaneously make their first scribbles on a piece of paper their acts are an expression of their individual creativeness. No matter that these first scribbles, like the first halting, imbalanced steps of the child learning to walk, are a universal human phenomenon. To each child, they are unique at that moment in time. The experience of pleasure that this typical act of creative synthesis engenders impels the child to continue exploration and experimentation that may lead to discoveries of the nuances of control, until at some point or another basic mastery is attained. At this point the experience/ expression loses the novelty of the creative. At this plateau the child is practicing. However, generally before this juncture, new discoveries overlap the old pushing the drawing experience forward. Somewhere hidden within those very early scribbles are the rudiments of first the egg-shape, then the circle, square, etc., each discovery of which will be a basic creative act or experience and an expression of creativeness, with each discovery accompanied by a sense of excitement and satisfaction. These are the very same rudiments first at two, then at three and later at six years of age that pull the child towards the elements of design, composition and pictorial representation. Once the basic shapes have been mastered and incorporated, they will never be forgotten. This is the same process which produces the five-year-old's potato-and-stick self-portrait and which produced paintings by

Vermeer. The major difference is the highly sophisticated combination and recombination of basic elements found in the latter's renditions.

As Kellog (1967) has astutely and handsomely pointed out, there is a universality to all children's art. No matter the country of origin, all children develop the same graphic configurations, the same basic representations and at about the same age levels. This process parallels the manner in which all children learn to walk at roughly the same age (whether cradleboarded, bound or free) and go about the process in about the same manner. It is this same universal elegance embellished with simple touches of individuality that make children's art so appealing and communicative. These are the same features evident in cave paintings and in folk art around the world, and we are only just beginning to understand their fundamental creativity.

Frequently, folk art is referred to as *primitive* art — in my opinion a deceptive misnomer. In these works, there is simultaneity of earnestness and playfulness that conveys a uniquely personal message. Often, perspective and natural size relationships are ignored. Colors may have little to do with those found in nature. Realistic depiction is secondary to self-expression. It appears that the artists — be they caveman, peasant, or child — are endeavoring to please themselves first and foremost. That the results may or may not be pleasing or communicative to others is secondary. The locus of evaluation seems to be the self, not society. As children grow more sophisticated (i.e., become socialized) they become aware, often through unempathic criticism, that in the graphic arts there are naturalistic rules which are to be obeyed. The individual's locus of evaluation at this juncture often begins shifting from internal to external. Too frequently, this shift occurs in the early school years coincident with the time when children's art begins losing some of its characteristic uniqueness. Children learn to *adjust* their artistic productions to that which becomes expected of them. They soon may deem themselves good or bad artists which, when paired with innate and developmental differences in visual motor coordination may erode the potential for deriving joy in like activities and thereby deflect pleasure and additional exploration in this sphere. One may shift to another area of endeavor (e.g., music, sports, language) if supported. The analogue between artistic reproduction and psychological development appears plain. Too often we stress conformity or adjusting as opposed to creative adaptation in our approach to children's art.

If children are dealt with empathically and warmly in their early years, the actualizing tendency continues from one synthesizing creative act to the next to sustain itself. The child is impelled forward with regular progression. As physical competence and a sense of psychological well-being increase, the child's creativeness is enhanced and vice versa. One reinforces the other much like a chain reaction creating a perpetuation of the actualizing process. These individuals are more likely to produce creatively. They are not afraid to do something that is different. They are not afraid to combine elements that appear to be contradictory. They are not afraid to stand alone at times, yet take satisfaction from contact with others. The threat of failure has little meaning or impact upon such a person's self esteem, because failure is more of an experiment leading to creative synthesis and from which something is to be learned. For such an individual the simple may become infinitely complex and the complex merge into benign simplicity, each with its own inherent fascination. They may grow where they are planted or transplant themselves elsewhere if enhancement in their present spot does not materialize.

This is not to imply that creative endeavors take no training. Mastery over techniques, knowledge of tonal scales, chemical balances, and blending of pigments require certain degrees of training. But like simpler creative acts, these become (to borrow from Hartmann, 1958) *automatized* — second nature. As in walking, there was creative synthesis first. However, through repetition and consequential incorporation into the organism's repertoire, the originally creative acts become rather the enlarged foundation from which the self may actualize.

Toward validation and application

Mental illness is far easier to examine than mental health, let alone the notion of psychological well-being. For investigative purposes, mental-illness investigators have a readily available population, captive in mental hospitals and/or in clinic offices. Usually a relatively well-defined group of people, their behavior is either crazy enough to get them put away or sufficiently self-distressing to cause them to seek help and relief. Therefore they are either unable to protest their being studied or so much in need of help that they will put up with a lot, perhaps even welcome the psychological poking and prodding of psychodiagnosticians. Furthermore, they generally present a relatively easy-to-describe set of behaviors (symptoms) which are labeled *maladjusted,* the elimination or reduction of which serves as evidence of therapeutic effectiveness.

With regard to creativity, there are generally two investigative tracks. The first includes investigations of character traits of successful artists, writers, scientists, etc. These are exemplified by such studies as those of Roe (1946 and 1960), Drevdahl and Cattell (1958), Eiduson (1958), Hammer (1961) and Myden (1960). There are problems, however, with this approach as noted by Barron (1963) and Kubie (1958). Often those actively engaged in the creative arts and sciences are concerned that the dissection and understanding of their gift might dissipate it in some way or another and are, therefore, reluctant to participate. In the minds of many, such concern is an extension of the continued association between neurosis and talent with the former considered the wellspring of the latter. Further, this kind of research again focuses on creativity (i.e., *special talent creativeness*) confounding the process with evidence of tangible products in combination with notions of special talents and skills rather than elucidating the kind of creativeness discussed in the preceding section.

The other tack has been to study *normal* groups such as high school and college students (also in part because of their availability and captive quality). In these studies, creativity is first operationally defined by some parameter such as originality in problem solving, and an appropriate corroborative test is then administered. These studies are best exemplified by the work of Getzels and Jackson (1962), Barron (1957), and Maddi et al. (1962). Problems here center on the validity of the defining parameters: measures of creativity vary widely, with subjects required to perform a spectrum of tasks from choosing the more aesthetic of a pair in a series of drawings to listing as many conceivable uses for a simple object, such as a brick.

None of these approaches can be faulted, considering our lack of knowledge concerning both the creative process and states of psychological well-being. And while consistencies are few and contradictions abound, from the results of one study to the next there *are* certain consistencies that recur with relative frequency. For example, observations persist among investigators using a variety of techniques that common to most individuals deemed as creative there exists a group of factors that include *memory*, *imagery*, *originality*, *organization*, (including organizational complexity) and *energy* (Barron, 1957, 1958; Brittain and Beittel, 1960; Drevdahl and Cattell, 1958; Ehrenzweig, 1957; Guilford, 1957; Hart, 1950; Horney, 1947; Porterfield, 1941; Spearman, 1931; Stein and Meer, 1954). These five qualities recur in the literature regardless of the diverse vocations of the individuals under study (e.g., artists, business executives, and scientists).

Let us assume that the five qualities noted by behavioral scientists under numerous conditions are indeed identifiers of creativity (which, in turn, is a special form of creativeness) and that we can measure these qualities in some way in all people. Furthermore let us assume, as has been contended in the previous section, that psychological well-being and creativeness are intrinsically related and positively correlated. Could we not then anticipate these same qualities to become even more evident for individuals who can in some way increase their level of psychological well-being?

On the basis of the continued popularity of psychotherapy as a means of easing psychological distress, it appears to be a safe assumption, too, that psychotherapy is a means of increasing psychological well-being. Studies that validate this claim are far too numerous to cite here but the interested reader is referred to Rogers and Dymond (1954), Strupp (1963), and Shlien (1964) as starting points. Given all of the above assumptions, we might then examine a number of people undergoing psychotherapy and assess the degree of improvement in level of psychological well being before and after therapy. At the same time we could also assess the creativeness of those individuals before and after therapy to determine if the proposed relationship between psychological well being and creativness does, in fact, exist.

Such a study was performed at the University of Chicago Counseling and Psychotherapy Research Center. It was part of a larger research design determining the effects of short-term (20 sessions, generally twice a week) psychotherapy (see Butler, Rice and Dicken, 1960). Prior to entering, and following 20 sessions of person-centered psychotherapy, a battery of tests was administered to each individual from a group of clients who had applied for outpatient psychotherapy. The standard Rorschach Test, the Butler-Haigh Q-Sort, and the Therapists' Rating

Scale were among the tests administered to these clients. The last of these was administered only at the end of 20 sessions.

Although elaborate detail is inappropriate here, a brief description of the methods is in order. The Rorschach (inkblot) test derives a composite of complex scores designed to obtain a total picture of the subject's personality functioning (Beck, 1950). Some of the scoring is heavily loaded with what are considered normative-adjustment criteria; these are called *structure scores*. On the other hand, there is another group of scores that places little emphasis upon normative-adjustment criteria but rather has been shown to tap and measure the same five qualities associated with creativity listed above (i.e., memory, imagery, originality, organization, and energy). These latter scores are called *function scores*. Previous to the study under discussion here, little attempt to distinguish selectively or separate these two kinds of scores had previously been made.

To assess change in level of psychological well-being, two other measures were employed. The first of these was an *ipsative* measure, the Butler-Haigh 100-item Q-sort (see Chapter 13). The Q-sort compares clients' sorting of adjectives which describe their actual perceptions of self — S, and their image of an ideal self — I, thus obtaining a measure of self-comfort. These Self-Ideal (S-I) sort correlations, like the Rorschach, were obtained before their participation in person-centered therapy and again upon the completion of 20 sessions. Thus, clients assessed their own level of self-comfort by delineating how they felt about themselves against how they felt they should be. Note that the concern was with improvement for each individual rather than any specific level that might be considered psychologically healthy or conversely psychologically ill. To obtain a measure of change in level of psychological well-being, the S-I correlations obtained before the onset of therapy were subtracted from those obtained after 20 sessions. The same procedure was followed for the Rorschach *function* (creativeness) scores and the Rorschach *structure* (adjustment) scores. Therapists' Rating Scale, the final measure administered, is a simple nine-point scale on which each subject's therapist was asked to rate the amount of gain made by his or her client at the end of 20 sessions of psychotherapy.

Two groups of clients were arrived at: one group who had significantly increased their levels of psychological well-being (according to themselves and their therapists) and one group who (on the same basis) had not. The success group contained 20 people, the failure group 13. By and large the groups were quite similar and there seemed little to distinguish them from the usual outpatient clinic population. Furthermore there were no significant differences found among the groups in their pre-therapy adjustment or creativeness scores. Thus any changes found in the scores could be attributed solely to the clients' changed levels of psychological well-being. The pre-therapy/post-twentieth session Rorschach change scores were then compared for the groups.

Analysis of the data revealed that although the failure group showed no change in their creativeness scores, the success group showed large positive gains in creativeness (and in only two and one half months of therapy). These results were obtained at statistical levels well beyond those deemed acceptable for such research. Furthermore — and this was not anticipated — the Rorschach adjustment scores showed not only little change, they demonstrated a slight (though not statistically significant) downward shift for both the successful and unsuccessful clients. Lastly, when the creativeness and adjustment scores were combined, the dramatic positive results for successful psychotherapy clients were minimized to an almost negligible change. The actions of these two scores tended to cancel each other out.

The results of this study demonstrated a positive relationship between psychological well-being and creativeness. Furthermore, these factors had little to do with adjustment criteria heretofore commonly used to determine psychological health and improvement in psychotherapy. Indeed, it could be argued from these results that the healing force — that which enhances people's growth towards a higher level of functioning — lies somewhere in their innate creativeness and its push towards expression. Thus, the process of psychotherapy in some way (and for some clients) may be seen as freeing or mobilizing this force, rather than facilitating an adjustment or fit into the world. In summary, self-actualization and creativeness seem virtually synonymous and the maximization of both leads to increased psychological well-being.

We generally think of psychotherapy as starting from a negative base: a means of alleviating psychological distress, of making the impaired more normal. But if the psychotherapy process can augment creativeness in clients who, by definition, are experiencing psychological distress, what might be the potential for these techniques when used with people who are already moderately well-functioning, productive individuals? Perhaps we should begin conceptualizing an applied psychology of human potential rather than one solely of deficit.

From a human potential vantage point, we might begin to explore the relationship between creativeness and creativity and the eventual manner and modes in which creativeness can and does express itself through creativity. How does a Mozart, Planck, or Michelangelo come to be? It is in these individuals that the interplay of constitutional and social factors is inextricably woven with the psychological to produce a tapestry that we call personality. Herewith are a few speculations on this interplay, among some other concluding considerations.

Strong evidence (e.g., Getzels and Jackson, 1962; and Chess et al. 1965) supports the position that there are genetic and constitutional givens with which individuals begin life. Not only do these constitutional parameters help determine certain directions that shape people's lives, from birth on they cause unique, reciprocal relationships with the environment. Thus, that which has been referred to as *talent* may well be an inherent biological disposition towards certain sensory modalities (see Meier, 1939). For example, in the musician, the auditory-vocal modality may take precedence over the visual-motor. Such dispositions are encouraged through exploration at first by the organism and then by the environment (both interpersonal and physical). If, for instance, a child learns to distinguish tones, begins humming and derives pleasure from it, he or she may take pleasure in music, if encouraged. If not, such embryonic talent may indeed become submerged in favor of other modalities which *are* responded to. Undoubtedly, in the worst of circumstances, such inclinations may be lost altogether if actively suppressed or if creativeness is not enhanced along with them. Talent without creativeness may lead to craftsmanship but not creativity. Possibly, if the thrust of these dispositions is great enough and the environment continually thwarts them, the result may be an unhappy marriage between creativity and psychological distress.

On the other extreme, little has been said heretofore about the severe pathological limits of human behavior — those which are so bizarre that they fall beyond the range of acceptable — e.g., the psychotic. In part, I believe such psychopathology resides in a totally different realm of study from that of psychological well-being. Discoveries regarding brain activity and chemistry continue to reveal biological bases for mental illness (in the narrowest sense of the word) just as was the case for general paresis in the nineteenth century (Rose, 1995). Likewise, studies of early childhood autism are beginning to disclose previously unnoticed perceptual imbalances, both structural and biochemical, which may soon better account for schizophrenic-like behavior in children (Happÿe and Frith, 1996). Indeed, even our conceptualization of mental retardation is beginning to shift its emphasis from a once hopeless wastebasket to a differentiated schematization regarding remediation and enhancement of human potential (Verdugo, 2000).

Conclusion

Our world is shrinking and simultaneously growing more complex. We have gained immense technical capacities in but a short period of time. Yet lagging far behind is knowledge about ourselves and how we function when at our best. How little we understand the process of our maturation as individuals; even thinner is our understanding of ourselves when functioning at our noblest and most creative best. The process of psychotherapy is not simply one of removing infirmity: it is one that makes transparent the process of our self-actualization, our becoming more fully functioning, more open to our experience and more creative. In our frenetic need to cope with and maintain the pace of modern existence, we have tended to ignore the fact that humankind is more than an appendage to the machinery it has created. Indeed, we are people in search of our creativeness and ourselves.

Moral Aspects of Psychotherapy

7

The Moral man is not the one who merely wants to do the right thing and does it, nor the man without guilt, but he who is conscious of what he is doing.
Hegel, *The Philosophy of Right*.

Introduction

Efforts to salve the troubled spirit have existed since before recorded history. Until the modern era, the practice of healing the soul or psyche (once synonyms) fell under the purview of religion or philosophy, as did discussions of human nature and behavior. In the twentieth century, psychotherapy came under the aegis of the scientific study of behavior, namely psychology. The effort to make psychotherapy the applied arm of the science of psychology has effectively separated it from all branches of philosophical inquiry, including the study of ethics. We in the twentyfirst century are overdue in examining some of the dangers inherent in that separation.

Defining terms

In the behavioral sciences and common parlance, three related terms are sometimes used interchangeably: *values, morals, and ethics*. Although the differences among these ideas are sometimes subtle, their distinctions and interactions are focal to the study and practice of working with individuals and families in a psychotherapeutic context.

Values is the most circumscribed and mundane of the three terms. Values are more or less transitory; they are prized by an individual, group or a whole society at given times or in different eras. These values may be objects or qualities deemed desirable as a means or an end in themselves. Thus the term has a self or group-centered quality and a sense of the present. We speak easily of the values of an individual, a given era, a particular age, ethnic group or socio-economic class. In educational circles, particularly in the area of family study, it is common to discuss, evaluate, and analyze values. The social sciences have developed tests to measure them; parents, teachers, as well as theorists and policy makers discuss values frequently.

Of the three terms — *values, morals, and ethics* — ethics is the most overarching, abstract, and remote. One of the basic branches of general philosophy, ethics traditionally deals with the establishment and evaluation of rules of conduct and the general nature of moral decision-making by humankind. Today, we tend to think of ethics as codes of behavior ascribed to groups. The associations of all helping professions establish criteria for conduct that govern the ethical practices of those professions. These codes of conduct tend to be legalistic in nature and directed at professional, rather than personal, behavior. Perhaps because of their somewhat impersonal quality, we allude to them freely.

The term *morals*, on the other hand, has palpably different parameters from both *values* and *ethics*. Morals are the principles that govern human behavior in a much more universal and personal sense than either values or ethics. Morals force us to come to terms with black and white concepts such as *right* and *wrong*, *good* and *evil*. For westerners, morals are perhaps best embodied in the Decalogue — the Ten Commandments. Since their elaboration and exposition in the Old Testament (dated about 3,000 BCE — though there is evidence that as an unwritten moral code they were around at least 5,000 years prior to that) there has been relatively no change in them. In distinction to values, morals tend to be universal, timeless, and allocentric.

Today, we are often awkward in talking about morals and morality. In the behavioral sciences, discussions of morals are generally limited to their study in child development (e.g., Piaget, 1965, and Kohlberg, 1984). Much of modern post-technological society looks upon morality as an embodiment of simplistic, rather impractical issues to be reserved for the domains of philosophy and/or religion.

Religion, which once exercised powerful influence over the lives of many, has lost its place as a major institutional force in post-technological society. Furthermore, the separation of church and state has effectively precluded most discussions of morals and morality in our public schools. Therefore, for most of us, the transmission of those profound tenets that guide our moral behavior — bastions of humanitarian principles and foundations of great societies — is relegated solely to the family. Moreover, we expect that burdened institution to accomplish the job in about five years.

Clinical practice, morality, and evil

The clinical branch of the behavioral sciences has exacerbated the avoidance of morals as a legitimate consideration within its realm. Individual, group, and family therapists have been traditionally so concerned with the liberation of psychic functioning from *irrational* cultural constraints that the question of morality has become virtually taboo. In like fashion, the equating of morality (a general interpersonal code of civil behavior) with sexual moralism (rules defining sexual conduct) has reinforced the avoidance of this area of concern within the helping professions.

The continuing trend away from discussions of specific moral behaviors in favor of talk of ethics and values, I believe, is inherently dangerous and fraught with potential evil. My use of the word *evil* here is intentionally provocative. I want to make a case for infusing a moral stance to the theory, research, and practice of psychotherapy. Unlike words like *bad*, *wrongdoing*, or *malfeasance* which speak to the mind and the intellect, the word 'evil' also addresses our hearts and souls. Furthermore, the infusion of a moral base into our thinking about and practice of behavioral science allows us to work with clients from a position that we recognize as personal, intimate, and experiential, rather than distant and abstract.

I have a relatively simple, rule-of-thumb definition of evil that serves me both personally and professionally in and outside the therapy hour. *Evil is the self-serving deceit of others and/or the abuse of power.* Although actions that are blatantly malevolent are easily identified as evil by almost any definition, insidious deceptions and self-serving abuses of power are not always so easily discerned. They are therefore potentially more dangerous.

As a therapist I am *not* a moralist in the sense of believing that my clients must observe a specified and prescriptive code of conduct at all times which I then must evaluate in the therapy hour. The nonjudgmental stance of the therapist identified by Rogers (1957) is crucial to the therapeutic process. It is practiced in virtually all forms of psychotherapy. Thus, I do not consider it my place to condemn any behavior that a client may bring to me (whatever my own personal set of values may dictate). Neither, on the other hand, is it my prerogative to condone, let alone suggest, a given course of action based upon my own personal or professional persuasions. The latter, the avoidance of prescription, is a particularly difficult stance for many psychotherapists to maintain. Yet, even with the best of intentions, to do otherwise is to court the abuse of power and walk close to the specter of evil.

The role of the therapist

For many reasons, both professional and personal, therapists may feel impelled to prescribe a given course of action for a client. Historically, it is the manner in which our health professionals have been trained to operate: Find the cause of the problem and prescribe a cure. The cure is often based upon circumscribed limits of knowledge at the time. Herein lies the danger.

For therapists working with individual clients, the presumption of an appropriate course of action could be based on limited knowledge of their clients and/or their circumstances. Consider how exceedingly complex the human character is. We are each shaped uniquely by biology, myriad relationships we engage in, and experiences we encounter throughout our lives. Individuals slipping into and out of various unions may find their perceptions and world-views continually modified by not only these relationships but by other day-to-day alterations in personal and interpersonal histories and physical environments as well.

When working with families, the situation is even more complex and difficult. The marital relationship itself and the parent-child relationships which ensue from it create a hybrid, fluid set of interpersonal dynamics as unique and perhaps more delicate than each individual member's internal dynamics. How audacious to presume to dictate specific courses of action for these clients as individuals or as a unit — yet we do.

The potential danger for evil lies in therapists' needs to validate either (a) their own personal values or (b) the professional values (i.e., theory) by which they practice (see Fancher, 1995). Sometimes the two are difficult to separate because of the merging of personal and professional values. For example, I have seen marital therapists (with troubled marriages of their own) attempt to reconcile the rent marriages of clients by advocating questionable strategies from trial separations to extramarital affairs. I have known a therapist so invested in seeing 'mother-son symbiosis' as the root cause of a seven-year-old's reading difficulties that he totally ignored the boy's subtle but discernable congenital visual problem. I have watched a marital therapist so focused on the 'sexual dysfunction' of a welfare couple with five children that she totally ignored the father's anguish over being out of work and the mother's distress over being unable to feed her family.

The person-centered perspective
As discussed in the preceding chapter, the person-centered framework characterizes psychological well-being via the idea of the *fully functioning person*, one who is *open to experience*. Experiential openness means that both internal and external stimuli have entry to the individual's awareness without filtration or distortion. This includes one's perceptions of oneself, self-awareness.

Key to the alleviation of psychological distress in the person-centered framework is the concept of congruence where one's perception and experience of self are consonant. Although not identical to self-esteem, it shares similar parameters. Self-esteem contains two cognitive elements of self-awareness: it contrasts *perceptions of* self with *aspirations for* self (see Chapter 5). Congruence, like self-esteem, contains a cognitive element, but unlike self-esteem, it also incorporates a more fundamental *experiential* element: it juxtaposes *perception* of self against *experience* of self. In self-esteem both elements — self-evaluation and self-aspiration — are in the individual's field of awareness and can be expressed. Congruence is often a more primitive organismic sense. Ideally, congruence and self-esteem complement each other. But there are situations in which they do not, such as when a person has attained success, but is nonetheless disturbingly discontent.

Neither congruence nor self-esteem imply simply a state of self-satisfaction but, rather, an ever-fluctuating awareness of who one is in relationship to one's environment (both physical and interpersonal). They both are relative concepts in that the levels of tolerance for both vary from person to person. For both states there is always some discrepancy between their elements: when the discrepancy is tolerable the individual experiences psychological well-being (also relative); when intolerable, psychological anguish or distress is experienced. When one is sufficiently incongruent — when one's ideas regarding oneself and one's experience of oneself are greatly at odds — one may be impelled to seek help through psychotherapy. Incongruence may cause psychological discomfiture, the cause of which the person may or may not be aware. Also impelled to seek aid are those openly dissatisfied with themselves, i.e., whose self-esteem is intolerably low.

Despite close association with self-esteem, congruence is much more difficult to measure than self-esteem. Therefore, much of the outcome research in individual person-centered therapy rests upon a demonstrable change in positive self-regard throughout the course of counseling (Rogers and Dymond, 1954). Nonetheless, the concept of congruence continues to be considered a synonym for a sense of personal worth, or self-esteem.

However, neither congruence nor self-esteem imply a hedonistic or Epicurean view of the individual within society as many have inferred. Nowhere does they imply either a drive-reductionistic state of Nirvana, or the immediate gratification of needs. On the contrary, as noted in Chapter 6, Rogers held that congruent, fully functioning people would be flexible and adaptive, attempting to live as constructively as environments would allow. Rogers added that under certain circumstances those who are fully functioning might not be happy but would continuously strive to maximize their potential within their given circumstances.

The fully functioning person is always seen in cultural context. Implicit in this view are individuals' relationships with others and their capacity to act responsibly, defer gratification, and even cope with unhappiness and disappointment. Indeed, the whole concept of positive psychological growth and development is premised upon the continual examination and testing of experience with some conceptualization of self. When there is disparity between accurately symbolized experience and one's view of oneself there exists a state of incongruence. Simply put, we experience psychological distress. It might be mild discomfort or major anguish. That anguish may take many forms, e.g., anxiety, hurt, inferiority, rage, guilt.

Since therapists often see the removal of psychological distress as a major goal of therapy they pursue the removal of feelings of discomfort (particularly those presumed irrationally based) as a potentially positive end result. Not only is such a view of the therapeutic process naive, it can be dangerous and possibly destructive. The assuaging of incongruent feelings in another individual assumes a thorough knowledge of that individual's value orientation along with the assumption that the therapist has some absolute command of a positive course of action for the client(s). At this juncture in our profession, such a stance is absurd, especially when the client(s) and society's needs may be competing.

Thus mollifying another's sense of accountability over a given course of action — were it possible — suggests a lobotomizing of the character of the client. It is parallel to removing the kinesthetic senses of a person and then exposing the individual to fire. It destroys the organismic value processing of the individual and replaces it with only the prescriptions of an equally fallible expert, or perhaps worse, leaves only a sense of personal and social anomie. Although such a course of action may ameliorate a specific problem and its accompanying suffering at a given moment, its unintended impact may damage the growth potential of an individual, couple or family.

Psychological (like physical) discomfort can be organismically functional to client(s). In searching out the source of discomfort, individuals are compelled to pursue solutions within their repertoire of idiosyncratic experiences in their unique environmental contexts. The therapist is there to facilitate and enhance that process — nothing more.

Facilitating clients' quests may be best accomplished by accepting clients where they are, helping them to conceptualize their experience in their own existential vocabularies, and allowing them to come to grips with their experiences on their own terms. To the uninitiated beginning therapist, this prescription may seem unsophisticated and simplistic. Those of us who have listened for hours to expressions of widely ranging psychological distress and have interacted from a base of experience (and perhaps) pain can attest to the difficulties and pitfalls that attend even then.

First, there is the therapist's need to comfort and aid, both of which most of us who have entered the helping professions feel keenly. Accordingly, it is difficult to avoid the temptations of offering reassurance to the confused and license for the guilty. But experience teaches the futility of such attempts and their negative impact upon the client. However, the insensitive therapist may never perceive this lesson because simple endeavors to mollify the clients' concerns serve the therapist not the client. Reassurance or prescriptions meet therapists' needs to feel they are healing their clients.

But the greater pitfall is the one to which this chapter addresses itself. Like our clients, we therapists are also persons who are growing emotionally and intellectually, continually seeking our own answers to complex problems of living. Despite our best intentions, we all can have delusions about our objectivity and wisdom; all of us have the need to validate our own experience and values. The need for confirmation is most compelling for issues in which we may have invested the greatest energy but about which we remain least sure. Our own interpersonal relationships with spouses, children, parents, siblings, extended family and close friends, are cases in point. Particularly in these areas, we therapists must continually face the risk of our own incongruence, anguish and guilt. If, as therapists, we can face personal incongruence and confront the discrepancies between self and experience, the growth potential for both client and therapist is high. If, however, the risk feels too great and we as therapists continue to seek and find self-validation in our clients' lives, the growth of both client and therapist is seriously threatened, and the potential for harm — perhaps even evil — exists.

If we allow personal, professional or political prescriptions (that presume certainty of outcome) to direct clients' decision-making and problem analyses, we debase our professionalism. Furthermore, reliance on authority (either theoretical or institutional) can also be risky. For example, professional bodies develop standards to (a) ensure quality of service delivery and (b) articulate codes of ethics to protect the public and guide the practitioner regarding appropriate behavior. These promulgated professional criteria are inherently sterile and paradoxically perilous.

Depending too heavily upon rigorous standards can create hazards for clients, should the standards through time become rigid and unyielding. More often than not, many of them are based upon transitory values and/or models that are empirically unproven. Thus, there is the potential for reifying the past, wearing blinders and eschewing innovation and creativity. Professional guilds from their outset have fallen prey to this kind of mentality. Despite good intentions, a closed circle develops, replete with hazing of novitiates, which serves to circumscribe and protect the guild and its members. A hierarchy is established that may judge the behavior of members; deviance is often heavily sanctioned. Even the most famous and often cited professional code — the Hippocratic Oath — once past the opening line of 'first do no harm' would make many of us wince because of its temporal value orientation and guild-like emphasis.

The last century witnessed the technologizing of evil — the Holocaust. Our species has learned how to be brilliantly efficacious in its abuse of power. The Nuremberg trials forced us to come squarely to grips with the fact that institutions cannot be trusted to guide individual moral behavior, and each of us must stand alone, ready to answer to higher authorities than those found in extant bureaucracies. Following orders can no longer be considered a legitimate excuse for behavior — good or evil. Thus, personal morality is the source of truly ethical behavior: an internal sense of right and wrong that guides each individual. There can be no complacency, no automatization. Behaviors should be evaluated as life is lived, instance by instance. Morals that mediate between temporal values and institutional ethics are a shibboleth for intrinsic good and evil. They are also facilitators of growth for each of us as individuals and for all of us as humanity.

Although I do not know in any absolute sense what is right and what is wrong, what is good and what is evil, I firmly believe that there is good and there is evil; there is right and wrong. About some behaviors I am surer than others. The process of my becoming, my actualizing, seems contingent upon my continual exploration and clarification of the meaning of these concepts in my life, particularly in my relationships with others. Indeed, it is just this search that defines each of us as unique and growing persons and may be the root of our very humanness. Just as I would not allow anyone to deny me that search for meaning, neither would I deny it for another.

But where do I stand when I see or hear of someone abusing power and committing heinous acts? What do I do when I know a client is seriously contemplating suicide — or homicide? What is my stance professionally or personally when I hear that a father has been sexually abusing his daughter or a mother physically abusing her son? Is a morally neutral stance personally or professionally appropriate in these circumstances? These kinds of questions are moral imperatives. They require that individual and family psychotherapy alike always be viewed as a morally charged activity. In fact there are a multitude of decisions, often less dramatic than the aforementioned examples, which make a morally neutral stance in psychotherapy, if not impossible, difficult to maintain.

I recall Rogers, near the end of his life, musing at a conference in Chicago, that only recently had he felt the courage to accept a client's decision to commit suicide. I could not, even today, make that statement. Under virtually every circumstance I would certainly feel and express my empathy in general for people who contemplate taking their lives. I could not project, under most circumstances, my acceptance. Indeed, with my adolescent clients, my incongruence when they discuss suicide is so great that I am impelled to express my profound discomfort. I may go so far as to extract a promise from them to call me the moment that they feel so desperate. I have indicated that I am not sure I could continue to practice, knowing that I might have been able to prevent a suicide and did not. Thus, in such circumstances, I make a decision that I consider a moral one. I recognize that my client and I have a relationship, and that I am a growing part of that relationship. I know, too, that I have legitimate needs for safety in the relationship. I understand, as surely do my clients, that promises may be broken, but I am profoundly grateful that no one has, as yet, broken such a promise to me.

Conclusion

In only one century, humankind has effectively used its creative skills to augment technology in almost boundless ways. Yet in 30-fold that many years, not only have we found practically no way to improve our primal moral code, we even have trouble meeting its rather simplistic standards.

The person-centered approach emphasizes the process of becoming — of actualizing ourselves. For humankind, that process is always an interpersonal one: who each of us is in relation to the rest of us. While a search for a personal moral code helps actualize me as a person, so does our collective search actualize us as society. Put another way, the continued cultural attempt to refine a morality that all humans can decode and live by will define our social evolutionary progress.

The continual clash of values between individuals, within families, and among cultures necessitates our forging consensual validation and thereby refining the centrality and potential universality of our moral code. Such clashes involve tensions between rights and privileges juxtaposed against duties and obligations, tensions inherent in the creation of a civil society. There is something regressive in a moral anarchy of superficial prescriptions that can suspend such an evolutionary process. And if, as psychotherapists, we promulgate such an approach, I think the ethics of our profession are open to serious question.

PERSON-CENTERED FAMILY THERAPY[1]

8

No man is an island, entire of itself; every man is a piece of the continent, a part of the main . . .
John Donne, *Devotions.*

Introduction

Much as Carl Rogers clarified our understanding of *individual* psychotherapy, the person-centered philosophy provides a framework and context with which we can more easily understand *family* therapy. Yet despite the straightforward applicability of the person-centered approach to work with families, the *systems* perspective (which draws upon cybernetics theory that evolved in mid-twentieth century) continues to dominate the theory and practice of family therapy today. The basic assumption of a family systems orientation is that the family unit, rather than its individual members, is the primary focus of the therapeutic enterprise. Contrarily, person-centered family therapy sees each family member as part of a complexly interconnected milieu and proceeds to respond empathically to individuals in the context of their relationships within the family.

Because the family is the progenitor of all interpersonal relationships, working within the intimacy of the family enhances the potential for effective intra- and interpersonal growth. Person-centered family therapists augment their reflections of individuals' feelings by voicing interpersonal interactional processes, as well. Furthermore, by applying the methods of empathic responding within the presence of the family unit, the person-centered family therapist effects change. In addition to working one-on-one in the traditional manner, the person-centered family therapist facilitates change by modeling caring and empathic behaviors which may then be sustained within the family unit beyond the therapy session.

Family therapy and the Person-Centered Approach

During the last half of the twentieth century, family therapy evolved from somewhat fractured and relatively modest beginnings into an established discipline. In the early years, many viewed family therapy (introduced by practitioners in marital

---

1. First published in D. Brazier (Ed.), *Beyond Carl Rogers: Towards a psychotherapy for the twenty-first century.* London: Constable, (1993). Reprinted with permission of the publishers.

counseling, child guidance, child psychology, and sociology) as a rather marginal hybrid and/or an interesting and sometimes useful adjunct to traditional individual psychotherapy. In today's behavioral science and therapeutic communities, the discipline's main thrust has been towards a more comprehensive understanding and conceptualization of the intricate interactions between and among the individual members of a family.

In the process of establishing itself as a distinct discipline, family therapy embraced various *systems* models (see Nichols, 1984; Auerswald, 1987; Goldenberg and Goldenberg, 2000).[2] Despite their sometimes contradictory nature, all of the systems paradigms emphasize the family as a special unit, an entity far greater than simply the sum of its individual parts. In fact, one element common to virtually all family systems models is the avoidance, in both theory and practice, of focusing on the intrapersonal dynamics of individual family members.

Because systems models have provided family therapists with seemingly more efficient approaches to psychotherapy than those practiced by individual therapists, the models have had a dominant hold on the field of family therapy for the last 25 years. There are few voices, if any, which question the systems models and their ability to account adequately for the complex behaviors of individuals in a family context.[3]

On the other hand, the person-centered approach has traditionally emphasized the individual's internal dynamics. The individual's growth (or self-actualization) has been the primary concern of the therapy hour. The context in which that growth has taken place, which is invariably the family, merits focus only when the client brings it to the attention of the therapist. Although Rogers (1959, 1961, and 1977) occasionally alluded to the family and interactions among its members, such discussions were invariably brief and always couched in terms of the impact of familial interactions on the individual's actualizing tendency (either positive or negative). Ironically, Rogers' psychology, not unlike that of Freud's, clearly orients itself to the individual, with the context secondary, at best.

The evolution and subsequent eminence of individual psychotherapy in the twentieth century have simultaneously paved the way and presented detours to the theoretical and practical development of family therapy. As a result, vanguards like Haley (1963); Jackson (1965), and Minuchin (1964) intentionally tried to distinguish family from individual psychotherapy by suggesting that the former represented a unique, iconoclastic, and revolutionary approach to solving human problems. I suggest that the tension between individual and family therapy concepts

2. Twentieth-century family therapy evolved from underpinnings that embraced general systems theory, of Ludwig von Bertalanffy in the 1930s, and later the model and language of cybernetics of the 1940s. The use of the systems models enabled family therapy to differentiate itself from individual psychotherapy via the use of a new paradigm and accompanying nomenclature. Although this differentiation proved productive during family therapy's early growth in the middle of the twentieth century, it has since become a counterproductive distinction.

3. Some of the ideas basic to the person-centered approach have recently been finding their way into the family therapy literature under the name of *narrative* therapy (Anderson, 1997; White, 1995).

is a specious one arising, in part, from a reaction by family therapists to the earlier dominance of individual psychotherapy. Furthermore, I believe that person-centered family therapy represents an extension and progressive integration of the two positions into more consonant theory and practice. Person-centered family therapy respects the individual but also appreciates and respects the context of the individual's development. This context, for almost all of us, is the family.

Basic principles of the Person-Centered Approach

The person-centered approach and the practice of person-centered therapy derive from an experiential self-psychology. Thus, respect for the individual's experience and world-view is focal to the practice of person-centered psychotherapy.

During its heyday in the 1950s and 60s, person-centered therapy's great success enabled its tenets to be disseminated and applied throughout the United States and Europe. Today its major premises are presumed well understood by mental and allied health practitioners and the lay public alike. Further, virtually every mode of psychotherapy practiced today pays some homage to many of Rogers' contributions, particularly his articulation of the empathic stance of the therapist and the special relationship that exists between the client and therapist. Ironically, today these concepts seem so basic and rudimentary to the practice of psychotherapy that many consider them simplistic and thus unworthy of serious applied, theoretical, or empirical consideration. Summarily, most believe that the conditions inherent in the theory and practice of the person-centered approach are elemental to the practice of effective psychotherapy, but not sufficiently comprehensive.

Carl Rogers employed a few well-defined terms and parsimony of easy-to-understand postulates to describe the therapeutic process in an elegantly lean manner. Two years following the publication of his now classic *necessary and sufficient conditions* paper (Rogers, 1957, see Chapter 10), Rogers produced another seminal work, *A Theory of Therapy, Personality, and Interpersonal Relationships, As Developed in the Person-Centered Framework* (Rogers, 1959) which outlined a person-centered theory of personality. Nonetheless, person-centered theory clearly focuses more on therapeutic process than on the structure and organization of personality.

The individual's actualizing tendencies

Rogers' psychotherapeutic orientation was pragmatic and inductive: theory followed research on practice (Rogers, 1951, 1959). Rogers was not committed to a unified theory of personality and only developed one after his methods of therapy became established. He contributed to the professional community at large by cutting through the tangle of extant theory and empirically demonstrating a basic set of principles to explain the process of psychotherapeutic change.

One of the key elements and, for years, the only motive (or drive) postulated by the person-centered approach was that of the *actualizing tendency*. The actualizing tendency, assimilated from Kurt Goldstein's work with brain-damaged patients (1939, 1940), was biologically based and empirically grounded. From

Goldstein's organismic theory, Rogers (1951) borrowed the concept of the actualizing tendency to postulate the theoretical concept of *self-actualization*. Too often, however, the two ideas — those of the actualizing tendency of the organism (common to all organisms), and self-actualization (unique to the human organism) — are erroneously taken as synonymous.

The actualizing tendency is the universal press of all organisms to fulfill their destinies. For Homo sapiens, the actualizing tendency expresses itself in a manner distinct from all other beings. Children, in their earliest interactions with the environments (with significant others, in particular), begin to develop sentience and awareness of themselves as perceptual objects in their experience of the world (Rogers, 1959). This self-experience gives rise to a complex *self-system* from which the uniquely human process of *self-actualization* derives.

The actualizing tendency is the propensity of any organism to 'develop all of its capacities in ways which serve to maintain or enhance the organism' (Rogers, 1959, p. 196). The tendency towards self-actualization further requires the conceptualization of the self as distinct from others. Thus, the heart of Rogers' theory is the independent individual experience. For Rogers, as for the poet William Henley (1843–1903, *Invictus*), we are each the master of our fate, the captain of our soul.

A person's symbolization and actualization of the self as a separate and distinct individual make up the core concept for Rogers. However, there is good reason to believe that the self, like the concept of consciousness, is a relatively new social invention dating back, perhaps, only 400–500 years. Aries (1962), Jaynes (1976), and Stephenson (1980) all have made compelling arguments that the idea of an individual consciousness was preceded by a far longer period of group consciousness (see also Chapter 13). In a related, current exploration of these ideas, Sampson (1988) proposes as more explanatory of the human condition, the idea of an *ensembled* as opposed to that of a *self-contained* individualism. He suggests that there is no simple way to bridge the two positions because of basic ideological differences. I differ with that conclusion and believe that a person-centered family therapy is suggestive of such a bridge.

The family actualizing tendency
Not only *individual*, but also person-centered *family* theory rests upon the actualizing tendency of the organism, for the basic family unit is a true biological extension of the human organism. Moreover, the assumption of such an organismic base to person-centered family therapy easily allows for the incorporation of the *formative tendency*, one of Rogers' (1980) last major theoretical propositions. Accordingly, the formative tendency is the second basic human motive — the anti-entropic, creativeness motive.

Although the formative tendency might well be considered a metaphor for the creative endeavors of humankind, the concept does not quite work biologically as a construct for individual growth and development, which more accurately follow the entropy principle — at least for the majority of our adult lives. That is, from biological maturity onward, the individual is basically in a state of organic decline.

It is only through progenation that this decline is transcended. Thus, the formative tendency works with perfect validity when applied to the family, because the actualizing tendency of the family, by its very nature, includes the formative tendency: the primary goal of the family is the creation and maintenance of the next generation and the species.

The creation of offspring and assumption of responsibility for the next generation define the mature progenitor of any species. Human sentience, a special temporal awareness of our ancestral past and concern for our projected progeny and the progeny beyond, distinguish humankind from all other species. Furthermore, as individuals, we are aware of our biological destiny and this awareness is incorporated into our knowledge of self. These are some of the creative, anti-entropic or formative tendency fundamentals that define the family-actualizing tendency and make it inextricably linked to our self-actualization. Genetic and biologic proclivities aside, this premise of a self rooted in family is a natural one. Virtually all of us formulate our ideas about ourselves and who we are while growing up in a family. This is what makes the family so basic to who we are and what we do (Gaylin, 1985).

The family

The family unit is a living, organic whole that is never quite the same at any given moment in time. The family is continuously in flux because each person is composed of many self-elements (see Chapter 5) all of which are continuously experiencing change. These changes occur within individual members through development and experience. Interaction with other family members who similarly are experiencing changes can create often subtle — sometimes dramatic — relationship shifts within the family. However, the family's overall appearance and our sense of it maintain familiarity and integrity over time. Indeed, our expectation of our family's continuity and sameness may cause us to feel discomfort and distress when change, particularly abrupt change, occurs. Thus, metaphorically, the family may be seen as a kind of organic kaleidoscope composed of many selves, the elements of which are constantly changing in an interactive, fluid environment. Although the whole has an overall appearance that we all recognize, it is never really quite the same from moment to moment. The interactive patterns are constantly changing due to subtle shifts caused by both external and internal forces.

Thus, there are (at least) three apparent sources of change that constantly affect the family. These include:

1. intrapersonal dynamics of each of the individual family members which, by their nature, are fluid because of biological and intellectual maturation and the accretion of experience;
2. interpersonal interactions among the various family members; and
3. environmental forces (both natural and social interactional) outside the family.

While maintaining respect for the individual, person-centered family therapy also employs the context of the family's intimate interpersonal context. This context augments an understanding of the relevance of interpersonal interactions to each person's self-actualization by recognizing that the development of the self also occurs through interpersonal interactions. Such conceptualization leads to a better understanding of couples and family groups and sets the stage for a more efficacious form of psychotherapy.

The emergence of self in the family context

Crucial to understanding how the self develops is knowledge of how the individual is introduced to society. The family — the mediator between the individual and society — makes that introduction. Furthermore, the family initially swaddles the developing neonate in the conditions which Rogers (1957) deems necessary (as well as sufficient) for growth and change to take place, namely empathy and unconditional positive regard. As discussed in Chapter 3, these conditions define love and along with trust comprise the emotional bedrock of the family. Indeed, the therapeutic relationship pales by comparison with the actualizing power engendered by the family (Gaylin, 1990). Thus, according to person-centered therapy, the entire conceptualization of the therapeutic relationship is based upon the same psychologically nurturing elements that are found within the family milieu during the early months and years of an individual's experience. Ironically, although person-centered theory emphasizes empathic unconditional positive regard as the engendering force of psychotherapy, the theory tends not to recognize that force's kinship with the emotional power of early family dynamics.

Each of us has qualities determined by genetically different biologic constitutions that make us unique in temperament (Thomas and Chess, 1977). In turn, each of our temperaments interacts with our equally unique and complex familial environments to generate our evolving personalities. Alternatively, each of us from birth has a special impact on our familial environment and its members (Bell, 1971; Chess and Thomas, 1999). These reciprocally complex interactions shape us from birth (perhaps at conception). This sculpting continues throughout life.

The family, by its very nature, nurtures each person individually. Beginning with the first few days of life, each child in the family may be dealt with differently despite a context of unconditional positive regard and empathy. Disturbed parents and families excepted, the preponderance of new mothers and/or fathers provide a basic caring that is unconditional and deeply empathic of the child's needs.

However, with increasing maturation the child begins to perceive conditionality in the parent's love, often depending upon the child's behavior and the parent's mood. This change in parental behavior is the process of socialization at work: learning to live in concert along with specific rights and privileges but corresponding duties and obligations (Gaylin, 1980).[4] Thus, as the self emerges

---

4. Footnote 4 on next page.

and is fashioned within the familial environment, so does a sense of self-esteem. And the subtleties of individual differences and *goodness of fit* (Chess and Thomas, 1987, 1999) with the intimate environment of the family will have enormous impact on how each of us feels about ourselves within and in relation to the world around us throughout our lives.

Emergence of the self begins first through the process of self-awareness; it continues through self-differentiation during the first year (Brunner, 1986) and crystallizes by the end of the second year of life (Mahler, Pine, and Bergman, 1975). Through empathy which, from all indications, is innate and observable in the infant at birth (Sagi and Hoffman, 1976), the infant interacts with others, and the self emerges. By putting oneself in the place of another, sentience develops and true humanness is engendered. With the acquisition of speech and language in the first two years, babies naturally and gradually relate from the positions that they comprehend relative to the intimate members of their environment: they thereby establish a concept of their *self* in context. This contextual self is only the beginning of an amalgam of many *subselves* that the individual will continuously accrete throughout the life course.

As children we start out utterly dependent upon our primary caretakers. The dependent child self is the first of many that will emerge from the earliest awareness of the self as an acting and interacting entity. In families of two or more children, the addition and subsequent integration of a sibling will sooner or later expand this self. Thus, we begin amassing a set of *subselves* that creates a *self-complex* (see Chapter 5) by which we define ourselves And so we continue the lifelong process of defining ourselves by our interactions and relationships with others in our environment.

The self, the family, and psychotherapy
The family introduces the child to society. The shared meanings of the parents are conveyed to the child and help shape the child's view of the universe, including the child's view of self. Thus, one might say that within the family there is an amalgam of subjectivities which shapes our views of ourselves in the world around us. One might conjecture that the chances of having an adaptable, relatively happy individual develop is in some way contingent upon the roles played by the joint and individual congruences of the parents as they fashion an intimate environment for their developing family. The neonate's approach to the world cannot help being filtered, at first, through the individual and combined subjective perceptions of those interacting with them in their immediate interpersonal environment, i.e., parents, siblings, extended family, friends, and caretakers.

To understand the unique interactive ecosystem of any family, one must gain entrée to the shared meanings and values of the individuals within that system.

---

4. Rogers has alluded to this process as that of imposing *conditions of worth,* which he clearly construed as negative, and deleterious to healthy development and a 'psychologically adjusted' individual (Rogers, 1959, p. 224). Such ideation demonstrates Rogers' greater focus on the individual independent of the civil interaction of our species. See also Chapter 9.

The family therapist must be attentive to both the intra- and interpersonal elements that are presented during the family therapy hour. A more-finely tuned sense of integration and the well-being of each individual affect the well-being of the family system as a whole. Reflexively, interpersonal well-being has positive impact on the individual. Thus, a therapy model of the individual in intimate context holds promise of being more effective than one minimizing or ignoring that context.

The process of self-actualization is focal to all person-centered theory and practice. During this process, each of us acts in a manner that we believe will promote the realization of our potential. Our self-actualizing tendency 'may become deeply buried under layer after layer of encrusted psychological defenses; it may be hidden behind facades which deny its existence, but . . . it exists in every individual, and awaits only the proper conditions to be released and expressed' (Rogers, 1961, p. 351). Thus, we all strive to become ever more *fully functioning*.

However, there are times when our experience and conceptualization of self are at odds. At these times we feel threatened, vulnerable, and anxious — *incongruent*. Incongruence can cause us to lose our sense of integration and wholeness. We all feel incongruent at times. When this incongruence becomes so great that we feel discomfited and debilitated, we may seek relief through psychotherapy. Thus, the process of psychotherapy provides a climate of trust and warmth in which individuals may re-experience their views of self within and at large in the world. In this way, they become more congruent and integrated. Such wholeness in turn unencumbers the actualizing tendency heretofore impeded by personal incongruences.

Rogersian theory is, above all, based on the experience of clients: their reality what they perceive and experience. The therapist must understand, be empathic with, and reflect the client's reality to enable the client to *re-view*, *re-experience*, and *re-integrate* old experiences and thus become more open to new experiences. By this means the client's self-actualizing tendency is empowered, and the client becomes more fully functioning. Although greatly oversimplified, these are the primary elements of person-centered theory.

Individual and family incongruences

According to Rogers (1959, p. 203) individuals seek psychotherapeutic help because they are experiencing feelings of incongruence. Incongruence is a discrepancy between the actual experience of the individual and the individual's image of self. The reasons for the discrepancy may or may not be known by the individual. Incongruence may be mild and result in anxiety and/or other general psychological discomfort. When severe, however, incongruence invariably causes incapacitating anguish.

Comprehending the interaction among the subselves of a self-complex is crucial to extending an understanding of both intra- and interpersonal dynamics, particularly with regard to self-esteem and Rogers' focal concept of intrapersonal congruence and incongruence.[5] For example, feelings of worth regarding one or more of our various subselves could compensate for feelings of inadequacy or failure in other subselves.

Incongruence, often accompanied by feelings of anxiety and/or despair, may occur when: (a) a particular subself so dominates a self-complex that even small feelings of inadequacy about that particular subself can contaminate feelings of self-worth about all of the subselves or (b) virtually all subselves within the self-complex are felt to be lacking or inadequate. The incongruence that results (depending on severity and the individual's tolerance level) may move the individual to seek psychotherapy. In a similar fashion, a family may seek therapy when (a) any one if its members displays incongruence through dysfunctional behavior or (b) the whole system experiences incongruence. The following two chapters additionally explicate the concept of incongruence in the context of the other conditions Rogers deemed basic to the psychotherapy process.

Conclusion

Person-centered theory has extensively explored how the self operates *intra*personally and the application of person-centered psychotherapy to intervention with *individuals*. Lacking, however, is an examination of the intimate, interpersonal context in which the self evolves. Person-centered *family* therapy attends to both the intra- and interpersonal nature of the individual and does so within the family context. Despite differences that stem from the need to understand both the intra- and interpersonal nature of clients, the therapeutic approach in person-centered family therapy flows naturally from the same base as that of individual person-centered therapy. Empathic reflections remain the primary conduct of the therapist in both situations. However, the person-centered family therapist maintains and communicates a nonjudgmental, caring and empathic position with *each* family member in concert.

---

5. Rogers asserts that there exists an inverse relationship between the concepts of incongruence and self-acceptance. He further notes that the successful client 'not only accepts himself — a phrase which may carry the connotation of a grudging and reluctant acceptance of the inevitable — he actually comes to *like* himself', (1961, p. 87). Thus, although congruence and self-esteem are not synonymous, they seem to be strongly associated.

THE PSYCHOTHERAPY RELATIONSHIP: THE HEART OF THE MATTER[1]

9

There is no truth or reality for a living human being except as he participates in it, is conscious of it, has some relationship to it.
Rollo May, *Existential Psychology.*

Introduction

In 1957, Carl Rogers delineated six conditions he deemed both 'necessary and sufficient' for psychotherapeutic personality change. He thereby codified the underpinnings of the client-centered method and the very marrow of person-centered practice today. This chapter, and the next, review and re-examine the conditions and their application to both individual and family therapy. However, this chapter focuses primarily on the *bookend* conditions — namely the first and the last — which seem to be the least discussed and understood but the most important of the six.

The conditions[2]

The six conditions that Rogers deemed both necessary and sufficient for psychotherapeutic personality change are:

1. Two persons are in psychological contact.
2. The first, whom we shall term the client, is in a state of incongruence, being vulnerable or anxious.
3. The second person, whom we shall term the therapist, is congruent or integrated in the relationship.
4. The therapist experiences unconditional positive regard for the client.
5. The therapist experiences an empathic understanding of the client's frame of reference and endeavors to communicate this experience to the client.
6. The communication to the client of the therapist's empathic

---

1. Paper presented at the International Conference for Client-Centered and Experiential Psychotherapy, Chicago, June 2000.
2. It is noteworthy that a seminal paper by Jules Seeman (1951, reprinted 1994) pre-dates Rogers' and contains all of the therapist conditions.

> understanding and unconditional positive regard is to a
> minimal degree achieved.

> No other conditions are necessary. If these six conditions exist, and
> continue over a period of time, this is sufficient. The process of
> constructive personality change will follow (Rogers, 1957, p. 96).

My primary foci in this chapter are upon the first and last of the six conditions: respectively (a) psychological contact — the relationship and (b) the client's perception of that relationship. These two conditions have been, perhaps, the least scrutinized. Yet in my work with individuals and families they stand out as lynchpins for the other four. All six conditions guide all of my work as a therapist, both in individual and family sessions. Further, irrespective of the number of family members present in a session, I proceed from the same basic framework and relate in thought and attitude to each family member and the complex interrelationships.

The conditions are an integral whole, none separable from the others. Thus, I am taken aback when I see some theorists and practitioners telescope the classic six conditions into three (often termed the *core* conditions): genuineness, unconditional positive regard and empathy. What is omitted in this cryptic summary are the first two and last conditions. For me, these three neglected conditions — particularly the first and the last — are central to our understanding of how and why psychotherapy works.

The core conditions

I think we have focused on the conditions of genuineness, unconditional positive regard and empathy because they relate to the conduct of the therapist. Indeed, these three conditions encapsulate the single method of the person-centered approach. As therapists we are more or less in charge of these behaviors: we can observe them in research, teach them in training, and critique them in supervision or consultation. Thus, it makes sense to concentrate on those conditions that we are able to control and we presume drive the therapeutic process.[3]

Penultimately we attend to the second condition — that which impels our clients into therapy — their incongruence. However, we tend to disregard the first and the last conditions. So did Rogers. There is little elaboration of them in the original statement and little exegesis regarding them since.

The therapist in the relationship

About the first condition — 'psychological contact' — Rogers, in his classic 1957

---

3. A therapist variable, the condition of therapist congruence is an *inherent* characteristic and less obviously manipulable than both unconditional positive regard and empathy. It also is somewhat more vague. We attempt to explain it by calling it *genuineness, presence, transparency*, and if feeling unshakably incongruent in the hour, concern ourselves with the need for self-disclosure. It should be emphasized that even in this condition, the first is alluded to. It does not state that the therapist is congruent, but rather that the therapist is congruent *in the relationship*.

paper, mused that 'perhaps it should be labeled an assumption, or a precondition', for he noted that, without it, the others would have no meaning. Indeed, he went so far as to say that the following five conditions really define the first. In so doing he made the relationship (psychological contact) the pivotal condition. Until recently, I do not believe I had ever fully attended to Rogers' only statement that makes the first condition so interesting and complex. He notes that what he means by *psychological contact* is that client and therapist 'each makes some perceived difference in the experiential field of the other' (Rogers, 1957, p. 96). He later even qualifies the word *perceived*, settling for *subceived*. The essence is the reciprocal relationship between client and therapist.

By reciprocal I do not mean that the nature of the interaction is either parallel or equal. It is not. I am there to serve my clients in a professional capacity. There are generally rather formal contractual arrangements. We meet at a prescribed scheduled hour for a given period of time, and clients generally compensate me. All of these constraints, and more, set the therapeutic relationship apart from most others. But the key issue is not only how I respond to clients' concerns but my clients' impact upon my experiential field, as well. Despite the excellence of my didactic teachers, my clients were those from whom I learned the most.

Indeed, my first client at the University of Chicago Counseling Center was perhaps my best mentor. We were both graduate students, she in a different department than I. She was a couple of years ahead of me in school, a few years older, and a whole lot smarter. She continuously challenged my thinking about what I was doing and why. Shortly after we began our sessions together, one of her first admonishments was: 'You're nothing but a goddam whore — selling your love for money.' No matter that as an intern I received no money for my services; I felt hurt and humiliated. I was too young to realize that I should have been gratified that she sensed my caring, my *unconditional positive regard* for her. I remember going with anguish to Jack Butler, my supervisor at the time. He looked at me with a somewhat wry smile and unhelpfully replied, 'What's the matter with being a whore — if you're a good one?' My priggishness aside, it took a few years for me to come to grips with the fact that it was my time that was being procured. My love carried no price and could only be freely given. Nevertheless, questions of what the therapist does and what the therapeutic relationship is have led me to the conclusion that, among other things, psychotherapy clearly is an activity of very special and profound relationships, to say nothing of moral implications.

This same client also taught me about pacing. Following one of my overzealous reflections of feelings, she snapped, 'It took me 30 years to develop these problems. Who the hell do you think you are to try to solve them in 30 minutes?' Each client has a pace that is comfortable, and that pace varies, not just from client to client but for the same client at different times. The therapist needs to be empathic not only with the client's frame of reference or world-view but also the style and tempo of the client's readiness for hearing even empathic responses. This is a subtle point often lost on beginning therapists who are eager to effect change as rapidly as possible and for whom silence is consequently often unbearable.

Similarly, regarding style, pacing, and communication in the relationship, children are perhaps the best instructors of therapists. Even when disturbed, children usually exhibit little guile, though they may be wary. They can be very direct and, even when nonverbal, are very communicative. Thus, another of my best teachers was an 11-year-old boy, whom I will call Martin. Martin was referred because of his deteriorating school performance and growing aggressive behavior with age-mates and authority figures alike. He was a large lad entering adolescence — looking perhaps two or three years older than his 11 years. He was taciturn and wore a perpetual scowl. I can well imagine how he intimidated those around him. I was looking for another Dibs, a butterfly ready to emerge from its chrysalis. At the time, what I thought I got was a slug eating holes in my verdant fantasies about psychotherapy. It took a few years for me to realize that what I had, in actuality, was a young swan masquerading as an ugly ducking.

I saw Martin twice a week for over six months. During all of the time I was with him he said virtually nothing. In the first weeks, at the beginning of sessions, I would try reflecting what I thought was his mood which I interpreted from the expression on his face. He would neither validate nor invalidate this effort at reflection. Then we would sit. He would then test me. He would stretch out his legs — I would stretch mine. He would knock the soles of his shoes together — I would knock mine. It became a kind of elaborate nonverbal 'Simon Says'. And I was going crazy. Charlotte Ellinwood, my supervisor, would watch patiently behind the one-way mirror. After the sessions, when I started expressing my frustration, she would calm me by saying we were 'really establishing a relationship' and that I was 'developing rapport'. She apparently saw what I could not.

I had little idea what I was doing and what was happening. I was there — at his service. He never missed a session. As time progressed, reports from his mother indicated that things were improving both at home and school. Perhaps it was simply maturation. In working with children I have grown increasingly more humble, realizing that we often take credit for God's work. Indeed, the old saw about Virginia Axline and Dibs was that she was as good a diagnostician as therapist, plucking Dibs just at the moment of his flowering. Perhaps this was also true for Martin.[4]

For years after our formal work together, much to my amazement, Martin, who lived only blocks away from me in Hyde Park, would pop by my apartment on a Saturday or Sunday. First he came by to show me a new bike or a pair of athletic shoes, later to meet his friends — first male, then female. He still spoke little, but smiled more easily. I began feeling less awkward about our nonverbal interactions, taking pleasure in his initiative and demonstrated desire to have me continue to share in his life in some small way. Clearly, although I might neither have recognized nor understood it, something about my relationship with this lad

---

4. Perhaps it is true for the vast majority of our clients. After all, half improve just from being on the waiting list for therapy.

had meaning. The nonjudgmental stance took on new meaning.

The therapist learns to follow the client — in whatever way the client needs following. However, if therapists are servants, what rewards for them are inherent in the therapeutic relationship other than learning to serve well? Is the relationship entirely one-sided? Although therapists usually receive payment for their time and expertise, there are probably more remunerative and less taxing means of being gainfully employed.

As a teacher of therapists I am impressed first with the drive-like quality — the sense of *calling* — that impels our students to apprentice as therapists. The next quality that stands out is giftedness, or talent. Virtually all of our prospective students report experiences in which others have given our candidates positive feedback for their empathic interactions with them. In fact, friends and family continue to seek them out as 'good listeners'. Reciprocally, our candidates and beginning therapists report feeling good about doing good. There is an allocentric as opposed to egocentric quality that they convey; the most gifted radiate an almost grace-like quality.

I once asked one of Rogers' clients, a therapist himself, what he thought made Rogers such a great therapist. The response (through a telling anecdote) was Rogers' concentration and focus on the client. 'When Rogers is with you, you feel bathed by his attention: the world disappears — and you and he are alone in some special place.' I know that when I am deeply focused within the therapeutic relationship I am my best self; my dark side, my warts and scars, are sequestered. I am conscious of myself primarily as an amplifier of another, yet I feel whole, at one with myself and very much alive in the moment. It is exactly this quality of wholeness, integration — even at times a sense of *peak experience* — that I think the third condition alludes to when noting 'the therapist is congruent in the relationship'. Indeed, I can go into the hour feeling ill with a headache but if I can mobilize my concentration and focus entirely on the client, my headache disappears — I am not even aware that it has done so.[5] We sometimes refer to this quality of therapist congruence as *presence*. But there is vagueness to this term that somehow eludes me, whereas focus conveys an additional dimension that is easier to understand.

I note, too, that my memory is enhanced. In my personal life I have a terrible memory and it is growing worse. It has always been bad for remembering names and telephone numbers. I am loath to admit that at times I will walk into the therapy hour and, with horror, realize that momentarily I cannot retrieve my clients' names.[6] But I can remember details about their lives that amaze both them and me. This is true for clients who return even many years later. This is not a skill I have worked at or actively practice, in any way. It is there — sui generis. I do know that

---

5. This is a puzzling phenomenon. If my focus in the hour is true congruence — where I am freely and openly experiencing the totality of my being — then, at some level, I should be aware of my headache: Unless, of course, the headache was a symptom of my previous incongruence.
6. Should any clients see this I beg them not to take offense as even my children's names sometimes momentarily elude me.

such recall enhances my empathy and gives me a sense of closeness to my client, adding richness and depth to my feelings for them

Thus, when at my best in the therapy relationship, there is a sense of intimacy — a richness and reciprocity — a fulfillment as therapist that I experience during such periods. I do not believe that any of us can maintain such concentration for extensive periods. Rather, I think the time-limited nature of the therapy hour permits the exertion of a special congruence — a special focus or concentration. This kind of special ability to focus, I believe, is what makes being a therapist experientially gratifying. Such concentration may be similar to that of artists enrapt in the execution of their craft: be it sculpting, music-making, or whatever.

The importance of the relationship is augmented and takes on added dimension in the person-centered approach to working with families. But unlike other so-called *systems approaches,* genuine caring and empathic responding integrate to provide the sole method: there is no need, moreover, for an elaborate paradigmatic shift when working with individuals versus working with families. What changes is that the therapist relates to all family members as individuals present in the intimate context of their family. The therapist maintains empathy and caring for each individual both separately as well as collectively.

The client in the relationship

As therapists, we are expected to be in touch with who we are and what we feel during the therapy hour and in the therapy relationship, but what about the client in the relationship? From our clients' reports we know that they come to us troubled — incongruent. But we do not always know why. Indeed, some of our clients may not know why they are incongruent. Especially with young children and the severely disturbed, this is often the case. Even when clients do know why they are impelled to seek help, they do not always tell us — at least not right away. Many (perhaps most) clients may well delay sharing their deepest, darkest secrets until they assess the tenor of the relationship with their therapists and their respective therapists' trustworthiness (Rennie, 1990). Some clients have told me that they had *never* disclosed their heart of hearts to previous therapists.

Here is where the traditional core conditions — namely four and five, unconditional positive regard, and empathy — come into play. These two conditions are more complex than they appear at first glance. Condition four really is two conditions: true, it is unconditional regard — a nonjudgmental stance. But it is also *positive* regard, namely caring, or loving. I prefer to think of the two aspects of this condition separately, for I believe one can regard someone nonjudgmentally and dispassionately. That is, I can be fully open to someone, not place any valence on that person's behavior and simultaneously not care about her or him. Conversely I can love someone deeply and still be critical of specific qualities or behaviors. Thus, these two aspects coexisting within this condition give additive power to its totality. Empathy is interactional-nonphysical touching which conveys experiential understanding. Furthermore, we presume that the combination of these three qualities of the therapist's stance — nonjudgmental, caring, and (especially) empathic — establish a foundation and venue of trust which enable our clients to shed, or at least lower, their masks.

What is rarely discussed is *how* a relationship can enable healing for the client.[6] This process is articulated most clearly in Rogers' (1959) most comprehensive theory paper and one of the few theoretical statements that enunciate how deep-seated incongruences develop. The explanation requires the introduction of a key, though rarely discussed, concept in person-centered theory — namely, *conditions of worth*. Also, it assumes that we all require positive regard to thrive and the client in the psychotherapy relationship is no exception.

Early in life, the developing individual begins to recognize that certain behaviors elicit approbation — that is positive regard — and others elicit disapproval. Thus, there are circumstances in which the individual perceives that love is granted and others wherein a person believes love is withheld or denied. These opposing perceptions shape the person's feelings of self-worth or self-esteem. Though never stated directly, the implication is that within the therapy hour's interpersonal nonjudgmental, loving, empathic climate, early (previously instilled) *conditions of worth* can be mitigated and clients may feel free to be completely themselves without regard to disapproval or approbation. Hence, the importance of *unconditional* positive regard — love given unequivocally.

Herein lies one of my few difficulties with the person-centered framework. The inference too easily allowed for is that *conditions of worth* are inherently derogatory — always having negative impact which impairs the process of self-actualization. Contrarily I would argue that there may be greater danger in unconditional positive regard than in regard conditionally given. A civilized society and harmonious living impose conditions; without such conditions life would be anarchy — hell. Self-entitlement and self-indulgence lead to evil — the self-serving abuse of power. Human newborns, nonetheless, fully dependent for several months receive responsible care marked by *unconditional* positive regard and appropriately so. We indulge the neonate because of its total helplessness. Its survival depends upon our full and unreserved attention to its needs. Nature even helps by making the neonates of virtually all species utterly adorable.

The sense of total acceptance within the therapy hour may well be inherently reminiscent of those early months when caretakers unquestioningly and unqualifiedly gave nurture to the infant, and the infant experienced total acceptance and gratification of its every need. We infer the neonatal period to be one of virtual total self-centeredness. Perhaps the therapy hour emulates the ability of individuals to be totally and self-indulgently focused on their needs but in a manner that is simultaneously interpersonal within the therapeutic relationship. That was my experience of therapy as a client. I felt swaddled and protected emotionally. I could ramble, have a tantrum, cry (even though 'big boys don't') and feel and express anything, and my therapist would try — usually quite successfully — to

---

6. Rogers is clear that psychotherapy is not the only relationship which promotes healing (Rogers, 1961).

be there and make sense of what I was experiencing. I felt emotionally succored, even indulged. There were times I felt almost literally held and rocked by him.

However, from the client's perspective, there are experiences that are contradictory to the intense closeness described above. For example there is the *stranger-on-the-plane* phenomenon where, by dint of the knowledge that the fellow passenger is not a part of one's life, and one will never encounter that person again, one can unburden oneself of one's troubles. Can these experiences illuminate and suggest a parallel for the psychotherapeutic relationship? Here is another human being — one not anticipated ever again to be a part of one's life — acting as a sounding board and offering a measure of solace from emotional pain, just by being there. Some people report they feel the need to go into great detail. After their disclosures they say they feel unburdened and relieved. Ironically, it seems that what enables catharsis and relief is (in part) knowing that the relationship is circumscribed and quite limited. Perhaps it is the very circumscribed nature of the relationship and its promise of anonymity that, to some degree, enables its power. Although as therapists we respect and make every effort to vouchsafe the client's right of confidentiality, we do not explore it as a variable. Perhaps we should.

As a graduate student in Chicago over 40 years ago, I heard Stan Lipkin give a paper titled 'Round Robin Therapy'. that, like the *strangers-on-a-plane* phenomenon, struck at the heart of the notion of a long-term relationship being crucial to successful psychotherapy. A client who had asked Lipkin to be her therapist could not afford his fee. Rather than turn her down he offered her the opportunity to meet for 20 successive sessions with a different one of Chicago's most prestigious therapists for each session. The client reported the experience a great success. When questioned about having to tell her tale anew 20 times, she reported that she experienced no feelings of redundancy and, rather, learned something each time she met with a new therapist.

Similarly, from my training days at the Counseling Center, I recall how the *experienced clients* usually seen by the senior staff would accept an opportunity to meet gratis with a novice (but pronounced *ready*) therapist. After the pro bono session the clients invariably reported the experiences as positive and often requested — sometimes to the experienced therapists' chagrin — additional sessions with the novitiate. Indeed, it may be that a fresh therapeutic presence may offer the client new experiential data via the novel interaction. Furthermore, like Lipkin's round robin therapy, the new therapist may in fact validate the client's recognition that the healing force — i.e., self-actualization — resides within the client rather than results from the expertise of the therapist!

One final piece of anecdotal data regards clients' reports of their therapy and therapists in a study I read many years ago about therapeutic behavior modification. This was the period when behaviorists held that a neutral stance was de rigueur, and they prided themselves on the objective, aloof posture of scientists. Conditioning was the definitive behavioral method — the person of the therapist and the relationship were considered confounding rather than facilitative variables. Assiduous recording and note-taking regarding the clients' behavior were mandatory. Clients debriefed following a successful course of therapy reported that what was important to them was their therapist's position of concern and caring evidenced by their intense attention to the clients and their behavior.

This brings us to the seemingly most obvious throwaway condition, the sixth, wherein the client perceives (at least to some degree) the therapist's empathy and positive regard. One might add, even if it isn't there! Or maybe it is there even when the therapist believes it is not.

This last condition is truly the heart of the matter. It is the last condition that makes *all* therapy *client*-centered. Lest we forget, the conditions do not define the person-centered approach. Rather, we have adapted our approach to the knowledge that these conditions *alone* are both necessary and sufficient for psychotherapeutic change to take place. What other therapy approaches struggle with is the sufficiency of the conditions — their necessity has generally been conceded. That the world-view of the client is paramount — even when others may consider it distorted or erroneous — is what most other therapy models contest.

I remember working with a young 20-year-old man, diagnosed as schizophrenic. When he first came to my office he claimed to have visions of Jesus Christ, who spoke with him. The client asked me if I believed him. I hesitated, but answered by explaining that he and I had two problems. The first was that I was Jewish and had a difficult time accepting the fact that Jesus was, indeed, the messiah. The second problem was that I had never had such a vision and found it difficult to put myself in his shoes. But I added that I truly believed that he did have these visions and that I was interested in their meaning to him — as I truly was, even though I did not understand them. I worried that my response would alienate or offend him. It did not. Rather, he proceeded to talk to me about problems he was having with his girlfriend.

If clients believe that their therapist is working on their behalf — if they perceive caring and understanding — then therapy is likely to be successful. It is the condition of attachment and the perception of connection that have the power to release the faltered actualizing of the self. We all need to feel connected, prized — loved. We are a species born into mutual interdependence, and there can be no self outside the context of others. Loneliness is dehumanizing and isolation anathema to the human condition. The relationship is what psychotherapy is about.

Conclusion

The human condition is one of relationships and mutual interdependence. There have been healers of the troubled spirit as far back as we know. Their power may have been attributed to magic, the divine, or science. We, as psychotherapists, are but the most recent iteration of such healers. It behooves us to recognize that our clients' mending is a result of a growth motive internal to them; our presence is important only insofar as our clients recognize it as important. Thus, the source of our power resides in our clients and our relationship with them: in their belief in our belief in them.

The Necessary and Sufficient Conditions for Psychotherapeutic Change in Individual and Family Therapy[1]

10

> *The external realities . . . stand waiting in the mind, forming a beautiful ideal network; and the most we can say is that we hope to discover outer realities over which the network may be flung so that ideal and real may coincide.*
> William James, *Principles of Psychology.*

Introduction

Despite the fact that on the surface person-centered family therapy appears very different from individual therapy, methodologically it is not. My work with children, couples and families is methodologically the same as my work with adult individuals. What *is* different is a conceptual extension of the six *necessary and sufficient conditions* as they apply to more than one person in the intimate context of the family. This conceptual variance amends my focus and attitude even as I consider the essentials of person-centered theory. The more I explore the conditions' meaning and ramifications the more they continue to expand my understanding of psychotherapy practice and theory. Thus, I begin virtually all of my writing, teaching, and supervision by reconsidering them.

This chapter reviews and expands the original conditions in an effort to demonstrate their relevance to the practice of family psychotherapy. The similarities and differences of the conditions between the individual and family contexts are explored. The general intent of this endeavor is to identify and define elements common to all forms of psychotherapy regardless of context, in order to maximize the understanding and efficacy of individual and family therapy. In the end, I hope that the division between individual and family therapy will dissolve and the inherent (heretofore neglected) application of the person-centered approach to family therapy will prevail.

Background

Rogers' objectives in delineating the six conditions he judged 'necessary and

---

1. First published as 'The necessary and sufficient conditions for change: Individual versus family therapy' in *The Person Centered Review, 4* (3), (1989), 263–79.

sufficient' for therapeutic personality change (Rogers, 1957) was to discern an inherent unity within the process of psychotherapy, regardless of the psychotherapeutic persuasion practiced. His conceptualization was seminal in that it led, briefly, to a golden era of rigorous, empirical examination of the process of psychotherapy. It facilitated research primarily for two reasons: (a) his model had an elegant parsimony and (b) the conditions could fairly readily be operationalized. The conditions Rogers delineated helped distinguish those elements common to all therapeutic practices from those variables primarily stylistic in nature. By and large, despite some minor modifications (e.g., Rogers, Gendlin, Kiesler, and Truax, 1967), Rogers' six conditions for therapeutic change have withstood the test of time and clinical practice with individuals. However, it is primarily in the person-centered community that the conditions retain their import to this day.

The increasing professional acceptance and growing popularity of marriage and family therapy have spawned a plethora of schools of practice, but there has been little coherent, theoretically based, empirical research actually focusing on the process in family therapy that effects change. For students, practitioners, theorists, and researchers alike, the situation is at best confusing. Scant available literature (e.g., van der Veen, 1965; Levant, 1978, 1984; Thayer, 1982, and O'Leary, 1999) reveals that although some therapists have attempted to apply the basic principles of person-centered theory to the practice of family therapy, the person-centered approach has had little impact on the family therapy community. Therefore, Rogers' conditions are herewith reexamined and elaborated upon to elucidate their validity, relevance, and modification for applicability to the practice of family therapy.

The conditions
1. Psychological contact: the therapeutic relationship
In the practice of individual psychotherapy, Rogers assumed a priori the first condition of therapeutic change: psychological contact between the client and therapist. Little explication is offered. This lack of explanation is somewhat deceptive, however, as the quality of the client-therapist relationship is really delineated in the last three conditions: unconditional positive regard, empathic understanding, and the client's perception of the therapist. Thus Rogers really suggests that the client will at least *subceive* the therapist as engaged in the relationship, and this engagement will enable the client to perceive the therapist as both caring and understanding.

Therefore, even without elaboration, the assumption of psychological contact in individual therapy seems straightforward and obvious. In family therapy, however, the therapeutic relationship is neither obvious nor simple and requires explanation. The relationship between the therapist and client is complex in family therapy because the psychological contact almost always includes more than one client. The issue, however, is one about which theorists and practitioners of family therapy are divided.

For therapeutic change to take place in family therapy, many maintain that the therapist must sustain a relationship with the system as a whole (i.e., the couple or family). Some (e.g., Minuchin, 1964) believe that the entire therapeutic process is likely to be far more effective if the therapist not only relates to the system but to some extent becomes part of that system, as well. Still others (e.g., Bowen, 1975) maintain that family therapy may be accomplished if a relationship exists between at least one member of the family system and the therapist.

How the family system is defined becomes an issue for some family therapists. For example, Barrett-Lennard (1984) delineates a range of complex inter-relationships in various nuclear family constellations with which the family therapist must deal, while Speck and Rueveni (1969) propose that the nuclear family should be enlarged to include extended kin and even quasi-kin (e.g., neighbors) in the system.

Despite the debate, it becomes clear that therapists who work with families conceive of and relate to clients differently from therapists who work with individuals. To begin with, the family therapist is given entrée to the multiple perspectives of the various family members present. This affords the family therapist a rich multidimensional view of the individual members and their intimate environment, one to another or to the full family as an interactive whole — a view rarely available to the therapist working with an individual client. Thus, in contrast to the therapist who has the one-point perspective of a single client, the family therapist becomes aware of and attentive to the subtle ecology of the family context through the complex interactions played out directly in the therapy hour. It is common for therapists who begin doing family therapy (after they have practiced individual therapy for a while) to report that immersion in the family therapy process subtly but significantly alters the manner in which they think about and do therapy, even with individuals.

Thus, psychological contact between therapist and client, on the surface a relatively simple variable in individual therapy, becomes in family therapy a multifaceted and potentially investigable variable by which the effectiveness of intervention strategies may be evaluated. As noted in the previous chapter, this very basic condition is perhaps one of the least explored in either individual or family therapy. Possibly, investigation of this variable in family therapy might augment our understanding of its power in both individual and family therapy.

2. Incongruence: the state of the client

The state of the client, perhaps more than any of the other five conditions, differentiates individual from family therapy. The concept of incongruence as used by Rogers in the context of individual psychotherapy defines psychological distress as resulting from a disparity between the individual's actual experience of self versus the individual's perception or image of self.

Incongruence is relative (as are all of the conditions) in the sense that few, if any, of us, fully meet our expectations of ourselves. When this discrepancy is within tolerable bounds we may experience mild dissatisfaction, vulnerability, anxiety, or guilt. Such states may indeed be functional in that they may motivate us to reconsider and move in more appropriate directions as we endeavor to achieve our aspirations. On the other hand, when the discrepancy is more severe, we may experience anguish to the point of incapacitating psychological distress. The reasons for, or even the extent of, the distress may or may not be conceptualized fully by the individual. More simply put, this condition states that for therapy to be effective, the client must experience a degree of psychological distress that reaches some idiosyncratic threshold of discomfort. Although Rogers never explicitly articulated it, he certainly implied that personal incongruity urges the client to seek change.

Transposing the concept of incongruence to the milieu of the family extends the concept's richness. The concept of familial incongruence to some degree parallels personal incongruence since the incongruence of each family member, as well as the incongruence of the family system as a whole (or in various chunks), requires therapeutic attention. Van der Veen (1965) demonstrated that, like a concept of self, each of us has a personal concept of family (a similar concept has been discussed more recently by Reiss and Klein, 1987, called a *family paradigm*).

To some extent all family members' perceptions of their family is a shared experience. However, each individual's perception is also colored by the unique experiences of that individual family member, e.g., histories of the spouses' extended families and differences created by children's birth order (Toman, 1969). These experiences are augmented by the individual's separate observation of other families both real (extended families, friends, and neighbors), and unreal (those read about in books and seen in movies and on television).[2]

Thus, one form of familial incongruence exists when there is a discrepancy between how one or more family members *perceive* and *experience* the family. A common example of this discrepancy occurs when a spousal relationship begins deteriorating. Children, believing (or needing to believe) that their parents care about each other and that the relationship is repairable, often attribute the parents' disharmony to the children's behavior. Thus children often believe that if they had behaved better, performed better in school, or related better to their siblings, etc., the marriage would not be troubled.

In turn, the child may withdraw, refuse to go to school, fight with siblings, or exhibit other antisocial behaviors — any or all of which might create an incongruence (e.g., anguish, pain, distress) for virtually all family members and consequently impel the family to seek help. The latter condition, where there is consensual distress, may be termed *familial* or *system* incongruence. Thus, a family may seek therapy because of the distress (i.e., severe incongruence) of one or more of its individual members, an incongruence within one of the familial subsystems (i.e., spousal, parent-child, or sibling) and/or a generalized incongruence within the system as a whole.

Systemic incongruence may result from temporary acute stress placed on an individual or the system (e.g., severe illness, financial difficulty, death). Alternately,

---

2. Furthermore, the real and ideal family concepts are not mere analogues to the self and ideal self-concepts but are actually primary concepts from which the self-concepts emanate.

the incongruence may be chronic, having developed over a long period of time (e.g., a husband's and wife's disaffection, a child's failure to meet parental expectations, etc.). It is not unusual for one individual member's incongruence to lead to and essentially create a familial incongruence. Moreover, when the incongruence of an individual family member appears to be the presenting problem for family therapy, the therapist may question whether the individual's incongruence is primary or, alternatively, if it is an expression of the incongruence of the entire family system.

This last situation is a common occurrence in family therapy. An individual is presented as the *family's problem* when, in fact, the individual may actually be one of the more congruent family members who is being used, perhaps inadvertently, by the family to deflect or express the incongruence of the system. Such might well be the case when children blame themselves for their parents' marital problems and begin to withdraw or become otherwise dysfunctional. In this situation, the individual who impels the family to seek therapy is commonly referred to as a *lightning rod* or *scapegoat*.[3] However, the mechanism that may have begun as a temporary measure to maintain family congruence may since have become fixed due to its initial success. So reinforced, the lightning rod or scapegoat becomes entrenched in the role, thus creating a new set of problems with which the family must come to grips.

Similarly, the individual who symbolizes and outwardly bears the incongruence of the family may be analogous to an individual who suffers a psychosomatic disorder. The 'identified patient' may indeed be incongruent, but his or her incongruence may be the result of, and/or in conjunction with, the familial incongruence. In this case, the individual bearing the symptom may be the most vulnerable member of the family and thus the expresser of both the individual and the family's incongruence.

Another example is a family with a handicapped member. In this complex situation, the issues may include (a) the individual's incongruence related to the handicap itself; (b) the corresponding incongruences of other members surrounding their relationship to the handicapped individual; and (c) the incongruence of the family system. It should be noted that these last two examples sharply contrast with the family in which a relatively strong individual serves as the family scapegoat or lightning rod.

The discovery and unraveling of these incongruences by the family are a vital part of family therapy. As a result, it proves more complex than individual therapy and provides a greater challenge for the therapist. In individual therapy, as clients begin to feel more congruent they experience an assuaging of psychological distress and feel freer, more integrated, etc. This increased congruence is often accomplished

---

3. I have introduced the term *lightning rod* in lieu of the more commonly used *scapegoat*. Scapegoating implies burdening the designated target and driving it from the system, thus obviating its function. Contrarily the lightning rod remains to serve as the mechanism of discharge. Scapegoating is common in groups (where the target may, indeed, be driven out), but is rare in families.

by coming to terms (i.e., becoming more realistic — see Chapter 5) with expectations of oneself and establishing an internal rather than an external locus of evaluation. However, in the family session such simple congruence seldom suffices. Rather, the family often seeks a kind of consensual congruence consistent with each individual member's internal locus of evaluation. Consensual congruence is much more difficult to accomplish than mitigation of the incongruence sought by the client in individual therapy. The interplay of individual family members' states of congruence affords continually changing patterns (in response to both internal and external forces) that become the essence of the family therapy process.

Accordingly, although family therapy may reduce specific problems and conflicts that originally brought the family to seek help, certain family members may experience greater discomfort and distress than they did at the outset of therapy. Much of this has to do with individual family member's differing levels of frustration tolerance, the timing of change, and the lowering of individual protective defenses (see Gaylin, 1966). Indeed, apparent therapeutic *failure* or abortion of therapy may actually be engineered (often imperceptibly and/or unknowingly) by one or more family member(s) for whom the process may be too frightening or going too slowly or rapidly. Thus, for example, when the lightning rod is removed, other difficulties — including those for which the lightning rod may have been created — may become more easily discernable. This point in the therapeutic process is often a critical juncture. Here, the family must decide to tolerate the potential anxiety of the unknown and create new and perhaps unfamiliar behavior patterns for dealing with each other and the world or return to former familiar (albeit dysfunctional) behavior patterns.

Awareness of these system dynamics and the differing responses of individual family members to them and the therapeutic process requires assiduous concentration as well as *openness to experience* (see section 3, below) on the part of the family therapist.[4] On balance this effort is rewarded by the rich opportunities for change afforded throughout the course of family therapy. Finally, dealing with the complexity of multiple levels of potential incongruence within the family may help clarify previously negative and/or equivocal family therapy outcome results by delineating and separating variables that have had counteracting influences.

3. Congruence: the genuineness of the therapist in the relationship[5]
Rogers defined therapist congruence in very personal terms, that is, as therapist, one must be freely *and deeply oneself*. Rogers recognized that the therapist comes to the therapeutic relationship as a person with a history, values, feelings, etc.

---

4. The compounded complexity of incongruence in family therapy (as compared to incongruence in individual therapy) tends to support the case for the use of co-therapist teams (as suggested by Napier and Whitaker, 1972; and Rubenstein and Weiner, 1967) or *multiple impact family therapy* (McGregor, 1971). This complexity may also account for the extensive use of *live supervision* (through a one-way mirror with telephone contact) in the training and practice of family therapy.
5. Aspects of the self of the therapist and therapist congruence are dealt with again and more fully in Chapter 12.

Implicit in the notion of therapist congruence is the concept of *openness to experience* — the obverse of defensiveness — a key concept introduced and elaborated upon by Rogers in 1959. Therapists must be able to perceive both themselves and their clients as accurately as possible. As in the other conditions, the degree of a given therapist's congruence is relative. However, the contrast between the extent of the incongruence of the client (condition 2, above) and the degree of congruence of the therapist is focal. This relative absence of defensiveness and facade on the part of the therapist is considered to be a powerful force for therapeutic change. Although Rogers never really elucidated the reason for its power, part of the therapeutic process may be the client's subsequent emulation of the therapist's genuineness.

Therapist congruence is often more difficult to achieve and maintain in family therapy than in individual therapy. Family therapists must communicate openly with more than one individual — often simultaneously. Ideally, the family therapist needs to feel and express a genuine prizing and empathy (see next two conditions) for each family member — even though these individuals may be in open conflict with one another. A family therapist must be able to draw upon many aspects of the therapist's own history and experience (i.e., subselves, see Chapter 5) in order to empathize with individuals of different gender, age, and life experience. Moreover, family therapists must do this even when faced with feelings that may surface surrounding their own unresolved family conflicts evoked by client family members' interactions. Indeed, I have found this relatively unexplored therapeutic variable the lynchpin of the supervisory process. When I am in doubt about a problem presented by a therapist consultee, I seek out the potential incongruence of the therapist.[6]

4. Unconditional positive regard: prizing the client
Perhaps none of the six conditions has been so poorly understood as the need for the therapist to maintain unconditional positive regard for the client. Part of this misunderstanding may originate in the apparent absolute nature of the terminology. Once again, like all of the other conditions, unconditional positive regard is relative. It is therefore perhaps not quite so *unconditional*. Rather, Rogers meant that in therapy the client should experience an acceptance that is much less conditional than that which the client is likely to experience outside therapy. For clients to experience such acceptance requires that therapists suspend their personal values (to the extent possible) in order to maintain a nonjudgmental stance toward the client. Unconditional positive regard should be read as a caring or prizing attitude towards clients, regardless of the feelings clients present. In other words, a negative

---

6. A cautionary note is in order here. The concept of genuineness (later used and extended by Jourard, 1971, and Gendlin, 1978, as *transparency* and self-*disclosure*) should not be taken to mean that therapists must act upon or even express perceived incongruences within themselves. What is important is that therapists be aware of their reactions and feelings and continuously be in touch with their own internal frames of reference. Chapter 12 elaborates on this very important issue.

or even neutral therapist stance is one unlikely to effect therapeutic change on the part of the client.

Unconditional positive regard by the therapist for the client(s) is especially complex in family therapy. The therapist must maintain a prizing attitude towards more than one individual. It is not unusual for the therapist to have to maintain this attitude in the face of expressions of acrimony by family members towards one another. Thus, there is a contrast presented to family members when the therapist expresses feelings of unconditional positive regard to individuals who claim to have lost any positive regard for each other and where feelings of caring and prizing have been replaced by those of judgment and condemnation, even expressed loathing. As in the preceding condition, therapists may serve, in part, as role models for their clients. In so doing, they may also remind individuals of their positive attributes and worth.

A further complication arises (often in the case of marital discord or parent-child conflict) when one or more family members attempt(s) to place the family therapist in the role of arbiter. In these cases, family members may be locked into a struggle in which validation of one member's position may require the invalidation of another's. Further, initial resistance by family members to the nonjudgmental stance of the therapist is not at all unusual. It is rather natural to seek validation for one's position in a conflict; family therapy is no exception. If the family therapist can maintain a nonjudgmental stance towards all parties, the family may be able to *reframe* the situation from a winner-take-all conquest to a new and (ideally) mutually acceptable view of the situation (see Watzlawick,Weakland, and Fisch, 1974). Especially in these circumstances, unconditional positive regard is closely related to empathy.

5. Empathic understanding

The therapist's ability to maintain an empathic stance towards the client is undoubtedly the most widely accepted and commonly discussed of Rogers' six conditions. Rogers elegantly described empathy as follows:

> To sense the client's private world as if it were your own, but without ever losing the 'as if' quality . . . When the client's world is this clear to the therapist, and he moves about in it freely, then he can both communicate his understanding of what is clearly known to the client and can also voice meanings in the client's experience of which the client is barely aware (1957, p.99).

Ironically, empathy has become so accepted a concept in psychotherapy that few appreciate the intricacies of its nuances and power. It is neither so simple nor so easily accomplished as many beginning therapists suppose. Empathy requires rigorous attention and concentration to foster and maintain. While some come by it more naturally than others, empathic ability is nonetheless a skill that cannot be taken for granted. It, like musical virtuosity, requires both talent and continuous practice.

One of the difficulties in dealing with empathy as an identifiable (and therefore researchable) variable is its easy confusion with its isomorphs: sympathy and identification. Sympathetic observers maintain distance, not allowing themselves to enter the internal frame of reference of the other person. Identifiers, on the other hand, maintain *no* distance and presume to know another person on the basis of self-knowledge and the assumption that their own experience and that of the other's are identical. Although sympathy rarely engenders therapeutic change, identification can. However, it does so in a potentially dangerous manner because it permits the therapist to project motivations onto the client that may be outside the client's frame of reference. It is the delicate balance of significant but separate understanding that defines the empathic stance and gives it its power. Empathy also empowers metaphor as a therapeutic tool (Watzlawick, 1978) just as the empathic communication of metaphor enables poetry to express the universality of the human condition.

Although it is difficult enough for a therapist working with individuals to maintain an empathic stance in the therapeutic hour, it is far more difficult for a therapist to achieve and maintain this condition effectively in family therapy. However, if the therapist is able to convey empathy for each individual, family members may be led to the inevitable conclusion that separate realities may indeed exist, and that each person sees through lenses which have been uniquely colored by his or her experience. If family members can recognize and accept these separate realities, then rich complementarity can supplant clashing polarity. Thus, a reconceptualization of the situation is made possible, one which may engender greater empathy among family members.

The family therapist's ability to empathically experience the internal frame of reference of each family member not only facilitates intrafamilial empathy but also sheds new light on apparent *unresolvable* conflicts. When a family member concurs with the therapist's reflection of his or her internal frame of reference, it is not uncommon for another member — who is listening to the therapist — to exclaim in wonder, 'I never realized you felt that way!' or, 'I never understood what you meant when you said that before!' Johnson and Greenberg (1988) have identified this 'increased accessibility and responsiveness' and labeled it *softening*.

Furthermore, in the family therapy session, the therapist may often have an empathic understanding of the entire system, an understanding not easily available to family members since they are emotionally involved and invested. In such cases the therapist's reflection of a systemic vantage point may have the impact of holding up a mirror to the family, ideally enabling the family members to see their interactions in a new light. Often such re-perceiving can help cut through (or at least loosen) the family's Gordian knot.

6. The client's perception of the therapist
The final condition posits that the client must perceive, to some degree, therapist's acceptance and empathy. This last condition hearkens back to the first in that it delineates the special boundaries of the therapeutic relationship. Here, finally, the

family therapist may have it easier than the therapist working with individuals. Insofar as the condition indicates at least a minimal perception by the client(s), it may be sufficient if at certain times only some members perceive the therapist as caring and understanding. However, as noted throughout the preceding discussion, the more the therapist can communicate these positive attitudes to each family member and thus to the family at large, the more likely the therapist will be able to facilitate change. Conversely, when some family members experience the therapist as the obverse (i.e., insensitive and condemning) the likelihood of an abortion of the therapeutic process is increased because the alienated family member(s) may resort to withdrawal and/or sabotage. However, even when only parts of the system sense the therapist's prizing, additional change may be facilitated from within after the direct relationship with the therapist has ended, prematurely or not. That is, once the family experiences its actualizing potential, a process of growth has been set in motion and is likely to continue.

Conclusion

The six conditions reviewed above are the only conditions postulated by Rogers. In the years I have applied them to the practice, consultation, teaching, and supervision of family therapy, I have found the conditions to be a good foundation for refining and clarifying the processes occurring within the family therapy hour. I have further found them useful for identifying dimensions for research into the process of family therapy. Thus, neither this chapter — nor this book for that matter — is intended to suggest yet another form of family therapy. Rather it is an attempt to identify those elements common to all psychotherapeutic endeavors regardless of model and context — individual, group, or family. The expansion of the six conditions to encompass the practice of family therapy is both right and natural and clarifies not only our understanding of family therapy dynamics but those of individual therapy as well.

Family Therapy Process[1]

The word therapy *has no verb in English, for which I am grateful; it cannot do anything to anybody, hence can better represent a process going on, observed perhaps, understood perhaps, assisted perhaps, but not applied.*
Jesse Taft, *TheDynamics of Therapy in a Controlled Relationship.*

Introduction

The unappreciated brilliance of the person-centered therapy with clients is that only one method is applied: empathic, nonjudgmental, and caring reflection of feeling. This method is applicable no matter who the *client* — child, adult, couple, or family. However, to novice or even experienced therapists from other theoretical orientations, this single method often seems simplistic and inadequate to do the complex job of salving the troubled psyches of individuals and families. Thus, elaborate formulaic manuals have become popular, in part because they offer more complex explanations of psychopathology and techniques for rehabilitation. However, these books seem to miss the point that person-centered therapy's single method is sufficient for psychotherapeutic change to take place.

The basic method with families

Through repeated shared experiences, the family accretes an experiential history which, in turn, creates a culture filled with shared meanings, inculcated values, and expectations. In addition to being an internal part of the family community with its shared meanings, each family member is also a unique individual who interacts with the world at large in a manner that complements his or her own personality. These family histories replete with both shared and idiosyncratic meaning, are the life voyages, the odysseys that the families bring to therapy.

The therapist maintains an empathic stance with each family member's separate

---

1. Paper presented as 'Family centered therapy' at the International Conference of Client-Centered and Experiential Psychotherapy, Leuven, Belgium, September 1988. First published in Lietaer, G., Rombauts, J., and Van Balen: *Client-Centered and Experiential Psychotherapy towards the Nineties.* Leuven: University of Leuven Press, 1990. Reprinted by permission of the publishers and editors.

world-view and attending attitudes and feelings. With caring empathy, the therapist listens and reflects his or her understanding of each individual member's experiences surrounding various events that comprise the family's history. Through such empathic reflection, an atmosphere of trust and safety is created wherein all members can have their individual world-views validated, each in turn. As each member begins to trust the therapist's nonjudgmental empathic caring, as well as the therapist's ability to create an atmosphere in which the speaker is protected from other members' potential attributions or attacks, individual *intra*personal incongruences begin to surface.

Furthermore, as the various tales unfold, the therapist and family itself become privy to many contradictory perceptions that have become imbedded within the commonly shared but often misunderstood experiences. These contradictory experiences invariably define the interpersonal incongruences that have led to other previous misunderstandings that, in turn, have created hurt, anger, and conflict within the family. This usually gradual (though sometimes dramatic) unfolding process is what enables the family to work through conflicts that have heretofore disabled the family and its individual members from functioning effectively.

As family members begin the disclosing process, the therapist first gleans a sense of the whole and then offers it back to the family. This unfolding via reflections of both intra- and interpersonal incongruences and associated conflictive interaction patterns enables each member to revise perceptions and experience and see each other and the family differently. Through this process, barriers to the individual's and the family's actualizing tendencies may be attenuated.

With family members witnessing the revealing of various personal incongruences in an empathic atmosphere, mutual empathy and understanding for each other that had been waning may now be rekindled. The loosening of conflictive knots pulled tight over the years facilitates the family's own habilitative powers. In turn, the therapy process becomes a part of the family's history to be drawn upon as a restorative experience.

The presentation of self in individual and family therapy

One might suppose that clients would begin therapy by presenting the most pressing aspects of their incongruence, that is, those causing the most pain and debilitation. Evidence exists, however, that clients are far more likely to ease into the therapeutic process by presenting a generalized state of anxiety and only gradually revealing their self-complex to the therapist (Rennie, 1990). Knowingly or unknowingly, clients may hold back some of the more painful aspects of their self-incongruence until they feel emotionally safe with the therapist and the therapeutic relationship (Frank, 1961).

Such entrances into therapy are natural in individual person-centered therapy; the client is more or less in control of the initiation, direction, and pace of the therapy session. Accordingly, a client may talk initially about his or her difficulties as a parent and defer disclosure of felt inadequacies as a mate or lover, perhaps until the client feels less vulnerable and at risk within the therapeutic relationship.

Thus, invariably, individual clients will reveal incongruence surrounding a particular subself aspect of the self-complex or a generalized sense of incongruence of the total self-complex, and the therapist will not immediately be aware of the full scope of the presenting problem. This miasma may result from any or all of the following: (a) the client's own lack of awareness; (b) the client's editing; (c) the therapist's incongruence; (d) the therapist's inadequate empathy for the client.

In the context of person-centered family therapy, each family member brings to the session his or her individual incongruence along with those contributed by the entire family system (Gaylin, 1989, 1990). Revealed incongruence experienced solo by any family member, may create additional individual and familial incongruence.

These process complexities within the family session highlight some focal and functional distinctions between individual person-centered and person-centered family therapy. In family therapy, for example, a husband or wife may suddenly experience incongruences with regard to his or her spousal subselves as a result of challenging or contradictory data (perceptions, experiences, etc.) presented by the mate in the joint therapy session. Similarly, in multiple-generation family therapy, parents may find themselves compelled to confront an insecurity of their parental subselves upon hearing their child's experience of them as parents. The parent may have sensed this insecurity but never openly dealt with it. On the other hand, it may have been totally unidentified or honestly denied by the parent because of the parent's lack of awareness or comprehension. The situation can become even more complex when another family member (e.g., a sibling) challenges a parent or other sibling either of whom exhibits subself incongruence and appears not to sense this disparity from within.

Therapist stance and response differences in individual and family therapy
Although distinct process differences between individual and person-centered family therapy do not require a change in the therapist's orientation and practice, the complexity of the therapist's task is exponentially extended in the family therapy session. The dynamics of family therapy demand that the person-centered family therapist be in tune with the frames of reference of every family member, and simultaneously maintain an empathic position with each.

Indeed, person-centered family therapists listen in a somewhat different fashion from their individual person-centered therapist counterparts. The therapist must hear and empathically process what each family member is saying not only from that member's and therapist's respective vantage points but from the perspective of each of the various other family members as well. Thus, family therapists listen and empathically reflect as they criss-cross back and forth among the frames of reference of all family members. The family therapist must be ready and able to be empathic with the potential impact that any family member's verbal or nonverbal expressions may have on each and all of the other family members, each of whom is present with his or her own functional or dysfunctional self-complex.

Although the method of reflection of feelings in family therapy differs little from that practiced in individual therapy, there are subtle extensions of the empathic method when moving from the individual to the family context. Individual therapy is primarily a form of introspection in which the therapist acts as an interpersonal mirror to the individual client. In contrast, clients in family therapy are clearly in an interpersonal venue. Thus, internal dialogue is often supplanted by dialogue directed at others in a communal, albeit intimate, space. The family therapist is continuously shuttling between the intra- and interpersonal dynamics presented in the family therapy hour.

Those reflections of the dialogic interactions within the family therapy hour I have called *interspace reflections* (Gaylin, 1990). Although, certainly, interspace reflections are made to voice the shared meaning or interpersonal agreement among family members, they are also made when there is an interpersonal incongruence — a conflict between the experiences and perceptions of two or more member's perspectives of a given situation. When, for example, two or more family members are engaged in a dialogue, after empathically addressing each, the therapist may deal with the interaction between them.

The following scenario between a father and son demonstrates first the reflection of each family member's feelings and then an interspace reflection.

Father: I am sick and tired of having to remind him to do his chores.

Therapist: You are exasperated that he never remembers his jobs.

Son: He never gives me a chance. He wants me to do them on his schedule.

Therapist: Dad is impatient and unreasonable.

Father: If I don't keep after him all the time the jobs just don't get done.

Son: They'd get done if you'd give me a chance

Therapist: It seems that it's hard for the two of you to have confidence and respect for each other.

Often family members realize that they share responsibility for a problem once another person lays out and reflects the difficulties. Furthermore, the empathic responses to each member enlighten and help validate not only each speaker's feelings but also facilitate communication and understanding between the members.[2] Reflecting the interactive process provides an additional step in defusing an incendiary situation. It is crucial that the therapist be evenly empathic and maintain a nonjudgmental stance lest any party feel that the therapist is taking sides, which would mitigate the therapist's effectiveness in dealing with the party who felt slighted.

---

2. In the early part of the dialogue both father and son address their comments to the therapist (seemingly as arbiter), referring to the other family member in the third person. Near the end of the interchange, following individual reflection of feeling, the son addresses the father directly. This evolutionary process of the dialogue is a marker of potential for shared meaning.

The following is another brief scenario of an interspace reflection between a husband and wife.

Wife: You have never understood how I felt when your mother comes to stay with us.

At first the therapist simply reflects the client's feelings.

Therapist: When you try and tell Dan about your feelings when your mother-in-law visits, it seems he never understands you.

Husband: I want to understand, but every time I try and talk about it, she just walks away.

Reciprocally, the therapist attends to the husband.

Therapist: When you try and understand what Joan's concerns are about your mother, you feel she does not listen to your prodding.

At this juncture the therapist is in the position of reflecting the interspace, accordingly:

Therapist: Whenever you two try to talk about Danny's mom's relationship with Joan there seems to be some kind of barrier between you.

Thus the therapist hears and reflects each member's position but goes on to reflect the interpersonal or interface incongruence. Ideally, each family member feels heard and can go beyond simply accusing the other or feeling blamed by the other while the situation is outlined as a shared problem. Although interspace reflections seem simple — almost obvious — the immediate reduction of attribution and blame-laying with the principals sitting together creates an atmosphere of greater understanding. Then the couple's actualizing tendencies (both individually and in concert) can be unencumbered and change facilitated.

The following is an excerpt from an interview with an eight-year-old boy and his single mother. The mother has brought the child for therapy because of (a) a growing power struggle between her and the boy and (b) his growing stubbornness both at home and at school. The boy is sitting in the back of the room, out of range of the video camera. The mother knows that the therapist is recording and that the boy is not in camera range. At the outset of the interview the therapist is unaware of the mother's motivation.

Mother: LeRoy, sit over here (motioning to a chair next to hers — L. doesn't move.) LeRoy, I told you to sit over here!

Son: (mumbles) I don't wanna, I wanna sit here.

Therapist: Mom, you want LeRoy to sit next to you, but LeRoy, you want to sit in the back.

Mother: (Seeming to ignore therapist's interspace reflection),[3] LeRoy,

---

3. Note that in this first interspace reflection, there is no response on the part of either family member. As with any empathic response, the therapist may not get it right the first time. The validation of the accuracy of response is in the client process which follows. When the therapist tries again, he seems to get it right, and the interspace reflection is affirmed.

	I'm not playing with you — come sit over here by me. (L. folds his arms in defiance. Mother gets up and physically drags him to the chair and forces him into it. L. gets out of the seat of the chair and half stands, half sits on the arm. Mo. does not react to L.'s continued minor defiance, but seems satisfied with the outcome.)
Therapist	(Recognizing that mother wanted L. in camera range for the videotape). Mom, I guess you just wanted LeRoy to sit where he would be on camera (Mo. nods yes), but LeRoy didn't know that, did you?
Son:	(Shakes his head 'no', and slides down into the seat of the chair. Both seem more relaxed.)
Therapist:	I guess it's easy to get into a snit when you don't know why another person wants you to do something a certain way.

The foregoing demonstrates that simply reflecting the interaction is often sufficient to discharge a potentially escalating misunderstanding. Such reflecting clarifies meaning for the individual family members while offering empathy with both.

This interactive process reflection generated by person-centered family therapy may have potential for application to individual therapy as well. There may, in fact, be an analogue between the potential intrapersonal incongruence among the subselves of an individual and the incongruences that occur between and among family members. Although, on the surface, the client's awareness of subself incongruence may not appear to directly affect the behavior of the therapist working with such an individual, such awareness can create a heightened sensitivity to the individual client's struggle. Consequently, the capacity for empathic understanding of the complexity of the internal dialogues among a given individual's subselves may be increased.

Finally, there are some interesting dynamics within the family therapy session that bridge intra- and interpersonal dimensions. Thus, as the process unfolds in the family therapy session, a parent may empathize with his or her child — even identify with the child's expressed anguish, perhaps relating it to similarly stressful incidents in the parent's own childhood experience. Within the family therapy session, this empathy may play out openly as a mutually therapeutic engagement between the child and the parent and even extend itself to other if not all family members, thereby changing the entire family dynamic.

However, an alternate and more subtle possibility exists, in which the effect of interpersonal therapeutic interaction between or among family members regarding intrapersonal dynamics may be neither openly expressed nor apparent. This can happen when, under certain circumstances and for various reasons, a family member (or members) may have an investment in a given self-stance or position. For example, a stoic responsible father might feel the need to maintain a certain degree of opacity, despite his resonance with the pain that his child has expressed in the therapy hour (Stein and Markus, 1994; Straumann, 1994). The vicarious empathic healing of the father while observing and processing the interaction between the therapist and the child (or between/among other family members) may not be able to be shared openly at the time with those present. But this does not alter its impact: On many levels the unblocking of the self-actualizing process and the reassessment of self-worth is occurring through both intrapersonal and interpersonal means.

Other special processes within the family therapy hour

Subsumed in empathic reflection are related phenomena: *ghosting* and *intergenerational echoing* (Gaylin, 1993). Both phenomena appear to emanate naturally when family members interact in a therapeutic milieu.

Ghosting.[4]

Ghosting (Gaylin, 1993) is a means of empathizing with an absent family member. I accidentally stumbled upon this method when I taught an introductory marriage and family therapy course to graduate students. Not infrequently, after class, individual participants would come to my office to discuss problems they were having with a spouse, parent, or other intimate. They would ask my advice about what to do while relating some incident or problem in the relationship. Although I usually deferred, suggesting that they seek professional counseling, I still would try to be empathic with the student and his or her anguish in the interpersonal situation. I then might add some comment such as, 'You know, if you had said such and such to me, I might have felt hurt or upset, although I might not have been able to tell you so at the time.' Frequently, I would hear from these students that having related my statement back to the person with whom they were having difficulty, the person agreed with what I had said with respect to their probable feelings. The student would often go on to note that meaningful conversations ensued which resolved the difficulty.

Although sometimes useful in individual therapy, the empathic stance with an absent member is often more meaningful and powerful in marital or family therapy when, on occasion, I have been asked to see one member of the family at a time that the other member(s) could not be present.[5] Having worked with the absent member and established an ongoing relationship with that person, I have established an empathic position with him or her. As a consequence, I am free to say something in response to the present client such as 'You know, I think I understand how you feel about such and such' (being more empathically specific). Then I might continue, 'and I wonder if John were here, whether he might see things differently,

---

4. I have been told that some of these ideas are reminiscent of the *empty chair* and *doubling* techniques used in psychodrama (Moreno, 1947). I prefer, however, not to think of this way of working as a technique but, rather, an indigenous outgrowth of the empathic stance.

5. Seeing a family member without the rest of the family (or a partner without the spouse) is a practice I avoid — particularly in the beginning of therapy. However, on occasion, such as when a spouse has to be out of town and supports such an arrangement, I may agree to see the remaining partner alone with the caveat that the seen partner will convey what transpired to the absent one. I follow a similar procedure regarding telephone calls from a family member.

more like this'(and proceed to make a hypothetical empathic comment about John's possible feelings), thus *ghosting* the absent member. To such a comment the partner present will often cock his or her head (literally or figuratively), and process this new data in a manner that, reportedly, offers new insight into the situation. Furthermore, the present person would, invariably, report the episode to the absent member. This, in turn, would result in continued: (a) clarifying exchanges between the partners and (b) building of trust with me as a result of my maintaining empathy with both members, even when one was absent

Indeed, I have even used this empathic method when a family member not actively participating in the therapy (e.g., a grandparent) was talked about in the session. I might hazard an empathic guess as to how I would feel in a given situation were I that family member. I find that participant members are usually intrigued with my reactions. They then often report the incident to the nonparticipating member, who may validate my reactions as accurate. Not infrequently, family members are surprised to learn that the nonparticipating member is grateful for absentee representation. Thus, I believe standing in for absent members enhances my credibility with all family members who know that I make an effort to represent them empathically even when they are not there to speak for themselves. The process also encourages facilitative dialogues outside of family sessions.[6]

Finally, though not strictly a form of ghosting, a similar practice may be used when the therapist feels impelled to speak empathically for family members who, while present, may not for whatever reasons, seem able to speak for themselves. Thus, I might reply to a father who has just called his son a 'lazy good-for-nothing bum,' accordingly: 'You must be very hurt or angry with your son,' empathizing with the father. I might then continue 'and if I were sitting in his chair I guess I would be pretty hurt hearing my dad call me names like that.' I have watched the mask of anger on both faces melt into tears of recognition, which additionally enable an empathic interspace reflection.

It is important to note that I do not look upon ghosting simply as a technique but, rather, as a natural extension of the person-centered approach. Thus, ghosting employs empathy and prizing in the therapeutic relationship, along with the subtle distinction that the therapist is continuously aware of the explicit interpersonal elements that ongoing person-centered family therapy brings into focus.

Intergenerational echoing

Intergenerational echoing (Gaylin, 1993) is another phenomenon unique to the family therapy hour. On occasions when I am working with parents and children, a parent will have a dramatic gestalt recall of a parallel experience between the parent (when the parent was a child) and the parent's parent(s). These powerful and emotional moments often surround childhood feelings of resentment towards the parent regarding felt injustices. These echoes often signal a turning point in

---

6. Ghosting an absent member is not something that I do often. I believe I am impelled to do so when the client paints a very vivid picture of the absent member — often infusing that person's presence in the room: this, in turn, enables my empathy.

therapy whereby the parent recognizes a personal, experiential empathy for the child. Moments like these, in turn, greatly facilitate mutual respect and understanding between parent and child: shared meaning through parallel experience.

Thus, work with families allows for observation of the empathic resonance of family members for one another. Such observation may ensue as the empathic process between the therapist and a given family member takes place. As the therapy unfolds, one can see how this echoing, this intergenerational resonance, infuses the family process over time and allows the actualizing tendency of the family as a whole to mobilize (Gaylin, 1990).

Via an incident that occurred over a generation ago, I personally experienced the power of this kind of resonance. My father died when I was a young, married man without children. My father was a wonderful and gentle man but, as many other of his generation of Polish-Russian immigrants, rather stern and authoritative. He died, only as I was beginning to appreciate him as a person, not simply a loving authority figure. About ten years later an incident saturated with profound personal emotion occurred when one of our sons (the youngest of our four children) was about four years old. This son bears the same relational position to me as I have to my father. Both of us are youngest sons. I had been born when my father was in early middle age and my son arrived at a similar time in my life, etc. On this particular day, I was minding the children while my wife was running errands, and this youngest of our four children was playing near me as I worked at my desk.

Out of the corner of one eye (I had learned to look out of the corner of my eye when this son was particularly quiet), I noticed that he somehow had managed to pull the uppermost file drawer out of a very heavy, old oak, four-drawer file cabinet. He had begun to swing on it. The cabinet began to lean and topple and held the inevitable conclusion that it would soon fall squarely on him. Terrified, I leaped out of my chair just in time to grab him and slam the drawer shut so that the cabinet would remain upright. Adrenalized and shaking, my fear converted to anger now that the catastrophe had been avoided, I began shouting at my four-year-old son, who stood in front of me, not quite comprehending all that had transpired in those frightening seconds.

Now furious at him for his lack of care (and certainly at myself for the same reason), I excoriated him. As I felt ugly words tumble from my mouth, I saw tears well up in my son's eyes. The image triggered a memory trace never before retrieved. At that instant, two other people who lived in my mind's eye joined us. These apparitions were the four-year-old me (now standing next to my son) and my middle-aged father standing just to the right and behind me.

As I saw my words hit their mark, I saw and felt the four-year-old me crying alongside my tearful son. I knew exactly what my son was experiencing, and a part of me wanted to grab him and hug him and tell him how much I loved him and explain that I was angry at him because I was so frightened for both of us. But I could neither say these things nor stop the abusive words hurled at him from my mouth. I felt tears well up in my own eyes and grieved, wanting also to embrace my father and tell him I finally understood.

That moment was an experiential fulcrum in my life. I realized that many subselves maintained themselves in my *stream of consciousness* and would continue to do so now and into the future as I related to significant others in my life space — the living and the dead. This awakening has reasserted itself in my memory many times during therapy with individuals, but far more so in family therapy sessions because as I watch children and their parents struggling to understand each other, my empathy for each of them is enabled.

Working with children

Working with children entails special consideration, both when they are seen individually in therapy and when they are a part of the family therapy session. My entry into the practice of psychotherapy began with children, and I believe that there is no better training for therapists. Troubled young people are often wary of strange adults. Before they entrust adults with their deeply personal thoughts and feelings they need to believe the adults are worthy of that trust. Children are masters of nonverbal communication — more so than adults — and thus can sense deception and guile. Simply put, young people of all ages demand congruence in their therapists if therapy is to be effective.

Individual therapy with children

Traditionally, when we think of children in therapy — particularly young children — we think of play therapy. Indeed, the most popular book on the subject is from the person-centered approach. It is entitled *Play Therapy* (Axline, 1947). Play, be it fantastic, imaginary, role-taking, playground focused, competitive, etc., may be seen as the child's experiential experimentation. In therapy this play often expresses the child's feelings of incongruence and hungered congruence.

Unfortunately, many (both professionals and nonprofessionals) view psychotherapy with children as a palpably different psychotherapeutic endeavor from that with adults. Calling psychotherapy with children *play* therapy exacerbates the chasm between the two endeavors. The inference, too often drawn, is that therapy with children requires a special venue or environment, exotic equipment such as a sandbox, special dolls, puppets, etc. Such prejudice tends to deflect many from working with children. Although such items may be valuable additions to the therapy environment, few are crucial or essential.

In actuality, all that therapy with children requires is a comfort with and sensitivity to children, a willingness and ability to engage intimately with a child on the child's terms, and an internal integrity that permit therapists to access recollections of their own experiences during the growing-up years. Indeed, doing therapy with children helps therapists develop congruence by sharpening internal self-awareness that characterizes and is required for a therapeutic stance. Therefore, child therapy provides a sound foundation for therapists working with any population.

Children of all ages are amazingly resilient and inventive in creating toys out of virtually nothing. Indeed, parents who are concerned about encouraging violence often forbid their children to play with guns. These same parents are aghast when they see the children on the playground playing cops and robbers, thumb erect and forefinger extended, proclaiming to their playmates 'Pow! Pow! You're dead.' Very young children will often reject designer toys for simple household objects like pots, pans, and keys. Almost all children love to be read to and look at books. Similarly, most children like to draw and make up stories about their drawings. Thus, a therapist's office with a few interesting books, pencil and paper or crayons and other similar simple interesting objects are sufficient tools with which to begin engaging children.

By nature, children are usually eager to relate to adults and gain their attention. Like the young of most other mammalian species, children need and generally look to adults for guidance and approbation, significant primers of their actualizing tendency. However, when children become troubled, typical functional patterns of relating to others may break down. Troubled children may withdraw into themselves, act out, or generally behave in antisocial ways. When such behavior is severe enough, they are often brought for psychotherapy. Thus, an attentive, patient, and caring adult may create an interpersonal environment in which the child's trust in others, particularly adults, may be established (or re-established) so that functional developmentally-appropriate interaction may resume.

Work with any client, particularly those who have not yet reached adulthood, makes evident that clients may not use spoken language as the primary vehicle for conveying their inner experiences. Thus, therapists must additionally and actively attend to their younger clients' nonverbal behaviors. Therapists who can grasp the meaning of clients' inner experiences through those nonverbal behaviors should thus be able to reflect empathic understanding to their young clients. Reciprocally, sometimes those reflections are offered nonverbally and parallel the behavior of the child.

Working with children makes therapists aware of the need for keeping the client's agenda primary, allowing the client to lead. Language often acts as an accompaniment to the broader range of activities mentioned above, and therapists need to be prepared to engage in the child's repertoire of activities. The following is an excerpt from a session with an 11-year-old boy referred because of a mild learning disability and subsequent anxiety about his performance at school.

Andrew came into the therapist's office smirking broadly and carrying a large paper bag.

Therapist:	Hi Andrew. From the look on your face I would guess you have something very special in that bag.
Client:	(Grin broadening.) Guess!
Therapist:	You want me to figure out what you brought here today.
Client:	(Nods animatedly.)
Therapist:	Hmm, it must be something very special — a treasure.
Client:	Yeah, but what? *Guess*!

Therapist:	It's a treasure, but something more . . .
Client:	(Interrupting excitedly.) Something I made.
Therapist:	Something you made at school?
Client:	No, no — at home. (Dumping the contents on the coffee table.) It's origami!
Therapist:	(Truly impressed by the amount and complexity of the paper-folded objects.) Wow! Look at all those things! Looks like animals, *lots* of animals, and . . .
Client:	Balls and jumping frogs (demonstrating how to make the frog jump).
Therapist:	They really *do* jump like frogs.
Client:	Want me to show you how to make one?
Therapist:	You want to teach me how to make a jumping frog.
Client:	(Nods) Sure, they're easy . . . (catching the look of skepticism on the therapist's face) . . . it's not that hard — really!
Therapist:	You think I could learn; they're easy when you know how to do it, eh?
Client:	Yeah (hands the therapist a piece of origami paper from the pile on the table and takes another piece for himself, beginning, almost at once, to fold it). First you fold it in half, like this.
Therapist:	(Following instructions, folding the paper as the client.) So far so good.
Client:	(Folding increasingly more rapidly as he gets engrossed in the task) then like this, then like that, then turn it over and . . . (noticing the therapist is hopelessly lost) . . . here, let me help you (taking the paper from the therapist).
Therapist:	I guess it would be easier to do it yourself rather than teach a dummy like me.
Client:	You're not a dummy! You just never did origami before, did you?
Therapist:	Not really, I think I tried once but didn't have the patience. It's hard to try and learn to do something new, eh?
Client:	Yeah, I know (looks wistful). Maybe we could do something simpler, like a boat — they're *real* easy.
Therapist:	We should start with something simple like a boat and work up to something complicated like a frog.
Client:	Yeah. (Smiling, taking another piece of paper for himself and handing one to the therapist.)

The client then proceeds in a much slower fashion than before and checks the therapist's progress more carefully as he succeeds in helping the therapist make a boat.

The foregoing represents role-taking by both client and therapist that facilitates the learning (and perhaps healing) for this learning-disabled client who, in this situation, is in charge of a task at which he is competent and the therapist is not. The role reversal appears satisfying to the child and enables him to display both a sense of mastery as well as empathy with the (sincerely) inept therapist. Led by the client, the therapist's ability to engage and express real feelings of ineptitude, involve the client in a healing process that simply *talking* about his difficulties with new learning situations probably could not.

Children in the family session

I generally like to see children without other family members present at the beginning of the session. I explain to the parents and the child at the outset that my sessions with children are confidential: the parents may ask the child what transpired in our sessions, and I explain that the child should feel free to reply or not, but I do not divulge session content. The exception to this rule occurs when I believe there may be potential for exposing the child or the community to danger. Parents must be informed if the child is using drugs, harming or contemplating harming himself or others. Should I learn of problems of this nature, I encourage the child to share this information with parents, explaining the importance of the disclosure. I also say that if the child finds it difficult to reveal such information to parents single-handedly, I will be there to help. Otherwise I will have to disclose the information myself. With this understanding at the beginning of the therapy relationship, I rarely have had a problem establishing trust with all family members.

At the beginning of therapy with children I ask them if they have any concerns and/or what events of the week may have been problematic. In these initial stages, children generally say little, e.g., 'Things were OK.' I then suggest we bring the parents in. Invariably one of the parents will say something like 'Did Johnny tell you what happened in school this week?'(implying a negative happenstance of some kind). I wait for a moment to let the child speak but, if nothing is forthcoming, I then reply that if they want to know what Johnny did or did not tell me that they need to ask Johnny. Children become better observers when they realize what to expect from psychotherapy sessions. They begin to realize that, not only can the therapist facilitate communication between them and their parents, he or she can even act as a friend and ally. Children begin sharing their concerns when they experience the empathic and facilitative role of the therapist.

One final point: neither the person-centered approach in general nor family therapy in specific, sees individual diagnosis as facilitative of the treatment of either individuals or families. However, in working with children there are some exceptions and caveats. Children with learning and other developmental disabilities may be suffering from constitutional problems, e.g., visual, auditory, or central nervous system. Although therapy may help them deal with the secondary emotional distress that these disabilities create, therapy alone cannot mitigate the basic problem. Psychotherapy alone, no matter how inspired, is not likely to make a reader of a dyslexic child. The reading problem must be addressed directly. Therefore, with some children, a psycho-educational diagnostic evaluation from an outside source may well be in order. Likewise, it is desirable for those working extensively with children to have a basic knowledge of child development to better ascertain if children may need referrals for special academic help, corrective lenses, hearing aids, etc.

Thus, in work with families in which a child suffers a developmental disability, I distinguish between the processes of *child guidance* and psychotherapy. In child guidance there are certain developmental norms, which, if not attended to, can adversely affect the child's future development and well-being. The identification and discussion of such issues differs greatly from the therapy process described above. For example, it is one thing to listen empathically to distraught parents lament their felt sense of inadequacy and express concern for their offspring. It is another story to hear the complaint that the child at a year and a half is 'willful' because he or she will not succumb to the parents' directives to become toilet trained.

There are relatively immutable normative developmental parameters regarding biological, physical, and neurological functions such as sphincter control (or talking, walking, reading, etc.). To ignore these parameters may support unrealistic parental expectations that could, indeed, have deleterious effects on all family members in this situation. Thus, I make a clear distinction in my work with families as to when I am doing child guidance and when I am doing family therapy.

Evidence from research
There is not a great deal of research on the process of individual psychotherapy. Among investigative efforts of the last half-century, vocal quality was one of the few research measures that held promise for evaluating client process in individual psychotherapy (Rice and Wagstaff, 1967). The measure, which identified four, typical, client vocal patterns within the therapy session, revealed *focused* pattern as the voice quality indicative of therapeutic activity leading to change. It was also the pattern highly associated with success in individual psychotherapy. Described by Rice and Gaylin (1973) as a sense in the vocal patterning that the client's 'eyeballs are turned inward', the pattern might be seen as that of an inner conversation among the subselves that has the potential for knitting up an otherwise unraveling self-complex.

Process research in family therapy, by dint of the number and complexity of interpersonal interactions involved, has been correspondingly rare. In an effort to determine whether or not a similar process indicator could be discerned within the family therapy session, Kilcarr (1987) evaluated the vocal quality of family members during several families' therapy sessions. He found a dearth of focused voice quality in family therapy sessions, even in those cases deemed successful. These findings suggest that the family therapy process may be somehow different from that of the individual therapy. Upon reflection, there is an obviousness to this observation. The family therapy session is at least on the surface less devoted to inner exploration than to the interactions among the family members. Although it is certain that complex intrapersonal processes are simultaneously taking place, person-centered family therapy is still a more public forum than that of individual therapy. However, as previously noted (Rennie, 1990), much goes on within clients to which the therapist is not privy.

Employing measures similar to those of Rice and Wagstaff (1967), Johnson and Greenberg (1988) identified a more interactive vocal quality in marital therapy that holds promise for identifying therapeutic change. They called this vocal quality *softening*, which they believed was indicative of greater 'accessibility and responsiveness' (i.e., empathy) between the marital partners. Thus, research suggests that one of the major healing forces within the interpersonal milieu is the process enabled by the self-complex whereby the many subselves of one person empathically interact with those of another.

Conclusion

Working with families within the person-centered approach is totally consistent with and a natural parallel to individual person-centered therapy. Theoretically and methodologically there are few differences except those subtle yet complex distinctions that result from the presence of more than one client. The person-centered family therapist attends to individual family members in a nonjudgmental, caring, and empathic manner. Additionally, the person-centered family therapist attends to and reflects the family members' interaction patterns. The application of the person-centered method in the family milieu enables a natural and efficacious process that helps people become more fully functioning as both individuals and families. Thus, the theory and practice of person-centered family therapy offers promise for enhanced understanding of people, both individually and in concert.

REFLECTIONS ON THE SELF OF THE THERAPIST[1]

12

This above all: to thine own self be true,
And it must follow, as the night the day,
Thou canst not then be false to any man.
Shakespeare, *Hamlet.*

Introduction

Having engaged in psychotherapy endeavors as a student, therapist, and teacher of therapists for nearly half a century, I have become increasingly convinced that therapists are born and not made by teachers or theorists. The best that education and training programs can do is offer student therapists experience under conditions in which they may safely experiment with who they are and how they may proceed in the therapeutic engagement. Therapy training programs and their teachers are merely the whetstones on which novice therapists hone their instruments. Those instruments are the selves of the therapist.

Talent

When I review the records of applicants to our family therapy training program, I am always impressed but not surprised by what has impelled them to want to become therapists. Despite widely differing ages, backgrounds and routes to our program, virtually all of the candidates mention that friends and relatives have already gratefully identified the candidates as good listeners and helpful friends. They, in return, admit that they have felt rewarded and validated and consequently have developed an aspect of their sense of self that one might call *helper*. For most of them, the formulation of this helper subself (see Chapter 5) actually began relatively early in their lives and has been continuously reaffirmed by others through the applicant's teenage years and beyond.

I, therefore, find ironic the anguish-laden puzzlement and frustration that beginning therapists invariably experience when they attempt to apply that helper aspect of self to the early stages of work in the professional therapy setting.

1. First published as 'Reflections on the self of the therapist', in Hutterer, R., Pawlowsky, G., Schmid, P. and Stipsits, R., (Eds.). *Client-centered and experiential psychotherapy: a paradigm in motion.* Frankfurt: Peter Lang, (1996). Reprinted with permission of the editors and publishers.

Somehow, in trying to analyze and enhance apparently innate therapeutic abilities, they become awkward, stiff, and often paralyzed. Where once they were intuitively empathic and helpful active listeners with friends, novice therapists interacting with their first clients often feel lost and devoid of the talent that gave rise to their helper subself in the first place. At this point, these apprentice therapists often become discouraged and bereft of confidence in that very ability that had worked so well and unquestioningly for them in the past.

This often terrifying sense of impotence — the clumsiness and corresponding loss of confidence — in large measure derives from the nature of our training programs. We have established a worship of theory and prematurely attempted to make scientific that which has been, and still is, primarily an art. Our assiduous attention to *pure* theoretical orientations in training (for years eclecticism was considered a dirty word) forces students to lay themselves on Procrustean training beds.

Theory as truth

In most therapy training programs, students must dutifully subscribe and adhere to the one *true* method propounded by the given psychotherapy program's model and its advocates. By dutifully emulating their trainers, trainees (the term *trainee* as distinct from *student* is purposive here) master the techniques espoused by the model. Trainees are rewarded for conformity and criticized for deviance. Training differs from education in which students assimilate and integrate new knowledge via encouraged inquiry and dialogue that include and elicit contrasting points of view.

Our reverence for the right theory reflects the general defensiveness of the behavioral sciences, particularly with regard to psychotherapy. In an effort to make psychotherapeutic practice more a behavioral science and less a behavioral art, we press to validate the effectiveness of psychotherapy by constructing theories that are replete with idiosyncratic nomenclatures and exotic techniques.

The construction, elaboration, and testing of theory in the behavioral sciences are, indeed, laudable and necessary to the understanding of psychotherapy, its practice and enhancement. However, except for a relatively few basic premises integral to all modes of psychotherapy, most theories have proven, at best, incomplete. Furthermore, virtually all extant theoretical models have been found flawed when put to the empirical test: we continuously rediscover that psychotherapy, regardless of theoretical orientation, has about a 60 percent success rate (Lambert and Bergin, 1994). This figure is undoubtedly inflated, for we have also learned that when prospective clients are put on waiting lists, about half those waiting report feeling better over time without benefit of actual psychotherapy services.

Nevertheless, despite empirical findings, staunch advocates of various theoretical persuasions abound. Such theoretical allegiance undoubtedly arises initially from personal, successful experiential validation of a chosen theory. Later, it becomes entrenched by the continuous investment and commitment of one's professional self to that choice. Such choices, usually made early in professional training, are perhaps the most important decisions that therapists make. They include decisions about: which psychotherapeutic methods are specifically right for them; which ones do or do not fit the therapist's natural personal style; which do and do not feel comfortable; which do and do not seem to work. Thus, at least in the best of situations, psychotherapy training is a laboratory for continuous discovery of the self of the therapist which, more than method or techniques, is the instrument of change in the practice of psychotherapy.

The inherent qualities of therapists and their training

Most training programs conceptually understand and respect the importance of the therapist as tool and, correspondingly, emphasize self-understanding on the part of the therapist as a meaningful aspect of training. However, herein lies another hazard of training. Too often, programs believe they are promoting such self-understanding by requiring that all of their trainees submit to therapy.

Certainly, it is not a bad idea for therapists to undergo their own self-exploration and experience the therapeutic process from the vantage point of the client, but I am not convinced that it is necessary for this experience to occur solely within the context of formal professional psychotherapy. Although I treasured my own experience as client during my training (and believe it has enhanced my empathy as a therapist), I do not believe that all therapists must undergo therapy themselves in order to be good therapists.

Pernicious dangers lurk in the situation where training programs require that students process self-issues in front of other students and their trainers. Even when handled discretely, self-discovery mandated by training institutions is problematic. Forced therapy is a contradiction in terms — more often traumatic than therapeutic — and does more harm than good. The process of self-discovery is one which is growth producing only if the individual is, to some degree, in charge of the process.

On the other hand, many experienced therapists believe that, in the course of providing therapy to others, we continuously learn about ourselves, even as we learn about our clients. I remember being supervised by Carl Whitaker towards the end of my graduate internship at a state agency in Chicago serving children and families. I naively asked him how he knew when therapy was over. Without hesitating, he responded, 'when the therapist stops growing in the relationship'.

As practitioners, our central focus is, of course, the client. But as theorists and empiricists, a shift from the traditional emphasis on the client to the therapist may be in order to understand better the qualities of the therapist, regardless of therapeutic model, which facilitate therapeutic growth in both client and therapist.

The therapist in the hour: process elements of the self-system

Since the inception of both psychodynamic and behavior-oriented therapies, the presumption of scientific neutrality has dominated thought about the therapeutic relationship. In 1957, borrowing from Jessie Taft, Carl Rogers virtually shocked the psychotherapy community by making the interpersonal relationship between the client and therapist basic and focal to his theory of therapy. Basically, Rogers' conditions for change center on the empathic caring of the therapist for the client and, reciprocally, the client's recognition of these feelings as the engine of change behind the psychotherapy process.

Despite Rogers having established the therapist's *personhood* as a central element in his model for change, most of the research that emanated from his theory emphasized aspects of the client rather than those of the therapist. This client emphasis is true for virtually all other psychotherapy models as well. There has been relatively little research on how the personal qualities of therapists (viz. their aspects of self) affect their behavior and influence their clients in the therapy session. Recently, interest in this area has been growing.

Thirty years after his initial, simple statement regarding the condition of the therapist, in an informal interview with Baldwin (1987), Rogers discussed growing awareness of his use of himself — his person — in the therapy hour. Basically, these comments (well towards the end of his life) reflect an earlier notion that Rogers proffered regarding therapist genuineness or authenticity. From the very outset, what is clear to Rogers is that the therapist is fully present as a person in the therapeutic encounter, and that encounter is clearly an interpersonal relationship of two (or more) people engaging each other. The deeply interpersonal nature of the therapist-client relationship is unique to the person-centered philosophy.

Not at all clear, however, is Rogers' meaning of the presence of the therapist and the ramifications of that presence upon the client. The entire second chapter of *Client-Centered Therapy* (Rogers, 1951), although nominally dedicated to the personal qualities of the therapist, addresses only the therapist's ability to adhere to and maintain the classic necessary and sufficient conditions of nonjudgmental, empathic regard.[2]

---

2. Later, in Chapter Ten, on training therapists, Rogers returns to the idea of the personal qualities of the therapist. Here, too, however, he never describes or explores these qualities, but rather concurs with the APA list regarding *Who Should Be Selected for Training* (APA, 1947, pp. 434–5). The list of qualities follows:
1. Superior intellectual ability and judgement.
2. Originality, resourcefulness, and versatility.
3. 'Fresh and satiable' curiosity; 'self-learner'.
4. 'Interest in persons as individuals rather than as material for manipulation — a regard for the integrity of other persons.'
5. Insight into own personality characteristics; sense of humor.
6. Sensitivity to the complexities of motivation.
7. Tolerance: 'unarrogance'.
8. Ability to adopt a 'therapeutic' attitude; ability to establish warm and effective relationship with others.
9. Industry; methodical work habits; ability to tolerate pressure.
10. Acceptance of responsibility.
11. Tact and cooperativeness.
12. Integrity, self-control, and stability.
13. Discriminating sense of ethical values.
14. Breadth of cultural background — 'educated man'.
15. Deep interest in psychology, especially in its clinical aspects.

What are the qualities, attributes, or characteristics of therapists and the special nature of psychotherapeutic relationships that set them apart from other interpersonal relationships? First of all, the therapeutic relationship is highly circumscribed and artificially structured. Generally, (a) meetings are fixed at mutually agreed-upon beginning and ending times; (b) therapist-client social contact is limited to the prescribed hours; and (c) therapists are remunerated in some fashion for their time and skill.

Like few other relationships, there is an intensity and one-sidedness to the psychotherapeutic relationship. The well-being of the client virtually always takes precedence over the well-being of the therapist. To modify Buber (1937) slightly, the therapy relationship is intensely *Thou-I*. The therapist's feelings and emotions are backdrop to the service of the client. The focus or *center* is the client. Buber and later Friedman (1992) employ the word *inclusion* in lieu of Rogers' *empathy*. Inclusion by the therapist appears to mean a more intense stance than that of empathy and emphasizes the *I-Thou* relationship of Buber. Theologians are less awkward than behavioral scientists in using intimate terms to describe relationships.

The therapist's ability to risk being intimate, engage, or even to embrace the client *yet not make demands for reciprocity*, may be another important and little-understood feature of healing relationships. Thus, *love* according to Fromm (1956), wherein the well-being of the other takes precedent over one's own well-being may, indeed, be the appropriate word. Maybe it is time to examine the caring or loving nature of the therapist as an indigenous aspect of the psychotherapy process.

Along with unselfish caring, there is intensity of focus and concentration that make the therapist-client relationship unique and, with few exceptions, unsustainable in normal social intercourse. In the session, the therapist gives over his or her entire concentration to comprehending and helping the client understand his or her experiences and the feelings that surround them. These qualities of concentration and focus taken together with the caring nature of the therapist define the special *presence* of the therapist in the psychotherapy hour.[3]

There are qualities to this special presence that complement and articulate with an empathic stance. An attribute that distinguishes truly effective therapists from others is a unique self-awareness that can be called self-availability. That is, the therapist has a repertory of experienced subselves, any of which may awaken in response to clients recounting of their experiences. Thus, as I listen to a young client relate a hurtful engagement with a parent, I find I begin to *subceive* or sense in myself a parallel childhood encounter which evoked similar feelings within me. The word *sense* refers to the fact that I do not actively search my memory, but rather my focus on the client somehow elicits the recall which emerges along with some re-experiencing. The feelings, freshly revived, enable me to relate quite actively to the feelings the client reports experiencing. This special kind of memory or awareness breathes dimension into understanding and communicates itself to

---

3. The above qualities of the psychotherapeutic relationship have few parallels in social intercourse, those few being that of loving parent, and perhaps, loving mate. Such a parallel allows for the *transfer of training* (or *transference*) phenomenon, far more understandable.

the client as active experiential understanding — empathy.

Thus, not only is reliance on theory alone unhelpful in facilitating the therapy process, it actually may hinder it. In attending to theory rather than using it as an infrastructure, focus and concentration are drawn away from the client, and the therapist's self-availability in service of the client is supplanted by concern for theoretical validation. When working with beginning therapists, who are often hungry for theoretical principles and accompanying techniques, I put it to them this way:

> *Forget what you have learned and sharpen your listening skills. The*
> *client is the theory, and each client is different. Thus, your theory is*
> *constantly undergoing change. You are, therefore, to learn the theory*
> *from its source — the client in the hour. So, too, are you responsible*
> *for learning the client's language, not vice versa.*

Furthermore, I do not allow my students to plan the next session and I enjoin them not to review their videotapes or notes of previous sessions on the day of the forthcoming session with a given client. At first, these dicta tend to be distressing for beginning therapists who have spent much of their time steeping themselves in the theoretical methods and techniques of various models. Furthermore, such edicts can be particularly distressing because virtually all of the students' other professors and supervisors (my colleagues) insist upon a strategy and therapeutic plan for at least the next session.

Certainly my students and I debrief on sessions but never on the day of the client's succeeding session. The major reason for this is a relatively simple one that I discovered during my own training. Therapists, particularly eager beginners, are prone to over-focus on their clients' problems as revealed during a given hour. For the therapist, a specific problem too easily can become a fixed point of reference and often obfuscate the totality of the client's distress. People are far more intricate than just the sum of their problems; even the most distressing problems are only part of a complex life moving in various directions through time.

Listening to or discussing a previous hour tends to fix the issues of that hour in the therapist's mind. Entering a new session with a focus on the concerns of the previous hour can, like a preoccupation with theory, distract the therapist from being fully present for the client at any given moment. Regardless of the amount of time between sessions, the client has had a multitude of experiences outside the clinical hour. This is true even in classical psychoanalysis where session frequency can often be three to five times per week. Many of these new experiences may take precedence for clients over what was bothering them during the previous session (which, indeed, the client may have forgotten or even resolved). With the previous hour fresh in the therapist's mind, the new session begins with the therapist out of sync with the client's needs at that moment. Therefore, it behooves the therapist to let the client set the agenda: it is the therapist's job to follow the client, not vice versa.

In addition to the requirements that the therapist care and have empathy for the client, Rogers (1957) in his conditions for psychotherapeutic change (see also Chapters 9 and 10) adds that the therapist must be *congruent* within the therapy relationship. The ramifications of therapist congruence on the therapy process are vast. Therapist congruence implies that the many subselves of the therapist are integrated in such a way as to be accessible during the hour, enabling the therapist to listen, empathize, and respond to clients as they explore their own subself complex. Furthermore, in family therapy (as noted in Chapter 10), this particular meaning of congruence is of special importance. Here the therapist must be in touch with, not just one individual's world-view (composed of the subself amalgam) but the multiple and often conflicting world-views of various family members. To complicate the therapist's task, these world-views are often transtemporal and thus transgenerational.

The concept of therapist congruence also implies another quality: genuineness or authenticity. This quality adds to the aforementioned special presence, caring, concentration, and focus of the therapist in the hour. The therapist needs to be available: continuously in touch with his or her feelings and reactions to the client. Accordingly, if the therapist is congruent, integrated, fully present, and genuine, the therapist becomes intuitively free to react to the total person of the client. In this manner, the therapist's empathy for the client becomes heightened and shared meaning is enhanced. It is this process that gives clients perspective on their lives and increases their own sense of personhood through feelings of shared meaning with the therapist. These are the attributes — the availability of the therapist, the caring and focused presence, and the shared meaning within the relationship — that mitigate the existential despair and loneliness that often impel clients to seek therapy in the first place.

Presence

The therapist's concentration on and empathy for the client make the therapist something of a lens. This lens-like quality enables the client to focus internal processes that may have led to the client's incongruence, the discrepancy between experience and perception of self. Blurring and confusion of subselves and generalized anxieties have hampered the client's natural growth or actualizing processes. Assisted by the therapist's caring, concentration, focus and empathic reflection of feelings, the client's self-awareness is heightened and aspects of the client's self can emerge for re-experiencing and eventual self-integration.

Most therapists become aware of certain markers during the therapy session, places where the therapist's attention is piqued. One such marker is the client's self-judgment that seems to interfere with the client's self-exploratory process. Thus, a client in the process of exploring some incongruent behavior may say something like, 'I don't know why I do such crazy things — they make no sense, they just aren't like me, etc.' Therapists in their nonjudgmental stance act as models, their acceptance encouraging the client's explorations of self. Most importantly, these explorations should include those *ugly* or otherwise unacceptable aspects of self which tend to act as a kind of black hole, drawing energy away from the actualizing process either through over-attention or by attempts to suppress such aspects from awareness.

Especially during those times when the client is in an overly self-critical (and thus incongruent) mode, descriptive detail becomes a vital tool in aiding the therapist's and therefore the client's understanding of the client's incongruence and self-blame. Such circumstances are generally situation specific, and clients typically note they cannot remember the details of a given incident. However, the therapist's empathy can facilitate experiential recounting (often through the elicitation of some small particular), and additional details begin to surface with exquisite minutiae and vivid clarity, often to the client's surprise. This unfolding of detail is usually accompanied by the sensation of relief, much like that experienced when a long-mislaid object is finally recovered.

Herein lie some of the elements requisite to the experiencing and re-experiencing of a given event. There is a sense of ordering that is prelude to the internal integration of the experience in a new manner.[4] Working with couples and/or families makes such ordering and re-experiencing clear. The couple often begins recounting a heated disagreement that was hurtful to both. Typically there will be a difference of opinion attended with confusion and puzzlement as to how the disagreement began. For me this is a marker. At such times I ask the couple to 'back up the tape' to a point somewhere before the dispute occurred. Generally what happens is aspects of some barely subceived umbrage are unearthed. Somehow (for a variety of reasons) the remembered dispute had eclipsed the previous intrapersonal and interpersonal incongruence. Such re-experiencing and reintegration are generally followed by a sense of discovery, relief, and lightening of the mood and gravity of the schism, not infrequently accompanied by amazement and laughter. Invariably the discovery leads to a revelation of additional subtle difficulties within the relationship that can be dealt with in the therapy. Though often less apparent during individual therapy, the sense of relief in resolving an intrapersonal incongruence is the same.

The parameters and ethics of self-disclosure

With regard to the impact of the personhood of the therapist on the therapy process, perhaps no one concept causes more anxiety for practitioners, theorists, and even researchers than that of self-disclosure wherein therapists share aspects of themselves with clients. (No matter how opaque or neutral one claims to be, there are always aspects of self that are disclosed, even to the casual observer.) The question is how much to disclose and when and why. I continuously struggle with how much of myself is appropriate to share with my clients and why and when I feel impelled to do so.

The obvious danger of self-disclosure is that it may lead to abuse of the client as discussed in Chapter 10. I define abuse of the client as that moment when the

---

4. This process is not unlike those of *assimilation* and *accommodation* discussed by Piaget (1963). Their relevance to the therapy hour is elaborated upon by Wexler (1974).

therapist's feelings for the client, either positive or negative, take the focus off the client and onto the therapist and, consequently, the activities of the therapist become self rather than client serving. The pursuit of therapist genuineness and transparency should never be construed as a license to use the client.

The most flagrant abuse of the client is as a sexual object. Clients, no matter how needy they may be for physical intimacy, are never well served by having their psychotherapist as a sexual partner. Thus, if a therapist is sexually attracted to a client, it behooves the therapist to search inside him or herself to discern the meaning of those feelings. In certain situations this search may warrant outside consultation, the use of a co-therapist and, if these steps are not sufficient, open and direct discussion between therapist and client, followed by referral to another therapist.

In maximizing one's self as the tool in therapy, responsible congruent therapists need to discern if they are bringing feelings incongruent with the therapeutic stance to the session or if, in some manner, the client is evoking them. Generally, in such circumstances, a complex combination of therapist and client interactive factors exists. Seasoned self-aware therapists will recognize their incongruence in situations that kindle strong personal responses. With continuous acknowledgment that the safety of the client is foremost, most can resolve their incongruence without use of disclosure. Furthermore, these circumstances, if dealt with properly, provide a powerful source of information that may facilitate the process of therapy.

Since the natural stance of the client is one of nonjudgmental caring, even mild dislike of a client is suspect. When I sense any alienation in myself towards the client — even something so little as my attention drifting — I generally find it mitigated by exerting greater concentration and empathic focus on the client(s).[5] Strong negative feelings such as anger, disgust, or disdain in response to a given client require even closer scrutiny and attention. Clients, no matter how interpersonally provocative and abrasive, are never deserving of verbal abuse by their therapists. It would seem gratuitous to add that physical abuse should be beyond the realm of the therapist's interactive repertoire.

Examples of therapists meeting their personal needs (e.g., intimacy, control) in the process of working with clients are generally obvious to all therapists except those who are severely incongruent and by definition do not fit the conditions of being facilitative of their clients' growth. A therapist's construction that such acts are performed in the service of his or her clients is indicative of the therapist's self-deception and corresponding incongruence.

More difficult to discern are the less obvious and more subtle forms of therapists' self-disclosure and their potential impact on clients. At some level, our style and the way we comport ourselves (our speech, smile, and the manner in which we dress) convey something about us and are, therefore, at some level, self-disclosing.

---

5. Difficulties with negative reactions are quite rare for me in individual therapy. However, in working with families I do sometimes find myself troubled by parents' offensive reactions to their children and struggle with how to deal with these feelings.

Consequently the more therapists are truly and utterly themselves, i.e., congruent in the therapy hour, the less confusing and abusive are they to their clients.

Nevertheless, no matter how congruent and integrated therapists may be, they will still encounter their own incongruences during therapy with clients. Often less dramatic and more transitory than sexual attraction or anger, a therapist may experience subtle incongruences either in relationship to a client with whom a therapist normally maintains congruence or with a given client who presents specific problems which elicit incongruent feelings within the therapist.

In 1990 I attended a workshop given by a very talented colleague at the annual meeting of the Association for the Development of the Person-Centered Approach (ADPCA).[6] The subject of the workshop was therapist incongruence, and the leader of the workshop reported on a client about whom she truly cared but with whom she was beginning to have trouble maintaining concentration. She felt increasingly bored as the client related happenings from his past. The therapist searched for a reason within herself. The client had rarely bored her for such a protracted period before. Yet despite her continuing efforts, she reported being unable to focus her concentration on the client. Finally, she gently and tenderly disclosed her feelings, took full ownership of them (i.e., did not blame the client for boring her) and noted that this response to the client was highly unusual.

The workshop leader then described how, in response to this self-disclosure, the client smiled good-naturedly and admitted that he did not think that what he was telling her about had much relevance to his concerns. However, because his previous therapist had considered the issues extremely important, the client thought it obligatory to share the incidents with her. In this case it became clear that the therapist's incongruence was a direct reflection of the incongruence of the client. The clearing of the air coupled with profound warmth, gentleness, and caring by the therapist allowed for an enhancement of the therapeutic relationship which in turn enabled the therapy to lift from a long-standing plateau.

The presumption that a good therapist is a unidimensional, unwavering paragon of caring, nonjudgmental, empathic understanding is not only inaccurate, it obfuscates valuable data regarding the instrument of the therapist. The ability to suspend judgment, care unconditionally, and remain intensely focused while conveying an understanding of the client's deepest meanings is the ideal from which we all deviate to some degree all of the time. With whom, how, when, why, and to what degree we stray from this ideal therapeutic stance can tell us much about the nature of therapists and the therapeutic process. Indeed, such questions form the foundation of my consultations with students.

When a student reports foundering or struggling with a client, I first ask 'Do you like this client?' and, depending upon the answer, then ask 'Why?' or 'Why not?' The answers to these questions invariably yield important information regarding the therapist, the client, and the nature of each idiosyncratic therapeutic

---

6. I am indebted to Jenny Biancardi for sharing this experience with me and for allowing me to report it here.

relationship. They shed light on the subtle intricacies of the intra- and interpersonal congruences of the relationship. The process of discovery thereby engendered enriches therapists' understanding of themselves as a unique and dynamic instrument in the therapy relationship and obviates the need for self-disclosure.

The therapist's environment

The therapist's environment is a related, even subtler and rarely discussed extension of therapist style and self-disclosure. This overlooked and important element of environmental ambience has proven to be a key issue in my own congruence during therapy sessions and, I believe, an equally important one to my clients.

In my early training I was fortunate. The Counseling and Psychotherapy Research Center at the University of Chicago granted its advanced interns their own offices. Indeed, each of the half-dozen or so of us was given $50.00 (at that time a worthy sum) to decorate our offices. For most of us, it meant putting a coat of paint on the decrepit oak desks and chairs and perhaps buying a rug, desk lamp, or curtains. Our offices became a sort of home for each of us, each quite different and a reflection of our personal styles.

I felt comfortable and secure in my little niche, as did my colleagues in theirs. Interestingly, I remember the therapy hours there vividly, in contrast to those of my internship the previous year at a state agency in Chicago. There, each therapist (including the senior staff) used common interviewing rooms on the second floor. Each had working offices on the floor above, so the need to conserve space was not an issue. Rather, this agency reflected its psychodynamic values regarding the clinical neutrality of its environment. By contrast, the University Counseling Center reflected its emphasis on the person and the personal. I do not think these policies were ever really consciously strategized by the staff of the two institutions but, rather, were a natural extension of their respective models and general orientations.

To this day, I find I do better therapy in my own personal environment. I lament the fact that our clinic at Maryland cannot afford the luxury of enabling our students to design an ambience more reflective of who they are so that their clients may benefit additionally from having their therapists feel truly at home in their environments. A small issue, perhaps, but one worthy of further exploration

In selecting materials for an office in which to engage children, I believe it is important for therapists to examine their own comfort levels in order to maintain congruence. When working with children, I have never been comfortable using plastic assembly models, overly competitive games, or a sandbox. Therapy rooms in many children's clinics include many of these materials de rigueur in an effort to enable the children to express themselves fully. My belief is that each therapist-child pairing is unique: if certain play materials compromise the therapist's congruence, they should not be used.

A small pilot study (Gaylin, Grebe, McCarrick, Millstein, and Werlinich, 1988) adds some credibility to this notion of therapeutic ambience. In this study conducted by a group of therapists, a consistent finding among clients seen in private practice was that they were very aware of and sensitive to the ambience of their therapists' offices. As one client noted, 'If she [the therapist] can't take care of her plants, what kind of care will she take of me?'

I have noted that the small garden that adjoins my office (and is my personal place of solace) attracts much attention from my clients. Not only do they comment about it, they will often arrive early and stroll or sit there before sessions. Sometimes, they will linger there after our session together. My garden is clearly an extension of my office, and it is clearly a reflection of me. It communicates something about me to my clients. It pleases me, both in and of itself as well and for the pleasure that it brings to others.

Just as I take joy in sharing the pleasures of my garden, I often will share relatively mundane things about myself with my clients. I have my degrees posted on my walls; it is no secret that I have a family. There are traces of the others who share my life throughout my environment. This is a form of self-disclosure that I believe humanizes and balances the therapist-client relationship. In many respects, I enjoy breaking the professional barrier that I believe many of us hide behind. Certainly I have boundaries and I believe they are clear. My clients respect them, as I respect theirs.

Conclusion

Healers of the soul and spirit (later to become the psyche) existed long before the age of psychology. Before the age of psychological *enlightenment* and the scientific era, these healers (e.g., prophets, priests, and shamans) were considered divinely inspired. In other words, they were believed to have *gifts* — talents beyond ordinary men and women. Although these individuals usually apprenticed under masters, they were considered *chosen* for such training.

Despite our present enlightenment, the situation today differs little. Although our metaphors have changed, those who are called to the helping professions are most probably impelled to do so by natural talents augmented by positive experiences in dealing with others: they like people; people like them. They are considered by themselves and others to be good listeners and, perhaps most important, they genuinely care for others.

Many attributes of potential psychotherapists are those traits listed by Rogers as the 'characteristics of the helping relationship', (Rogers, 1958). These characteristics, by and large, parallel Rogers' 'necessary and sufficient conditions' (Rogers, 1957) but go beyond them somewhat by exploring the notion of therapist congruence. Genuineness, transparency and overall personhood of the therapist become focal issues.

In our search for understanding the restorative nature of psychotherapy we have followed the medical tradition, focusing on either the *illness* and/or its repository, *the patient*. Perhaps it is time to focus on the restorative power of the client-therapist relationship, with particular emphasis on the integrated nature and self of the therapist.

IPSATIVE MEASURES: IN SEARCH OF PARADIGMATIC CHANGE AND A SCIENCE OF SUBJECTIVITY[1]

13

The empiricist . . . thinks he believes only what he sees, but he is much better at believing than at seeing.
Santayana, *Skepticism and Animal Faith.*

Introduction

For over a century the behavioral sciences have followed the tradition of twentieth century physical science and have attempted to develop a paradigm based upon objective and normative criteria. Although such a model is useful for sociologists trying to understand aggregate human behavior, the normative paradigm often falls short for psychologists endeavoring to study the behavior of individuals, couples, and families — particularly in a psychotherapy context. The human condition is that of the individual experience within the interpersonal or social context. As such, it demands scrutiny as the study of subjectivity and of shared meanings.

The *ipsative* is an alternative to the normative model and is gateway to a science of subjectivity. This chapter explores the advantages of the paradigmatic shift from the use of a normative to an ipsative-based model for examining human behavior. A science of subjectivity needs to view the individual in the context of the culture and thus needs also to include a concept of shared meanings. These ideas are particularly relevant to the study of psychotherapeutic change and emanate naturally from the person-centered approach.

Behavioral science in search of a paradigm

The physical scientist, Thomas Kuhn (1970), in his often cited essay on the history and development of science, has suggested that the social sciences are at the same kind of watershed that the natural sciences were 200 years ago. Social science observations are elaborate and extensive, but the models we have been employing to organize and analyze these observations are inadequate for the task of building a comprehensive understanding of human behavior. Kuhn notes that the social sciences have borrowed models or *paradigms* from the natural sciences — perhaps

---

1. First published in *The Person Centered Review, 4* (4), 429–45, (1989), Sage. Reprinted by permission of the Editor and publishers.

inappropriately so. Despite the validity of his observations, Kuhn offers few suggestions or alternatives.

This situation is perhaps most frustrating for those of us working clinically within the applied behavioral sciences. It is we who face the intra- and interpersonal anguish of our clients and struggle to find efficacious methods for facilitating change. Our negative-result studies are weighed in terms of human misery. Perhaps, as Albee (1970) has suggested, the clinician is a craftsman rather than a scientist, and the duality of craftsmanship and empiricism cannot exist simultaneously in the same individual. This stance (with which I adamantly disagree) is reflective of the tension between the clinical (translated as *art*) and the empirical (translated as *science*) aspects of psychotherapy. Such duality may result, in part, from the intellectual ecology of the twentieth century, which tended to view science as the salvation of humankind. We generally see the twentieth century as the fulmination of advanced technology via scientific discovery. Ironically, as the twentieth century drew to a close, we questioned the infallibility of technological science as it applied to the interpersonal aspects of our lives. With the dawning of the second millennium, perhaps we may be ready for a more person-centered or ipsative science of behavior to complement the normative approaches of the past.

On the nature of inquiry

Our species, more than any other on this planet, is unique: we have the ability to conceptualize our universe. That conceptualizing process requires and is enabled by our ability to categorize objects and events. Learning and the knowledge that is accrued in the learning process — everything from religion and philosophy to astrophysics, molecular biology, and family therapy — require a three-stage process: first observation and description, then categorization and nomenclature, and finally conceptualization of general principles.

Humankind by nature is a symmetrical, bilateral organism, and perhaps because of this, dichotomously orders its universe in dualities: male/female, right/left, good/bad, etc. Indeed, much attention has been given to the ramifications of the *bicameral* (i.e., left/right) nature of our brains on the way we perceive, think, and behave (Jaynes, 1976). One of the more complex dualities of human existence is the fact that we have both a social and an individual nature. That is, although our survival depends on our social or group orientation, our ability to shape our own behavior and respond idiosyncratically is integral to each human being's uniqueness. The duality makes the behavioral sciences different from just about any other branch of science and makes the study of ourselves by ourselves both fascinating and frustrating. Furthermore, in perhaps no other branch of the applied behavioral sciences are the dualities more germane than in the understanding and practice of psychotherapy in general and family therapy more specifically. Herein the interplay between intra- and interpersonal dynamics converges in an intimate social ecology which shuttles continuously between the rational and nonrational. It is just these complexities which require the family therapist to be simultaneously both artist and scientist (see L'Abate, 1985).

When studying ourselves, we are at our scientific best when we are studying our basic physical and biological parameters (e.g., height, weight, body temperature) and our subcortical, more animal-like behaviors (e.g., respiration, pulse rate, reflexes). We are most inept when it comes to the study of that which is uniquely human: (a) our ability to synthesize ideas which engenders our creativity, and (b) our attitudes and feelings which both create and are a result of our social nature.

The natural sciences (both physical and biological) now rely virtually entirely on absolute and normative measures and the methodologies they employ. Statistical inference enables predictive validity, the ultimate goal of science. Thus, by dint of repetitive observations, the scientist can make an *if-then* statement with a given degree of certainty. For example, one may predict (according to Boyle's law) how gases in a chamber will react to a change in temperature. More generally, by keeping certain variables constant and changing others, it is possible to predict how given elements in our environment will react. Such generalization of natural rule or law requires numerous observations under varying conditions. This approach is both absolute and normative in the sense that there are expectable phenomena measured in fixed terms (e.g., volume, pressure) and observed under defined normal conditions (e.g., temperature, altitude).

Normative measures have proven appropriate for certain aspects of the human condition, notably physical and biologically based variables. Thus, for example, when we obtain absolute measures on numerous individuals' physical characteristics such as height, weight, temperature, etc., we then aggregate and average the measures into group norms and make comparative statements about an individual's standing in relation to the group. Rarely, however, does the complexity of human behavior afford us, except under the narrowest limits, the luxury of comparative statements with regard to specific acts of the individual. With most animals, for example, one may assume with relative certainty that its drinking is in response to physiologically based thirst.[2] With a human being, however, even the simple act of drinking (although associated with physiological thirst) may be also the product of many psychological motivations: boredom, anxiety, sociability, etc. The problem is most accentuated when we attempt to generalize complex human behavior to the point of generating predictive validity for the behavior of a given individual or the complex interactions within a family. An extreme example would be the ability to predict the likelihood of a particular individual's attempting suicide within a given family context.

The more we aggregate the behavior of individuals, the more reliably we may predict the actions and performances of the group. For example, Emile Durkheim (1951), working from population statistics, developed his theory of anomie by examining the suicide rate of the French under varying conditions over time. He was therefore able to make general statements regarding the social and economic

---

2. One of the few interesting exceptions to this observation is the behavior of *domesticated* animals (i.e., cats and dogs) who will drink when anxious.

conditions under which suicide would be more likely to occur. By and large, within the behavioral sciences, sociologists (by definition) do not deal with individual behavior. They have been concerned virtually entirely with aggregate human behavior. Indeed, years ago it was fashionable for some sociologists to state provocatively, 'there is no such thing as a psychological fact'. Despite the umbrage that many of us working with individual behavior took at that comment, the statement is true as far as it goes.

Given the universal rules of science that we presently accept (i.e., a set of ordered postulates that parsimoniously accounts for all observations and thus enables predictability), we have little scientific theory or predictive validity for complex individual human behavior. Even behaviorists would agree that although one might reliably anticipate that a given individual will salivate on the presentation of a tasty morsel, it is quite another matter to predict that that same individual will attempt suicide under duress. Therefore with regard to complex psychological human behaviors we 'have no facts', Such a conclusion hardly affords comfort to those of us who work in the applied behavioral sciences — those of us who provide psychotherapy.

Ipsative versus normative measurement techniques

For the applied behavioral scientist who must evaluate, effect, and ideally predict changes in both behavior and attitude over time and/or through the introduction of programmatic variables such as education or treatment, one of the most important and overlooked techniques is the use of *ipsative* as opposed to normative measuring devices. The term *ipsative* was created and delineated by Cattell (1944) during the golden era of the development of personality theory in clinical psychology, psychiatry, and social work.[3] It was Stephenson (1953) who expanded and operationalized the concept through Q technique and methodology into a larger conceptualization — the scientific study of subjectivity. But until recently the concept never garnered much support.[4]

As conceived by Cattell, ipsative measures are those in which the referent is the individual rather than the population. This approach does not compare the individual to the group, nor make comparisons among groups of individuals. Its emphasis is the subjective viewpoint of the individual rather than the supposed objective vantage-point of the group or observers. Ipsative measures were not designed to determine an individual's standing or relationship to a given population, but they can ferret out certain attitudinal differences and changes within the individual. They are often relatively straightforward, simple to administer, easy

---

3. 'The term *ipsative* (Latin *ipse* = he, himself) is suggested as a convenient one for designating scale units relative to other measurements on the person himself . . . ' (Cattell, 1944, p. 294).

4. Despite their potential, surprisingly little has been written on ipsative techniques and their applicability to the study of behavior. When I first reviewed the literature a decade ago, I found only a handful of references since Cattell first introduced the term in 1944 (e.g., Cattell, 1951, 1957, 1958; Clemens, 1966; and Olson and Gravatt, 1968). A recent web search, however, revealed a number of unpublished studies (i.e., theses and dissertations) that may indicate renewed interest.

for the applied researcher and the lay public to understand, and often more relevant than normative measures in many applied situations. Ipsative devices can also be fun for research participants to use and interpret; therefore they can be employed as educative devices themselves, offering feedback to the participants in research.

Ipsative techniques and the Q-Sort

There are a number of evaluative instruments that employ an ipsative approach and many normative devices could easily be adapted to ipsative use. One of the most interesting, useful and paradigmatic ipsative measures is Stephenson's Q-sort technique (1953). Stephenson's methodological and statistical procedures are of interest, but space limits their elaboration here (the reader is referred to Stephenson, 1953 and Brown, 1993). The conceptualization, rationale, and technique are of greater import for the present discussion.

Stephenson came to psychology from that most *objective* of sciences, physics. Perhaps chagrined that his work had found little fertile soil in the nearly fifty years since he first propounded Q methodology, one of his last works (1980) is couched in the language of physics. '"Newton's Fifth Rule" gives priority to induction and subjectivity and leads to the conclusion that each person's own subjectivity is potentially more knowledgeable, by nature, than almost anyone has dared to believe', (1980, p. 882). Stephenson's invocation of the name of Newton (the father of modern science) is a powerful metaphor for the resistance he perceives in the behavioral sciences in accepting the subjective as a legitimate focus of inquiry.

Perhaps more than any other empiricist in modern psychology, Stephenson comes to grips with the question of epistemology in an operational, pragmatic manner. He directly attacks the centrality of the concept of consciousness in modern psychology as perhaps counterproductive or, at least, deflective in attempting to understand human motivation and interaction. Instead he introduces a word coined by Lewis (1967), *consciring*. Consciring means shared meaning. Consciring, or understanding through subjective interaction, creates a view of reality that is basically different from that created by a concept of consciousness which suggests a world of objective reality.[5]

Through this relatively simple view, Stephenson presents a revolutionary tool with which to study human interaction. It is a tool of a subjective, inductive, hypothesis generating (i.e., ipsative) science of behavior rather than that of an objective, deductive hypothesis testing (i.e., normative) one. Such a conceptualization creates a bridge between the person and the group that at the same time allows for the possibility of understanding intimate and intricate

---

5. As Stephenson (1980) notes, the concept of individual consciousness is a relatively new social invention dating back, perhaps, only 400–500 years. There is considerable evidence (Aries, 1962; Jaynes, 1976, that the idea of an individual consciousness was preceded by a far longer period of group consciousness. In a current exploration of these ideas, Sampson (1988) proposes as more explanatory of the human condition, the idea of 'ensembled' as opposed to 'self-contained' individualism.

interpersonal dynamics that comprise human interactions. Explication of the technique itself may serve to elucidate the ideas behind it.

Using the Q-Sort with individuals

Q-sorts consist of a number of items (either pictures or statements) that generally are self-referent, such as: 'I feel hopeless', 'I am optimistic', 'I am afraid of what others think about me'. Although the number of items may vary from as few as 12 to as many as 100 statements, most sorts are composed of 40–100 written statements.

One of the earliest and perhaps most productive applications of Q-sort technique to research in individual psychotherapy was conducted by Butler and Haigh (1954). The Butler-Haigh sort consisted of 100 self-referent statements culled from audio tape recordings of individual psychotherapy sessions. The sort was accomplished in two phases (although more could have been done). First, individuals were asked to sort selectively the total number of descriptive items, in a forced normal distribution from most like the way that they perceived themselves to least like the way they perceived themselves. This task was performed on a specially designed sorting-frame with individual spaces provided for the cards, each of which contained one of the 100 descriptive phrases called *descriptors*. (Although not absolutely necessary, data handling is made easier when these spaces are arranged in a normal distribution.) Next, the same individuals performed another sort with the same cards, but this time according to their ideal aspirations for themselves. Thus, the same descriptors were used to derive a *real self* and an *ideal self* profile for each individual. An index of association between individuals' actual perceptions of themselves and their ideal aspirations for themselves was then calculated from the two sorts. Butler and Haigh referred to this association as the *self-ideal correlation*. However, since the derivation does not follow all the rules required to calculate a correlation coefficient, some investigators have suggested the measure might instead (more appropriately) be called a *score* (see van der Veen, 1965). Regardless of label, what is obtained is an index of the individual's degree of self-satisfaction or dissatisfaction. More simply put, using Stephenson's Q technique, Butler and Haigh quantified an individual's self-esteem.

Butler and Haigh administered these Q-sorts before and after psychotherapy to clients at the University of Chicago Counseling and Psychotherapy Research Center. They discovered that self-ideal scores increased significantly (i.e., real and ideal matched more closely) for clients who experienced successful psychotherapy; for those who experienced low or no success, scores did not change. As might be anticipated, individuals who experienced successful psychotherapy shifted in their *real* self-descriptions towards those of their ideal. However, individuals (one from the other) may vary considerably with respect to that which they consider to be their real or ideal self, yet still display the same degree of satisfaction or Q-sort score. In this process and analysis of the Q-sort, there was no normative or standard ideal to which the individual was compared. Each client was his or her own self-referent regarding the measure of self-esteem.

In a later report of this study, Butler dealt with the concept of a *common ideal*. The aggregate of the ideal sorts he reported, 'remained remarkably stable over therapy for the clients (and) also for research controls' (Butler, 1972, p. 168). How can the concept of an ipsative, subjective methodology be reconciled with the concept of a *common ideal*? Note what Butler has done. He has shifted from an ipsative to a normative approach to his data. Both findings can and do exist simultaneously. It is like saying that there are broad similarities among all human beings when they are looked at in groups, yet subtle though distinct differences exist among all individuals when they are focused upon as individuals. But it should be emphasized that the data are still based upon the *subjective* perceptions of individuals. Butler's later findings point out not so much the superiority of the ipsative over the normative approach (or vice versa) but rather the complementary nature of the two approaches. Considering both the social and individual nature of the human organism, it would seem desirable to retain the advantages of both approaches, particularly when one is concerned about individual and group (e.g., family) change.·

What is discovered through factor analysis of various groups' *ideal* Q-sorts is that there is a factor loading (i.e., cluster of descriptors) that accounts for the similarities among individuals' *ideal* sorts. However, although this factor accounts for a percentage of the communality, it does not account for all of it. There is a significant amount of communality, yet sufficient variability among the *ideals* that they simultaneously display similarities and uniquenesses. More simply put, the comparison of *ideal* Q-sorts indicates both ipsative and normative qualities.

Ipsative measures in interpersonal contexts

In the study of intrapsychic phenomena, ipsative measures seem a natural choice, but it is in the interpersonal arena that ipsative and normative evaluations complement each other to form an advantageous merger. The field of marriage and family therapy seems to be a natural laboratory for this merging. However, research on marriage and family therapy has been plagued by the same kinds of difficulties, frustrations, and equivocal results as those of individual therapy (see Gurman and Kniskern, 1981; Jacobson, 1985; and Kniskern, 1985). Undoubtedly, the methodologies employed in both individual and family therapy research have derived from the same traditional investigative paradigms with similar less-than-satisfactory outcomes.

The idea of a combined ipsative and normative investigative and/or assessment approach affords exciting possibilities in marriage and family therapy research. We all enter marriage with expectations. Some are met; some are not. These congruities and incongruities may indeed define each couple's, as well as each spouse's, marital satisfaction or its converse, dissatisfaction. Analysis from these perspectives would constitute an ipsative approach. Thus one might ask a husband and wife to sort from a given concourse what each perceives their marriage to be (*actual marriage*) and also what each would like it to be (*ideal marriage*). A marriage or family-oriented Q-Sort might include such items as: 'I am honest with my spouse', 'We argue a lot', 'As a couple, we keep to ourselves'. Note, however, that in the case of a couple's evaluation of their own marriage, one extends the ipsative concept from an intrapersonal to an interpersonal one. The locus of evaluation is still ipsative in that each partner determines for him or herself what constitutes the experience and the aspiration. But now, in addition to getting a measure of intrapersonal congruence regarding the union (i.e., actual compared with ideal marriage) one may also compare the couple's actual perception of that marriage (husband's perceived actual/wife's perceived actual) and, at the same time, compare the couple's aspirations (husband's conceived ideal/wife's conceived ideal). In turn, this technique could be extended to the partners' perceptions of each other (see Luckey, 1961) and to families (see van der Veen, 1965).

Interestingly, it seems that partner satisfaction with the marriage (by definition an ipsative concept) is a natural means by which to evaluate the marital relationship as is demonstrated by the number of studies which have employed this approach (see Lewis and Spanier, 1979). Despite the application of ipsative concepts (e.g., happiness, satisfaction, congruence) to the study of marriage, they have found little favor in the study of either individuals or families. With both individuals and families, emphasis has tended to remain on the normative (e.g., the *healthy* or *adjusted* person or family type and their converses). Somehow, with the birth of the child and the creation of family from marriage, we focus more on normative considerations.

The family introduces the child to the society. The shared meanings of the parents are conveyed to the child and help shape the child's view of the universe — including the child's view of self. Thus, within the family there is an amalgam of subjectivities by which each person's view of him/herself and the world around him/her are shaped, at least in part. One might conjecture that the chances of having an adaptable, relatively happy individual develop may in some way be contingent upon the individual congruence of the parents and their joint congruence in shaping an environment for their developing family. Thus, each newborn's approach to the world (the manner in which reality is perceived) cannot help being filtered, at first, through the individual and combined subjective perceptions of those interacting with the infant in the immediate environment (i.e., parents, siblings, extended family and friends).[6]

The very basic relationship of the concept of subjectivity to family therapy theory, practice, and research is becoming a central issue for dialogue among practitioners and theorists in the field. From the therapy practice issues of working with families of differing subcultures (McGoldrick, Pearce, and Giordano, 1982) to the more abstract discussions of aesthetics (Allman, 1982; Keeney, 1983) and epistemology or *world-view* (Dell, 1982; Keeney and Sprenkle, 1982) the importance and appropriateness of subjective determinants to the study of family interaction and change have become focal. Indeed, all of the theories of

---

6. This assumes that each newborn enters the world with basic perceptual faculties relatively intact (note the normative suggestion: see Thomas and Chess, 1977).

communication deal with the basic question of shared subjectivity or shared meaning — *consciring*.

Despite the recent attention given to the importance of subjective knowing and interaction (e.g., White, 1995; Anderson, 1997), ipsative research in family therapy is dated and relatively rare (some notable exceptions are those of Luckey, 1961; van der Veen, 1965; and Cartwright, 1972). The reasons for this lack of enthusiasm are undoubtedly multicausal. One of the more obvious is that ipsative (Q) methodology, i.e., the study of subjective meaning, although no more complicated than that of its normative counterpart (R methodology), has never really been accepted by behavioral science researchers (see Brown, 1972; and Rozeboom, 1972).[7] But, indeed, that answer begs the question.

Why, then, has Q methodology never been accepted? In part the answer lies in our confusion with regard to basic questions of what psychotherapy — individual, group, or family — is really all about. These are the same concerns that individual psychotherapy practitioners, theorists, and researchers attempted to address over a generation ago (discussed in Chapter 6). What is normal? What is abnormal? What is mental health? What is mental illness? Answers to these questions have never been agreed upon, and they continue to haunt us. The retilling of the soil through the birth and growth of family therapy raises the questions again, this time in perhaps more fertile soil. The answers will demand a real paradigmatic shift in research approach, regardless of the therapeutic milieu.

Some concluding thoughts

The basic issues are whether to use a normative, adjustment-oriented, illness-health model or an ipsative, adaptive-oriented, well-being framework in the study of human behavior. Originally the argument was couched in the health versus illness context; prevailing normative psychology resulted in a pathology-oriented framework. Such generative forerunners as Allport (1955), Hartmann (1958), Jahoda (1958), Maslow (1962), Rogers (1961), Schachtel (1959) and Szasz (1960) all attempted to conceptualize a shift from an illness to a health model in psychological theory and practice. Although the positive approaches proffered by these theorists undoubtedly modified the way we thought about psychological development, we were still left with normatively based methods for assessing human behavior and a psychotherapy of psychopathology. Although mental health should imply a state of being more robust than that which is suggested by the mere absence of mental illness, we have been trained to see these concepts as simple reciprocals. In an attempt at reconceptualization (in Chapter 6) I proposed the alternative phrase, *psychological well-being* and paired it with a concept of *creativeness* in an effort to shift and refocus the goals of the psychotherapeutic endeavor.

---

7. '. . . the Q-methodology . . . studies a population of items in order to characterize an individual, the R-methodology . . . studies a population of people to see how they compare on some item' (Olson and Gravatt, 1968, p.13).

Since there is no ideal to aim for, no concretely specified or universally agreed upon ideal *healthy* state to which we direct ourselves and our clients, then it is the clients — the consumers themselves — who must decide. The ultimate test is our clients' satisfaction: Does therapy enable them to feel better? Of course feeling better is complicated; it involves feeling better about the details of one's interpersonal, loving, nurturing, professional and sexual life; kinship and friendship relations; childrearing; work; etc. But these life-span activities and aspirations can all be broken down, addressed, and researched. Such a process is exactly what goes on in the therapy hour. And such examination is exactly what makes the therapist the natural inductive researcher in the ipsative mode. If not addressing individual aspirations, the family therapist is working with family goals (which may also have mutually exclusive individual goals imbedded).

More importantly, ipsative thinking raises and resolves an issue with which family systems therapy has traditionally struggled. Systems therapists (e.g., Haley, 1963; Hoffman, 1971; Jackson, 1967; Rabkin, 1977) are often critical of others for not seeing and/or relating to the system as a whole. Although there is obvious truth to this notion of holism, to understand the interactive ecosystem as a whole one must gain entrée to that system's *consciring*: the shared (and conflicting) meanings and values of the individuals within that system. Thus, whatever terminology one uses (e.g., *congruence*, *reframing*, *detriangling*, etc.) the family therapist must shuttle back and forth between understanding the intra and interpersonal congruities and incongruities that are presented during the family therapy hour. More finely tuned congruence within each individual member positively effects the integrity of the system as a whole, and more broadly developed interpersonal congruence reciprocally affects intrapersonal congruence.

Expanding the view to a larger systems context, long and short-term aims of the therapeutic process generally must be in balance with the norms of society. There are exceptions, rare instances when the individual or system is healthier than the larger group, (as was the case, for example, in Nazi Germany when the collective subjectivity — the norm — was sick). That norm was then, in turn, subjectively assessed according to the shared meaning of many other individuals and found incongruent with the collective subjectivity of the rest of the world. Thus shared subjectivity gives all human systems, i.e., families, communities, cultures, etc., a sense of intimacy, safety, warmth, and trust. When these systems do not have this shared meaning there is incongruence and therefore stress. These cause family breakdown, divorce, even revolution and civil war.

Conclusion

Thus to be human is to be subjective; to be an examiner of human behavior is to know that normative and ipsative appraisals are synergistic — complementary rather than conflicting scientific approaches. Science has three components: subjective (ipsative), collective (normative) and absolute (universal). In the search for the last, we must never lose sight of the importance and interdependence of the first two.

The concept of *consciring*, or shared meaning, has enormous potential as a means of understanding the entire range of social interactions. Ceremonies, traditions, and rituals (both sacred and secular) are symbolic expressions of shared meaning. Such expressions transcend time and embellish communal life (e.g., familial, cultural, and religious) with a sense of cohesion. Shared meaning is what gives vitality and eloquence to great works of art — poetry, music, sculpture, dance. The greatest works are recognized for their evocative power to touch the emotions of people similarly, even across cultural boundaries. They thus speak to the universality of the human experience.

REFERENCES

Aberle, D. F. (1950). *The functional prerequisites of a society. 60,* 100–11.

Ables, B. S. and Brandsma, J. M. (1977). *Therapy for couples.* San Fransisco, CA: Josse-Bass.

Ackerman, N. W. (1938). The unity of the family. *Archives of Pediatrics, 55,* 51–62.

Ackerman, N. W. (1958). *The psychodynamics of family life.* New York: Basic Books.

Ackerman, N. W. (1970). Family psychotherapy today. *Family Process, 9,* 123–6.

Alexander, F. and Healy, W. (1935). *Roots of crime, psychoanalytic studies.* New York: Knopf.

Albee, G. W. (1970). The uncertain future of clinical psychology. *American Psychologist, 25,* 1071–80.

Allman, L. R. (1982). The aesthetic preference: Overcoming the pragmatic error. *Family Process, 21,* 43–56.

Allport, G. W. (1943). The ego in contemporary psychology. *Psychological Review, 50,* 451–78.

Allport, G. A. (1955). *Becoming.* New Haven: Yale University Press.

American Psychological Association. (1947). Report of the committee on training in clinical psychology of the American Psychological Association. *American Psychologist, 2,* 430–45.

Anderson, H. (1997). *Conversations, language, and possibilities.* New York: Basic Books.

Ardry, R. (1970). *The social contract: A personal inquiry into the evolutionary sources of order and disorder.* New York: Atheneum Press.

Aries, P. (1962). *Centuries of childhood: A social history of family life.* (R. Baldick, Trans.). New York: Alfred A. Knopf.

Aries, P. (1979). The family and the city in the old world and the new. In V. Tufte and B. Myerhoff (Eds.), *Changing image of the family* (pp. 29–42). New Haven: Yale University Press.

Auerswald, E. H. (1987). Epistemological confusion in family therapy research. *Family Process, 26,* 317–30.

Axline, V. M. (1947). *Play therapy.* Boston: Houghton Mifflin. (Reprinted in 1969.)

Axline, V. M. (1964). *Dibs in search of self.* Boston: Houghton Mifflin.

Bach, G. R. (1968). *The intimate enemy.* New York: Avon.

Baldwin, M. (1987). Interview with Carl Rogers on the use of self in therapy. In M.Baldwin and V. Satir (Eds.), *The use of self in therapy.* (pp. 47–57). New York: Haworth Press.

Bardis, P. (1964). Family forms and variations historically considered. In H. Christianson (ed), *Handbook of marriage and family.* Chaicago: Rand McNally.

Barrett-Lennard, G. T. (1984). The world of family relationships: A person-centered systems view. In R. F. Levant and J. M. Shlien (Eds.), *Client-centered therapy and the person-centered approach* (pp. 222–42). New York: Praeger.

Barron, F. (1957). Originality in relation to personality and intellect. *Journal of Personality, 25,* 730–42.

Barron, F. (1958). The psychology of imagination. *Scientific American, 199*(3), 150–70.

Barron, F. (1963). *Creativity and psychological health.* Princeton, NJ: Van Nostrand.

Bateson, G. (1936). *Naven.* Cambridge, MA: Cambridge University Press.

Bateson, G., and Reusch, J. (1951). *Communication: The social matrix of psychiatry.*

New York: Norton.

Bebout, J. (1974). It takes one to know one: Existential-Rogerian concepts in encounter groups. In L. N. Rice and D. Wexler (Eds.), *Innovations in client-centered therapy* (pp. 367–420). New York: John Wiley and Sons.

Beck, A. P. (1974). Phases in the development of structure in therapy and encounter groups. In L. N. Rice and D. Wexler (Eds.), *Innovations in client-centered therapy* (pp. 421–64). New York: John Wiley and Sons.

Beck, S. J. (1950). *Rorschach's test: Basic processes (2nd ed.).* New York: Grune and Stratton.

Bech, S. J. (1950). *Rorschach's test: basic processes. (2nd edition).* New York: Grune and Stratton.

Bell, R. Q. (1971). Stimulus control of parent or caretaker behavior by offspring. *Developmental Psychology, 4,* 63–72.

Belliveau, F., and Richter, L. (1970). *Understanding human sexual inadequacy.* New York: Bantam.

Benedict, R. (1938). Continuities and discontinuities in cultural conditioning. *Psychiatry, 1,* 161–7.

Berk, L. E. (1999). *Infants and children.* Boston: Allyn and Bacon.

Bertocci, P. A. (1945). The psychological self, the ego, and personality. *Psychological Review, 52,* 91–9.

Biegel, H. G. (1951). Romantic love. *American Sociological Review, 16,* 323–34.

Biesanz, J., and Biesanz, M. (1964). *Modern society.* Englewood Cliffs, NJ: Prentice-Hall.

Bossard, J. H., and Ball, E. S. (1950). *Ritual in family living: A contemporary study.* Philadelphia: University of Pennsylvania Press.

Bowen, M. (1961). Family psychotherapy. *American Journal of Orthopsychiatry, 31,* 41–60.

Bowen, M. (1965). Family psychotherapy with schizophrenia in the hospital and in private practice. In I. Boszormenyi-Nagy and J. Framo (Eds.), *Intensive family therapy* (pp. 213–44). New York: Harper and Row.

Bowen, M. (1975). Family therapy after twenty years. In S. Arieti, D. X. Freeman, and J. E. Dyrud (Eds.), *American handbook of psychiatry V: Treatment* (2nd ed.) (pp. 367–92). New York: Basic Books.

Bowlby, J. (1952). *Maternal care and mental health.* World Health Organization, Monograph no. 2., Geneva.

Brittain, W. L., and Beittel, K. R. (1960). Analysis of levels of creative performance in the visual arts. *Journal of Aesthetic Art Critique, 19,* 83–90.

Brown, S. R. (1972). A fundamental incommensurability between objectivity and subjectivity. In S. Brown and D. Brenner (Eds.), *Science, psychology, and communication: Essays honoring William Stephenson* (pp. 57–94). New York: Teachers College Press.

Brown, S.R. (1993). A primer on Q methodology. Operant Subjectivity, 16, 91–138.

Brunner, J. (1986). *Actual minds, possible worlds.* Cambridge: Harvard University Press.

Buber, M. (1937). *I and thou.* (R.G. Smith, T. Edinburgh, and T. Clark, Trans.). New York: Charles Scribner's Sons.

Burr, W. R., Day, R.D., and Bahr, K.S. (1993). *Family science.* Pacific Grove, CA: Brooks /Cole.

Butler, J. M. (1972). Self-concept change in psychotherapy. In S. Brown and D. Brenner (Eds.), *Science, psychology, and communication: Essays honoring William Stephenson* (pp. 141–71). New York: Teachers College Press.

Butler, J. M., and Haigh, G. V. (1954). Changes in the relationship between self-concepts and ideal concepts consequent upon client-centered counseling. In C. R. Rogers and R.Dymond (Eds.), *Psychotherapy and personality change.* Chicago: University of Chicago Press.

Butler, J. M., and Rice, L. N. (1960). Self-actualization, new experience, and psychotherapy. *Counseling Center Discussion Papers, 6,* 12–20.

Butler, J. M., Rice, L. N., and Dicken, C. F. (1960) Process and outcome in psychotherapy: a controlled study. *Counseling Center Discussion Pares, 6,* 30–45. Chicago Counseling Centre.

Carter, H., and Glick, P. C. (1970). *Marriage and divorce: A social and economic study.* Cambridge, Massachusetts: The Harvard University Press.

Cartwright, R. D. (1972). The Q method and the intrapersonal world. In S. Brown and D. Brenner (Eds.) *Science, psychology, and communication: Essays honoring William Stephenson* (pp. 172–99). New York: Teachers College Press.

Cattell, R. B. (1944). Psychological measurement: normative, ipsative, interactive. *Psychological Review, 44,* 292–303.

Cattell, R. B. (1951). On the disuse and misuse of P, Q, Qs and O techniques in clinical psychology. *Journal of Clinical Psychology, 7,* 203–14.

Cattell, R. B. (1957). *Personality and motivation: Structure and measurement.* Yonkers-on-Hudson, N.Y.: World Book Co.

Cattell, R. B. (1958). What is 'objective' in 'objective personality tests'? *Journal of Counseling Psychology, 5*(4), 283–9.

Cavan, R. S. (1969). The family life cycle. In R. S. Cavan (Ed.), *Marriage and family in the modern world* (pp. 28–38). New York: Thomas Y. Crowell.

Chance, E. (1959). *Families in treatment.* NewYork: Basic Books.

Cherlin, A. J. (1990). Recent changes in American fertility, marriage, and divorce. *Annals of the American Academy of Political and Social Science, 510,* 145–55.

Cherlin, A. J. (1999). *Public and private families.* Boston: McGraw-Hill.

Chess, S., and Thomas, A. (1987). *Know your child.* New York: Basic Books.

Chess, S., and Thomas, A. (1999). *Goodness of fit: Clinical applications from infancy through adult life.* Philadelphia: Brunner-Mazel.

Chess, S., Thomas, A., and Birch, H. G. (1965). *Your child is a person.* New York: Viking Press.

Chien, I. (1944). The awareness of self and the structure of the ego. *Psychological Review, 51,* 304–14.

Clayton, R. R. (1975). *The family, marriage, and social change.* Lexington, Massachusetts: D. C. Heath and Co.

Clayton, R. R., and Bokmeier, J. L. (1980). Premarital sex in the seventies. *Journal of Marriage and the Family, 42,* 759–76.

Clemens, W. V. (1966). An analytical and empirical examination of some properties of ipsative measures. *Psychometric Monographs, 14,* 30–45.

Collingwood, R. G. (1958). *The principles of art.* New York: Oxford University Press.

Condon, W. S., and Sander, L. M. (1974). Synchrony demonstrated between movement of the neonate and adult speech. *Child Development, 45,* 456–62.

Coopersmith, S. (1967). *The antecedents of self-esteem.* San Francisco: Freeman.

Darwin, C. (1952). *The origin of the species and the descent of man.* Chicago, IL: Encyclopedia Britannica, Inc.

Dell, P. F. (1982). Beyond homeostasis: Toward a concept of coherence. *Family Process, 21,* 21–41.

Dewey, J. (1939). *Intelligence in the modern world.* NewYork: Random House.

Drevdahl, J. E., and Cattell, R. B. (1958). Personality and creativity in artists and writers. *Journal of Clinical Psychology, 14,* 107–11.

Durkheim, E. (1951). *Suicide.* (J. Spaulding and G. Simpson, Trans.). New York: Free Press.

Duvall, E. M. (1971). *Family development* (4th ed). Philadelphia: Lippincott.

Edwards, J. N. (1967). The future of the family revisited. *Journal of Marriage and the Family, 8,* 505–11.

Ehrenzweig, A. (1957). The creative surrender. *American Imago, 14,* 193–210.

Eiduson, B. (1958). Artist and nonartist: A comparative study. *Journal of Personality, 26,* 13–28.

Elkind, D. (1981). *The hurried child: Growing up too fast too soon.* Reading, Mass.: Addison-Wesley.

Erikson, E. H. (1950). *Childhood and society.* New York: W. W. Norton.

Erikson, E. H. (1959). *Identity and the life cycle.* New York: International Universities Press.

Erikson, E. H. (1964). *Childhood and society* (Rev. ed.). New York: W.W. Norton and Co., Inc.

Fancher, R. (1995). *Cultures of healing.* New York: W. H. Freeman.

Figley, C. R., and McCubbin, H. I. (Eds.). (1983). *Stress and the family* (vols. 1–2). New York: Brunner-Mazel.

Fiske, D., and Maddi, S. (Eds.). (1961). *Functions of varied experience.* Homewood, Illinois: Dorsey Press.

Fox, J. (Ed.). (1987). *The essential Moreno: Writings on psychodrama, group method, and spontaneity by J. L. Moreno, M.D.* New York: Springer Publishing Company.

Frank, J. D. (1961). *Persuasion and healing.* Baltimore: Johns Hopkins University Press.

Freud, S. (1932). *Leonardo da Vinci: A psychosexual study of an infantile reminiscence.* New York: Dodd, Mead.

Freaud, A. (1935). Psychoanalysis and the training of the young child. *Psychoanalytic Quarterly, 4.*

Freud, A. (1946). *The ego and the mechanism of defense.* New York: International Universities Press.

Freud, S. (1956a). Dostoyevsky and parricide. *Collected papers* (pp. 222–42). London: Hogarth.

Freud, S. (1956b). The Moses of Michelangelo. *Collected papers* (pp. 257–87). London: Hogarth.

Freud, S. (1958). *Creativity and the unconscious.* New York: Harper.

Freud, S. (1959). *The interpretation of dreams.* New York: Basic Books. (Original work published 1900.)

Freud, S. (1962). *Three contributions to the theory of sex.* New York: Dutton.

Friedman, M. (1992). *Religion and psychology.* New York: Paragon House.

Fromm, E. (1956). *The art of loving.* New York: Harper and Brothers.

Gallup, C. (1977). Self-recognition in primates. *American Psychologist, 5,* 329–38.

Garber, S. N., Garber, M. D., and Spizman, R. F. (1996). *Beyond ritalin.* New York: Harper-Collins.

Gay, P. (1983). *The bourgeois experience: Victoria to Freud* (vol 1). London: Oxford Press.

Gaylin, N. L. (1966). Psychotherapy and psychological health: A Rorschach structure and function analysis. *Journal of Consulting Psychology, 30,* 494–500.

Gaylin, N. L. (1974). On creativeness and a psychology of well-being. In D. Wexler and L. Rice (Eds.), *Innovations in client centered therapy* (pp. 339–66). New York: John Wiley and Sons.

Gaylin, N. L. (1980). Rediscovering the family. In Stinett, N., Chesser, B., Defrain, J., and Knaub, B. (Eds.), *Family strengths: Positive models for family life.* Lincoln, Nebraska: University of Nebraska Press.

Gaylin, N. L. (1981). Family life education: Behavioral science wonderbread?. *Family Relations, 30,* 511–6.

Gaylin, N. L. (1985). Marriage: The civilizing of sexuality. In M. Farber (Ed.), *Human sexuality: Psychosexual effects of disease* (pp. 40–54). New York: Macmillan Publishing Co.

Gaylin, N. L. (1989a). The necessary and sufficient conditions for change: Individual versus family therapy. *Person-Centered Review, 4,* 263–9.

Gaylin, N. L. (1989b). Ipsative measures: In search of paradigmatic change and a science of subjectivity. *The Person-Centered Review, 4,* 429–45.

Gaylin, N. L. (1990). Family-centered therapy. In G. Lietaer, J. Rombauts, and R. Van Balen (Eds.) *Client-centered and experiential psychotherapy in the nineties* (pp. 813–28). Leuven, Belgium: Leuven University Press.

Gaylin, N. L. (1991). An intergenerational perspective of marriage: Love and trust in cultural context. In S. Pfiefer, and M. Sussman, (Eds.), *Families: Intergenerational and generational connections.* New York: Haworth Press.

Gaylin, N. L. (1993). On a person-centered family therapy. In D. Brazier (Ed.), *Beyond Carl Rogers: Towards a psychotherapy for the twenty-first century* (pp. 181–200). London: Constable.

Gaylin, N. L., Grebe, S. C., McCarrick, A., Millstein, F., and Werlinich, C. A. (1988). Looking in the mirror: A pilot study of family therapy research process and outcome in private practice. Unpublished study.

Gaylin, W. (1976). *Caring.* New York: Knopf.

Gendlin, E. (1978). *Focusing.* New York: Everest House.

Getzels, J. W., and Jackson, P. W. (1962). *Creativity and intelligence.* New York: John Wiley and Sons.

Gibson, E. (1993). Ontogenesis of the perceived self. In U. Neisser (Ed.), *The perceived self* (pp. 25–42). Cambridge: Cambridge University Press.

Gilbreth, F.B. (1911). *Motion study: a method for increasing the efficiency of the workman.* New York: D.Van Nostrand.

Goffman, E. (1971). *Relations in public.* New York: Harper and Row.

Goldenberg, I., and Goldenberg, H. (2000). *Family therapy: An overview.* Belmont, CA: Wadsworth.

Goldstein, K. (1939). *Human nature in light of psychopathology.* New York: Schoken Books.

Goldstein, K. (1940). *The organism.* Boston: Beacon Press.

Goldstein, K. (1963). *The organism.* (Rev. ed.). Boston: Beacon Press.

Goode, W. J. (1963). *World revolution and family patterns.* New York: Free Press of Glencoe.

Gordon, W. J. (1961). *Synetics.* New York: Harper.

Greenblatt, C. S. (1983). The salience of sexuality in the early years of marriage. *Journal of Marriage and the Family, 45,* 289–99.

Guilford, J. P. (1957). Creative abilities in the arts. *Psychological Review, 64,* 110–18.

Gurman, A., and Kniskern, D. (1981). Family therapy outcome research: Knowns and unknowns. In A. Gurman and D. Kniskern (Eds.), *Handbook of Family Therapy* (pp. 742–76). New York: Brunner-Mazel.

Haley, J. (1963). *Strategies of psychotherapy.* New York: Grune and Stratton.

Haley, J. (1976). *Problem-solving therapy: New strategies for effective family therapy.* San Francisco: Jossey-Bass.

Hammer, E. F. (1961). *Creativity: An exploratory investigation of the personalities of gifted adolescent artists.* New York: Random House.

Happÿe, F. G., and Frith, U. (1996). Theory of mind and social impairment in children with conduct disorder. *British Journal of Developmental Psychology, 14*(4), 385–98.

Harlow, H. F. (1959). Love in infant monkeys. *Scientific American, 200,* 68–74.

Harlow, H. F., and Harlow, M. K. (1962a). Social deprivation in monkeys. *Scientific American, 11,* 30–45.

Harlow, H. F. (1962b). The heterosexual affectional system in monkeys. *American Psychologist, 17,* 1–9.

Hart, H. H. (1950). The integrative function in creativity. *Psychiatry Quarterly, 13,* 1–16.

Hartmann, H. (1958). *Ego psychology and the problem of adaptation.* New York: International University Press.

Hartmann, H., and Kris, E. (1945). The genetic approach in psychoanalysis. In A. Freud (Ed.), *The psychoanalytic study of the child* (pp. 11–30). New York: International Universities Press.

Havighurst, R. J. (1971). *Developmental task and education.* New York: David McKay Co. (Original work published 1959).

Hoffman, L. (1971). Deviation-amplifying processes in natural groups. In J. Haley (Ed.), *Changing families.* New York: Grune and Stratton.

Horney, K. (1947). Inhibitions in work. *American Journal of Psychoanalysis, 6,* 18–25.

Huesman, L. R., and Miller, L. S. (1994). Long-term effects of repeated exposure to media violence in childhood. In L. R. Huesman (Ed.), *Aggressive behavior: Current perspectives* (pp. 153–86). New York: Plenum.

Huxley, A. (1932). *Brave new world.* New York: Harper Brothers.

Jackson, D. D. (1961). Family therapy in the family of the schizophrenic. In M. I. Stein (Ed.), *Contemporary Psychotherapies* (pp. 272–87). New York: Free Press of Glencoe.

Jackson, D. D. (1965). Family rules: Marital quid pro quo. *Archives of General Psychiatry, 1,* 618–21.

Jackson, D. D. (1967). Aspects of conjoint family therapy. In G. Zuk and I. Boszormenyi-Nagy (Eds.), *Family therapy and disturbed families* (pp. 28–40). Palo Alto: Science and Behavior.

Jacobson, N. (1985). Family therapy outcome research: Potential pitfalls and prospects. *Journal of Marriage and Family Therapy, 11*(2), 149–58.

Jahoda, M. (1958). *Current concepts in positive mental health.* New York: Basic Books.

James, W. (1890). *The principles of psychology.* New York: Holt.

James, W. (1892). *Textbook of psychology.* New York: Holt.

Jaynes, J. (1976). *The origins of consciousness in the breakdown of the bicameral mind.* Boston: Houghton Mifflin.

Johnson, S. M., and Greenberg, L. S. (1988). Relating process to outcome in marital therapy. *Journal of Marital and Family Therapy. 14,* 175–83.

Joint Commission on Mental Illness and Health (1961). *Action for mental health* (Final report of the Joint Commission on Mental Illness and Health). New York: Basic Books.

Jourard, S. (1971). *The transparent self* (Rev. ed.). New York: Van Nostrand Reinhold Co.

Kaufmann, W. (1958). *Critique of religion and philosophy.* New York: Harper and Brothers.

Keeney, B. P. (1983). *The aesthetics of change.* New York: Guilford Press.

Keeney, B. P., and Sprenkle, D. H. (1982). Ecosystemic epistemology: Critical implications for the aesthetics and pragmatics of family therapy. *Family Process, 21,* 1–19.

Kellog, R. (1967). *The psychology of children's art.* San Diego, California: CRM-Random House.

Keyes, R. (1973). *We are the lonely people: searching for community,* New york: Harper and Row.

Kilcarr, P. J. (1987). *Client vocal quality as a process measure in marriage and family therapy.* Unpublished master's thesis, University of Maryland, College Park, MD.

King, D., Balswick, J., and Robinson, I. (1977). The continuing premarital sexual revolution among college females. *Journal of Marriage and the Family, 39,* 455–9.

Kniskern, D. (1985). Climbing out of the pit: Further guidelines for family therapy research. *Journal of Marriage and Family Therapy, 11,*(2), 159–62.

Koffka, K. (1935). *Principles of gestalt psychology.* New York: Harcourt.

Kohlberg, L. (1984). *Essays on moral development* (vol. 2). San Francisco: Harper and Row.

Kris, E. (1952). *Psychoanalytic explorations in art.* International University Press.

Kubie, L. S. (1958). *Neurotic distortion of the creative process.* Kansas: University of Kansas Press.

Kubler-Ross, E. (1969). *On death and dying.* New York: Macmillan.

Kuhn, T. S. (1970). *The structure of scientific revolutions* (2nd ed.). Chicago: University of Chicago Press.

L'Abate, L. (1985). Permissiveness is out! Directiveness is in. *Contemporary Psychology, 30,* 23.

Lambert, M. J., and Bergin, A. E. (1994). The effectiveness of psychotherapy. In A. E. Bergin, and S. L. Garfield (Eds.), *Handbook of Psychotherapy and Behavior Change* (4th ed.) (pp. 143–89). New York: John Wiley and Sons.

Lasch, C. (1977). *Haven in a heartless world: The family besieged.* New York: Basic Books.

Lasch, C. (1978). *The culture of narcissism: American life in an age of diminishing expectations.* New York: Norton.

Lederer, W. J., and Jackson, D. D. (1968). *The mirages of marriage.* New York: W. W. Norton and Co.

Levant, R. F. (1978). Family therapy: A client-centered perspective. *Journal of Marital and Family Therapy, 2,* 30–45.

Levant, R. F. (1984). From person to system: Two perspectives. In R. F. Levant and J. M. Shlien (Eds.), *Client-centered therapy and the person-centered approach.* (pp. 243–60). New York: Praeger.

Levi-Strauss, C. (1969). *The raw and the cooked: Introduction to a science of mythology.* (J. Weightman and D. Weightman, Trans.). New York: Harper and Row.

Lewis, C. S. (1967). *Studies in words.* London: Cambridge University Press.

Lewis, R. A., and Spanier, G. B. (1979). In W. Burr, R. Hill, I. Nye, and I. Lewis (Eds.), *Contemporary theories about the family* (vol 1). New York: Free Press.

Lifton, R. J. (1968). Protean man, *Partisan Review, 35,* 13–27.

Lindsay, J. M. (2000). An ambiguous commitment: Moving into a cohabitating relationship. *Journal of Family Studies, 6*(1), 120–34.

Linton, R. R. (1936). *The study of man.* New York: Appleton-Century-Crofts.

Linton, R. R. (1949). The natural history of the family. In R. Anshen (Ed.), *The family: Its function and destiny* (pp. 18–38). New York: Harper.

Lorenz, K. (1952). *King Solomon's ring.* New York: Crowell.

Luckey, E. B. (1961). Perceptual congruence of self and family concepts as related to marital interaction. *Sociometry, 24,* 234–50.

Mace, D., and Mace, V. (1974). *We can have better marriages if we want them.* Nashville, Tennessee: Abingdon.

Macklin, E. D. (1980). Nontraditional family forms: A decade of research. *Journal of Marriage and the Family, 42,* 905–22.

Maddi, S. R., Charlens, A. M., Maddi, D., and Smith, A. (1962). Effects of monotony and novelty on imaginative productions. *Journal of Personality, 30,* 513–27.

Mahler, S. M., Pine, F., and Bergman, A. (1975). *The psychological birth of the human infant.* New York: Basic Books.

Maslow, A. H. (1954). *Motivation and personality.* New York: Harper.

Maslow, A. H. (1957). Cognition of being in the peak experience. *Counseling Center Discussion Papers, 8,* 14–30.

Maslow, A. H. (1962). *Toward a psychology of being.* Princeton, NJ: Van Nostrand.

Maslow, A. H. (1971). *The farther reaches of human nature.* New York: Viking Press.

McCubbin, H. I., Joy, C. B., Cauble, A. E., Comeau, J. K, Patterson, J. M., and Needle, R. H. (1980). Family stress and coping: A decade review. *Journal of Marriage and the Family, 42,* 855–71.

McGoldrick, M., Pearce, J., and Giordano, J. (Eds.). (1982). *Ethnicity and family therapy.* New York: Guilford.

McGregor, R. (1971). Multiple impact psychotherapy with families. In J. G. Howells (Ed.), *Theory and practice of family psychiatry* (pp. 890–902). New York: Brunner/Mazel.

Mead, G. H. (1934). *Mind, self, and society.* Chicago: University of Chicago Press.

Mead, M. (1970). *Culture and commitment: a study of the generation gap.* New York: Columbia Univ. Press.

Mead, M. (1950). *Sex and temperament in three primitive societies.* New York: Mentor.

Meier, N. C. (1939). Factors in artistic aptitude: Final summary of a ten-year study of special ability. *Psychological Monographs, 31*(5), 140–58.

Meltzoff, A. N., and Moore, M. K. (1977). Imitation of facial and manual gestures by human neonates. *Science, 198,* 75–85.

Minuchin, S. (1964). *Families and family therapy.* Cambridge, Mass: Harvard University Press.

Moreno, J. L. (1947). *The theater of spontaneity: An introduction to psychodrama.* New York: Beacon House.

Morris, D. (1967). *The naked ape.* New York: McGraw Hill.

Murdock, G. P. (1949). *Social structure.* New York: Macmillan.

Myden, W. (1960). An interpretation and evaluation of certain personality characteristics involved in creative production. In M. H. Sherman (Ed.), *A rorschach reader* (pp. 149–67). New York: International University Press.

Napier, A. Y., and Whitaker, C. A. (1972). A conversation about co-therapy. In A. Ferber, M. Mendelsohn, and A. Napier (Eds.), *The book of family therapy* (pp. 480–506). New York: Science House.

Natiello, P. (1987). The person-centered approach: From theory to practice. *Person-Centered Review, 2,* pp. 203–16.

Neisser, U. (1993). The self perceived. In U. Neisser (Ed.), *The perceived self.* Cambridge: Cambridge University Press.

Nichols, M. (1984). *Family therapy: Concepts and methods.* New York: Gardner Press.

Norton, A. J. (1983). Family life cycle. *Journal of Marriage and the Family, 45,* 267–75.

O'Leary, C. J. (1999). *Counseling couples and families: A Person-Centered approach.* London: Sage.

Olson, D. H., and Defrain, J. (2000). *Marriage and the family: Diversity and strengths.* Mountain View, CA: Mayfield Publishing Company.

Olson, D. H., and Gravatt, A. G. (1968). The Q-sort as an attitudinal measure. *College Student Survey, 2*(1), 13–22.

Orwell, G. (1949). *1984.* New York: Harcourt Brace.

Osmand, M. W., and Thorne, B. (1993). Feminist theories: The social construction of gender in families and society. In P. G. Boss, W. J. Doherty, R. LaRossa, W. R. Schumm, and S. K. Steinmetz (Eds.), *Sourcebook of family theories and methods* (pp. 591–622). New York: Plenum.

Oxford English Dictionary (Compact ed.). (1971). Oxford: Oxford University Press.

Parsons, T., and Bales, R. F. (1955). *Family, socialization and interaction process.* Glencoe, IL: Free Press.

Piaget, J. (1951). Principal factors determining intellectual evolution from childhood to adult life. In D. Rappaport (Ed.), *The organization and pathology of thought* (pp. 154–75). New York: Columbia University Press.

Piaget, J. (1963). *The origins of intelligence in children.* New York: Norton.

Piaget, J.(1965). *The moral judgment of the child.* New York: Free Press. (Original work published 1932).

Plato. (1952). *The dialogues of Plato.* In Hutchins, R. M. (Ed.), *Great books of the western world (V.7).* Chicago: Encyclopedia Britannica, Inc.

Platt, J. R. (1961). Beauty: Pattern and change. In D. W. Fiske and R. S. Maddi, *Functions of varied experience.* Homewood, Illinois: Dorsey Press.

Porterfield, A. L. (1941). *Creative factors in scientific research: A social psychology of scientific knowledge studying the interplay of psychology and cultural factors in science with emphasis upon imagination.* Durham, North Carolina: Duke University Press.

Prescott, S., and Letko, C. (1977). Battered women: a social psychological perspective. In M. Roy (Ed.), *Battered women: A psychological study of domestic violence* (pp. 72–96). New York: Van Nostrand Reinhold.

Price, S., McHenry, P., and Murphy, M. (2000). Families across time. In S. Price, P. McHenry, and M. Murphy (Eds.), *Families across time* (pp. 2–22). Los Angeles, CA: Roxbury Publishing Co.

Price-Bonham, S., and Balswick, J. O. (1980). The noninstitutions: Divorce, desertion, and remarriage. *Journal of Marriage and the Family, 42,* 959–72.

Pritchard, J. B. (Ed.). (1955). *Ancient near eastern texts relative to the old testament* (2nd ed.). Princeton: Princeton University Press.

Rabkin, R. (1977). *Strategic psychotherapy.* New York: Basic Books.

Redl, F., and Wineman, D. (1951). *Children who hate.* New York: Free Press.

Reiss, I. L. (1965). The universality of the family: A conceptual analysis. *Journal of Marriage and the Family, 27,* 443–53.

Reiss, I. L. (1980). *Family systems in America.* New York: Holt, Rinehart and Winston.

Reiss, D., and Klein, D. (1987). Paradigm and pathogenesis. In T. Jacob (Ed.), *Family interaction and psychopathology* (pp. 203–58). New York: Plenum Publishing Corporation.

Rennie, D. L. (1990). Toward a representation of the client's experience of the psychotherapy hour. In G. Lietaer, J. Rombauts, R. Van Balen (Eds.), *Client-centered and experiential psychotherapy in the nineties* (pp. 155–72). Leuven, Belgium: Leuven University Press.

Rice, L. N., and Gaylin, N. L. (1973). Personality processes reflected in client vocal style and Rorschach performance. *Journal of Consulting and Clinical Psychology, 40,* 133–8.

Rice, L. N., and Wagstaff, A. K. (1967). Client voice quality and expressive style as indexes of productive psychotherapy. *Journal of Consulting Psychology, 31,* 557–63.

Rodgers, R. (1962). *Improvements in the construction and analysis of family life cycle categories.* Kalamazoo, MI: Western Michigan University Press.

Rodman, H. (1965). Talcot Parsons' view of the changing American family. *Merrill-Palmer Quarterly of Behavior and Development, 11,* 209–27.

Roe, A. (1946). Artists and their work. *Journal of Personality, 15,* 1–40.

Roe, A. (1960). Painting and personality. In H. H. Sherman (Ed.). *A rorschach reader* (pp. 137–48). New York: International University.

Rogers, C. R. (1939). *The clinical treatment of the problem child.* Boston: Houghton Mifflin.

Rogers, C. R. (1942). *Counseling and psychotherapy: New concepts in practice.* Boston:

Houghton Mifflin.

Rogers, C. R. (1951). *Client-centered therapy: Its current practice, implications and theory.* Boston: Houghton Mifflin.

Rogers, C. R. (1953). The implications of client-centered therapy for family life. Paper presented to the Chicago chapter of the International Society for General Semantics, Chicago, IL.

Rogers, C. R. (1954). Toward a theory of creativity. *Etc., 11,* 249–60.

Rogers, C. R. (1957). The necessary and sufficient conditions of therapeutic personality change. *Journal of Consulting Psychology, 21*(2), 95–103.

Rogers, C. R. (1958). The characteristics of a helping relationship. *Personnel and Guidance Journal, 37*(1), 6–16.

Rogers, C. R. (1959). A theory of therapy, personality and interpersonal relationships, as developed in the client-centered framework. In S. Koch (Ed.), *Psychology: A study of a science* (vol. 3), (pp. 184–256). New York: McGraw Hill.

Rogers, C. R. (1961). *On becoming a person.* Boston: Houghton-Mifflin.

Rogers, C. R. (1977). *Carl Rogers on personal power.* New York: Dell.

Rogers, C. R. (1980). *A way of being.* Boston: Houghton Mifflin.

Rogers, C. R., and Dymond, R. F. (Eds.). (1954). *Psychotherapy and personality change.* Chicago: University of Chicago Press.

Rogers, C. R., Gendlin, E. T., Kiesler, D. J., and Truax, C. B. (1967). *The therapeutic relationship and its impact: A study of psychotherapy with schizophrenics.* Madison, WI: The University of Wisconsin Press.

Rollins, B., and Feldman, H. (1970). Marital satisfaction over the life cycle. *Journal of Marriage and the Family, 32,* 20–7.

Rose, R. J. (1995). Genes and behavior. *Annual Review of Psychology, 46,* 625–55.

Rozeboom, W. W. (1972). Scientific inference: The myth and the reality. In S. Brown and D. Brenner (Eds.), *Science, psychology, and communication: Essays honoring William Stephenson* (pp. 95–120). New York: Teachers College Press.

Rubenstein, D., and Weiner, O. R. (1967). Co-therapy teamwork relationships in family psychotherapy. In G. H. Zuk and I. Boszormeny-Nagy (Eds.), *Family therapy and disturbed families* (pp. 206–20). Palo Alto, CA: Science and Behavior Books.

Russell, C. S. (1974). Transition to parenthood: Problems and gratifications. *Journal of Marriage and Family, 36,* 294–302.

Sager, C. J., Brown, H. S., Crohn, H., Engel, T, Rodstein, E, and Walker, L. (1983). *Treating the remarried family.* New York: Brunner-Mazel.

Sagi, A., and Hoffman, M. L. (1976). Empathic distress in the newborn. *Developmental Psychology, 12,* 175–6.

Sampson, E. E. (1988). The debate on individualism. *American Psychologist, 43,* 15–22.

Schachtel, E. G. (1959). *Metamorphosis.* New York: Basic Books.

Schram, R. W. (1979). Marital satisfaction over the family life cycle: A critique and proposal. *Journal of Marriage and the Family, 41,* 7–12.

Seeman, J. (1988). The rediscovery of the self in American psychology. *Person-Centered Review, 3,* 134–65.

Seeman, J. (1994). Conceptual analysis of client and counselor activity in client-centered therapy. *The Person-Centered Journal, 1,* pp5–10.

Sells, S. B. (Ed.). (1968). *The definition and measurement of mental health.* Washington, DC: U.S. Dept. of Health, Education and Welfare.

Sherif, M., and Cantril, H. (1947). *The psychology of ego-involvements.* New York: Wiley.

Shlien, J. M. (1964). Comparison of results with different forms of psychotherapy. *American Journal of Psychotherapy, 28,* 15–22.

Skinner, B.F. (1948) *Walden II.* New York: MacMillan.

Skolnick, A. S., and Skolnick, J. H. (1971). *Family in transition.* Boston: Little, Brown and Company.

Slater, P. (1970). *The pursuit of loneliness: American culture at the breaking point.* Boston: Beacon Press.

Smith, M. B. (1968). Competence and 'mental health': Problems in conceptualizing human effectiveness. In S. B. Sells (Ed.), *The definition and measurement of mental health* (pp. 99–114). Washington, DC: U. S. Dept. of Health, Education and Welfare.

Spanier, G. B., and Lewis, R. A. (1980). Marital quality: A review of the seventies. *Journal of Marriage and the Family, 42,* 825–39.

Spanier, G. B., Lewis, R. A., and Cole, C. L. (1975). Marital adjustment over the life cycle: The issue of curvilinearity. *Journal of Marriage and the Family, 37,* 263–75.

Spearman, C. (1931). *The creative mind.* New York: Appleton.

Speck, R. V. and Rueveni, U. (1969).Network therapy: A developing concept. *Family Process, 8,* pp. 182–91.

Spitz, R. A. (1945). Hospitalism. An inquiry into the genesis of psychiatric conditions in early childhood. In A. Freud (Ed.), *The psychoanalytic study of the child* (vol. 1) (pp. 53–74). New York: International Universities Press.

Stein, K., and Markus, H. (1994). The organization of the self: An alternative focus for psychopathology and behavior change. *Journal of psychotherapy integration, 4,* 317–53.

Stein, M. I., and Meer, B. (1954). Perceptual organization in a study of creativity. *Journal of Psychology, 37,* 39–43.

Stephens, W. N. (1963). *The family in cross-cultural perspective.* New York: Holt Rinehart and Winston.

Stephenson, W. (1953). *The study of behavior: Q technique and its methodology.* Chicago: University of Chicago Press.

Stephenson, W. (1980). Newton's fifth rule and Q methodology. *American Psychologist, 10,* 882–9.

Straumann, T. (1994). Self-representations and the nature of cognitive change in psychotherapy. *Journal of Psychotherapy Integration, 4,* 291–315.

Strupp, H. H. (1963). Psychotherapy revisited: The problem of outcome. *Psychotherapy, 1,* 1–13.

Sullivan, H. S. (1947). Conceptions of modern psychiatry. *William Alanson White Memorial Lectures, 7,* 147 p.26.

Sullivan, H. S. (1953). *The interpersonal theory of psychiatry.* New York: W. W. Norton.

Symonds, P. M. (1951). *The ego and the self.* New York: Appleton-Century-Crofts.

Szasz, T. (1960). The myth of mental illness. *American Psychologist, 15,* 113–8.

Taft, J. (1933) *The Dynamics of Therapy in a Controlled Relationship.* New York: MacMillan

Thayer, L. (1982). A person-centered approach to family therapy. In A. M. Horne, and M. M. Ohlsen (Eds.), *Family counseling and therapy.* Itasca, Ill: F. E. Peacock.

Thomas, A., and Chess, S. (1977). *Temperament and development.* New York: Brunner/ Mazel.

Toffler, A. (1970). *Future shock.* New York: Random House.

Toman, W. (1969). *Family constellation: Its effects on personality and social behavior.* New York: Springer Publishing Co.

Trevarthen, C. (1993). The self born in intersubjectivity: The psychology of an infant communicating. In U. Neisser (Ed.), *The perceived self* (pp. 121–73). Cambridge: Cambridge University Press.

Turner, R. (1991). Many Canadian women are delaying marriage. *Family Planning Perspectives, 22*(6), 282.

Udry, J. (1971). *The social context of marriage.* Philadelphia: Lippincott.

Valenstein, E. S. (1998). *Blaming the brain.* New York: Simon and Schuster.

Van der Veen, F. (1965). The parent's concept of the family and child adjustment. *Journal of Counseling Psychology, 12,* 26–34.

Van der Veen, F., and Novak, A. L. (1969). Perceived parental attitudes and family concepts of disturbed adolescents, normal siblings and normal controls. *Family Process, 8,* 327–41.

Verdugo, M. A. (2000). Research on mental retardation: An agenda for the future. *Psychological Reports, 86*(3), 1189–2000.

Washburn, S. L., and DeVore, I. (1961). The social behavior of baboons an early man. In S. L. Washburn, (Ed.), *Social life of early man.* Chicago, IL: Aldine.

Watzlawick, P. (1978). *The language of change.* New York: Basic Books.

Watzlawick, P., Weakland, J., and Fisch, R. (1974). *Change: Principles of problem formation and problem resolution.* New York: W. W. Norton.

Weber, M. (1930). *The protestant ethic and the spirit of capitalism.* London: G. Allen.

Wells, C. A. (1971). Women's lib and the USSR experience. *Between the Lines, 30,* 30–45.

Werner, H. (1948). *The comparative psychology of mental development.* New York: International University Press.

Wexler, D. A. (1974). A cognitive theory of experiencing, self-actualization, and therapuetic process. In L. N. Rice and D. A. (Eds.), *Innovations in client-centered therapy* (pp.49–116). New York: John Wiley and Sons.

Whitaker, C., Felder, R. E., and Warkentin, J. (1965). Countertransference in the family treatment of schizophrenia. In I. Boszormenyi-Nagy, and J. L. Framo (Eds.), *Intensive Family Therapy* (pp. 323–42). New York: Harper and Row.

White, M. (1995). *Reauthoring lives.* Adelaide, Australia: Dulwhich Centre.

White, R. W. (1956). Motivation reconsidered: The concept of competence. *Psychology Review, 66,* 297–333.

White, R. W. (1959). *The abnormal personality.* New York: The Ronald Press Co.

Wilens, T. E. (1999). *Straight talk about psychiatric medications for kids.* New York: Guilford.

Wilson, E. O. (1980). *Sociobiology.* Cambridge, Massachusetts: Harvard University Press.

Zahn-Waxler, C., and Robinson, J. (1995). Empathy and guilt: Early origins of feelings of responsibility. In J. P. Tangney and K. W. Fischer (Eds.), *Self-conscious emotions* (pp. 143–73). New York: Guilford.

Zimring, F. M. (1988). Attaining mastery: The shift from the 'me' to the 'I'. *Person-Centered Review, 3,* 165–75.

Zubin, J. (1968). Clinical phenomenological, and biometric assessment of psycho-pathology with special reference to diagnosis. In S. B. Sells (Ed.), *The definition and measurement of mental health* (pp. 67–98). Washington, DC: U. S. Dept. of Health, Education, and Welfare.

Index of Names

Index of Main
Subjects

Person-Centred Approach
& Client-Centred Therapy
Essential Readers
Series editor Tony Merry

Person-Centred Therapy: *A Revolutionary Paradigm*

Jerold D. Bozarth 1998 ISBN 1 898059 22 5 234 x 156 pp 204 + vi £15.00

Jerold D. Bozarth is Professor Emeritus of the University of Georgia, where his tenure included Chair of the Department of Counseling and Human Development, Director of the Rehabilitation Counseling Program and Director of the Person-Centered Studies Project.

In this book Jerold Bozarth presents a collection of twenty revised papers and new writings on Person-Centred therapy representing over 40 years' work as an innovator and theoretician. The book is divided into five sections:

- Theory and Philosophy
- Applications of Practice
- Implications
- The Basics of Practice
- Research

This important book reflects upon Carl Rogers' theoretical foundations, emphasises the revolutionary nature of these foundations and offers extended frames for understanding this radical approach to therapy. This book will be essential reading for all with an interest in Client-Centred Therapy and the Person-Centred Approach.

——————— • • • ———————

Experiences in Relatedness:
Groupwork and the Person-Centred Approach
edited by **Colin Lago** and **Mhairi MacMillan**
1999 ISBN 1 898059 23 3 234 x 156 pp 182+iv £15.00

This book is an international collection of specially commissioned papers. Contributors include Ruth Sandford (USA); Peggy Natiello (USA); John K. Wood (Brazil); Peter Figge (Germany); Irene Fairhurst, Tony Merry, John Barkham, Alan Coulson and Jane Hoffman (UK). This is the first substantial book within the person-centred tradition on group work since Carl Rogers' *Encounter Groups*. Topics include the history of the development of small and large group work within the PCA; theoretical principles of person-centred groupwork; working with issues of sexuality and sexism; the use of the group in training, and groups, organisations and the Person-Centred Approach.

The authors have uniquely caught the spirit of the person-centred approach in their various writing styles, which combine personal expression with disciplined reflections on experience. References to research studies sit comfortably alongside personal testimonies; philosophical reflections are underpinned by a wide range of references from other disciplines.

——————— • • • ———————

Women Writing in the Person-Centred Approach
edited by **Irene Fairhurst**
1999 ISBN 1 898059 26 8 234 x 156 pp. 217+ii £15.00

Edited by the co-founder of the British Association for the Person-Centred Approach (BAPCA), this book is the first anthology of women's writing informed by and focusing on the Person-Centred Approach. This uniquely themed collection includes contributions from all over the world, representing the wide range of developments in client-centred therapy and the Person-Centred Approach.

In person-centred counselling and psychotherapy training courses, women outnumber men by about eight to one, yet in our literature the opposite is the case. This book is not written specifically for women, or about women — it redresses the balance — it is a place for women with something to say, to meet together, and for some, to find their voice. Twenty-one papers from an impressive international list of contributors.

Person-Centred Approach
& Client-Centred Therapy
Essential Readers
Series editor Tony Merry

Understanding Psychotherapy: *Fifty years of client-centred theory and practice*

by **C.H. 'Pat' Patterson** *foreword by John Shlien*

2000 ISBN 1 898059 28 4 234 x 156 pp. 338+iv £17.50

'This weighty volume, collection of a life-time of work, constitutes a whole course of instruction in theory and practice. But how does it look, feel, sound, in action? There is at hand a wonderful answer.'   John Shlien

'C.H.Patterson is one of the most productive and observant scholars of psychotherapy in the twentieth century. He continues such work into the twenty-first century with new publications and reiteration of some of his classic writings. **Understanding Psychotherapy** *contains the real 'gold standards' of psychotherapy and counseling.'*   Jerold Bozarth

Aimed at everyone with a scholarly interest in psychotherapy and counselling whether client-centred or not, this substantial volume is a mine of essential reading. The style is direct and accessible, inviting the reader to consider many theoretical, practical and contextual issues that have vexed therapists for the past 50 years.

• • •

The Person-Centred Approach: *A passionate presence*

by **Peggy Natiello** *foreword by Jules Seeman*

2001 ISBN 1 898059 20 9 234 x 156 pp. 190 £15.00

Extract from the foreword by Jules Seeman:
Peggy Natiello's depth and strength of conviction is illustrated with special fidelity in her discussion of collaborative power. To begin with, her view of its importance in client-centered therapy is indicated by the fact that she devotes an entire chapter to that topic. Beyond that, she applies the concept to client-centered therapy in such a fundamental way that she comes very close to advocating it as an additional necessary and sufficient condition, co-equal in importance to unconditional positive regard, empathy, and congruence. The crux of her argument is that the development of collaborative power within the relationship not only strengthens the relationship itself, but that it augments for each of the participants their own personal sense of power, presence, and effectiveness in the relationship.

In the end, I could understand and appreciate exactly why Peggy Natiello used the subtitle "A passionate presence." It is exactly that kind of book. And if you as reader match Peggy's passion with your presence, the experience may be one of rare stimulation.

Recommendations:
'For anyone seeking to understand the person-centred approach, this book will give a real insight into the rigour, discipline, courage and depth required. For those already committed, this timely book with its many examples deepens our understanding of the radical, political, yet deeply personal nature of this way of being. Not since reading my first Carl Rogers book, have I been so moved, empowered and affirmed.'   Jenny Biancardi

'Peggy Natiello's original voice strikes the same chords of excitement, empowerment and integrity stirred in me when sitting with her and Carl Rogers in their training program some twenty years ago. On reading this book I felt intellectually aroused, supported in deep reflection on my practice and passionate about doing this work. This level of introductory clarity and theoretical intricacy is hard to find. It is a gift.' Carol Wolter-Gustafson

DATE DUE

MAY 1 9 2003			
MAY 1 9 2003			
OCT 2 9 2003			
OCT 2 7 2004			
NOV 1 7 2004			
MAR 1 5 2006			
JUN 0 1 2009			
JUN 2 5 2009			
GAYLORD			PRINTED IN U.S.A.